THE
POPULATION
PROBLEM

Arthur McCormack

THE
POPULATION
PROBLEM

Thomas Y. Crowell Company

NEW YORK

ESTABLISHED 1834

Designed by Nancy Dale Muldoon

Manufactured in the United States of America

L.C. Card 74-109908

ISBN 0-690-64892-8

1 2 3 4 5 6 7 8 9 10

CONTENTS

"THE MOST URGENT CONFLICT CONFRONT-
ING THE WORLD TODAY IS NOT BETWEEN
NATIONS OR IDEOLOGIES, BUT BETWEEN THE
PACE OF GROWTH OF THE HUMAN RACE
AND THE INSUFFICIENT INCREASE IN RE-
SOURCES NECESSARY TO SUPPORT MANKIND
IN PEACE, PROSPERITY, AND DIGNITY."

—U THANT
Secretary-General of the United Nations

INTRODUCTION

IS MANKIND FACING DISASTER OR IS IT ON the threshold of a golden age of plenty such as the world has never seen? All the means are available to wipe poverty off the face of the earth—at least the grinding poverty that is the lot of millions of our fellow human beings. Yet at the same time the specter of the Third Horseman of the Apocalypse—famine—looms over the rosy prospects of the future. The unprecedented expansion of population in this century, especially in the second half, which is expected to continue virtually unchecked for the remainder of the century, might seem to give justification to the prophets of gloom.

Assessments of the future, based on estimates of world population, vary from optimistic appraisals of the bounty of the earth and of advances in technology to sensational, pessimistic prophecies of catastrophic famine within the next decade, which can be avoided only by crash programs of worldwide birth control, and in the view of some, not even by these.

The controversy between the exponents of one extreme or the other generates more heat than light. It is difficult for the nonexpert to form an intelligent opinion amid so much confusion. What is needed, it seems, is to give the facts stripped of the interpretations and theories and biases of particular extreme schools of thought. In this vital subject we must, as the famous English scientist T. H. Huxley said, "sit down like a child before the facts."

The purpose of this book is to attempt to suggest, in an intelligible and readable form, the answers to three questions: First, what are the facts about the population situation in the world today and in the foreseeable future? Second, can the resources of the world cope with this situation, not only with regard to food, but with regard to all the other elements of a decent life—and if so, how? Third, what part have population policies to play?

In order to achieve this purpose, I will rely heavily on primary sources, on the work of the United Nations Population Commission and the World Population Conference, on the figures made available by reputable bodies such as the World Bank, the Organization for Economic Cooperation and Development, the International Union for the Scientific Study of Population, the Population Council of New York, the Population Reference Bureau of Washington, and other institutions devoted to the in-depth study of the problems of population. In this way it is hoped to present an objective, scientifically based but popular study from which the reader can form his own assessment.

This might seem a well-nigh impossible task, however. First of all, the field is so vast. The realization of this is not without its merits. It is a good safeguard against the simplistic analyses and panaceas that are sometimes offered. Second, the population problem is a controversial issue, and it brings in many related issues on which people feel deeply—religion, social culture, basic philosophies of life, politics, economics, history, national prestige. It would be unrealistic for any writer on the subject to pretend that he is unbiased, even when he seeks to be completely objective. Third, after a number of years of engaging in population studies, I am bound to have formed certain definite lines of thought and to have become attached to certain theories.

Nevertheless, I hope to provide material for judgment rather than impose my own. I trust it is not arrogant to hope that the result will be of more value than a book written to propagate a certain line of thought or to indulge in special pleading by means of a weighted selection of facts and statistics. It is possible also, I believe, to present a consensus, or a movement toward a consensus, on a number of important points.

In a book on one of the most serious subjects of the day, use must be made of the quotations, references, statistics, and scientific data that are essential to ensure a balanced treatment, and sources must be supplied for those who wish to check or follow up the ideas and facts presented. However, I will endeavor to present the scientific impedimenta in a way that will slow up the pace of the book as little as possible and avoid a welter of figures, which most people find distasteful.

The scientific data will be supplemented with my own personal experiences gained from wide travels. I have been around the world twice in the past four years and have had the privilege of discussing problems on the spot with leading population experts in South America, East and West Africa, and the Far East, as well as in the United States and Europe.

The first book I wrote on this subject indicated the broad approach needed by its very title, *People, Space, Food!* [1] And "space" and "food" are only two of the related factors that need consideration. Indeed, population pressures such as these are but one aspect of the vast and poignant problem of world hunger and world poverty today. A glance at the *Proceedings of the World Population Conference* held in Belgrade in the summer of 1965 shows the tremendous range of multidisciplinary and interdisciplinary areas of knowledge and research required to cover adequately these complicated problems. A wide range of subjects was covered at this population conference; [2] for example, there were eighteen papers alone on demographic aspects of urban development and housing, only one of the important sections dealt with. Topics as widely diverse as fertility and demographic aspects of savings, investments, technological development, and industrialization were discussed and seen to be interrelated. Since 1965 considerable changes in the population situation, in food production, and in family-planning policies have taken place to make problems more complicated still, though they have brought more hope of solutions. Even since I started writing this book, new factors have emerged, such as the new ways of increasing food production that have modified the views of some population experts.

Naturally, it is difficult in a book such as this to bring the various aspects of the picture into focus without distortion and oversimplification. Yet this challenging and necessary task must be attempted, for distortion and oversimplification have been the bane of popular population books written from one angle or another.

I will try to disentangle the key issues from the mass of material and theory and limit myself to the more dramatic—and in my opinion more urgent—situations. For this reason, my main theme will not be internal demographic problems within developed countries, though these are interesting and serious. For this reason, also, I have not treated the effect of large populations and population increase on problems of environment and pollution, which are rightly but belatedly beginning to occupy the attention of

---

[1] McCormack, Arthur, *People, Space, Food.* London: Sheed & Ward, 1960.

[2] This conference began on August 30 and lasted until September 10, 1965. Its proceedings have been published in four volumes, on which I shall rely heavily in these chapters.

developed countries. I shall instead deal with worldwide population pressures especially as they affect the problems of poverty and hunger and all their concomitants in the developing countries. I shall try to provide material by means of which such statements as the following can be assessed and put into perspective:

A locomotive is roaring full throttle down the track. Just around the bend an impenetrable mud slide has oozed across the track. There it lies, inert, static, deadly. Nothing can stop the locomotive in time. Collision is inevitable; catastrophe is foredoomed. Miles back up the track the locomotive could have been warned and stopped. Years ago the mud-soaked hill could have been shored up to forestall the landslide. Now it is too late. The locomotive roaring straight at us is the population explosion. The immovable landslide across the tracks is the stagnant production of food in the under-developed nations, the nations where the population increases are the greatest. The collision is inevitable; famines are inevitable.

William and Paul Paddock, who make this prophecy in their book *Famine—1975*, also say:

The famines which are now approaching will not . . . be caused by weather variations and, therefore, will not be ended in a year or so by the return of normal rainfall. They will last for years, perhaps several decades, and they are for a surety inevitable. Ten years from now parts of the under-developed world will be suffering from famine. In fifteen years the famines will be catastrophic and revolutions and social turmoil and economic upheavals will sweep areas in Asia, Africa, and Latin America.[3]

Another pessimistic forecast has come from Professor P. R. Ehrlich of the Department of Biological Sciences, Stanford University, who states categorically:

The battle to feed humanity is over . . . . some time between 1970 and 1985 the world will undergo vast famines—hundreds of millions of people are going to starve to death . . . . unless plague, thermo-nuclear war, or some other agent kills them first . . . .
Population control is primarily a matter of human attitudes, not contraceptive technology, and human attitudes are not changing or being

[3] Paddock, William and Paul, *Famine—1975*, pp. 8, 9. Boston: Little, Brown and Company, 1967.

changed at anything like the rate necessary to minimize the coming catastrophe—a catastrophe which could not be avoided entirely even if men's minds were transformed tomorrow.[4]

A third, only slightly less pessimistic statement, by a distinguished scientist from a developing country, should also be mentioned. Abdus Salam, chief scientific adviser to President Ayub Khan of Pakistan, has commented:

I would like to live to regret my words, but twenty years from now I am positive the less developed world will be as hungry, as relatively undeveloped, and as desperately poor as today. And this despite the fact that we know the world has enough resources—technical, scientific, and material—to eliminate poverty, disease, and early death for the human race.[5]

Even greater dismay at the outlook on world hunger has been expressed by Lord C. P. Snow:

I have to say I have been nearer to despair this year than ever in my life. We may be moving, perhaps in ten years, into large-scale famine. Many millions of people are going to starve. We shall see them doing so upon our television sets.[6]

[4] *New Scientist,* December 14, 1967.
[5] Quoted in International Planned Parenthood Federation, *Family Planning: Vital Ingredient in 1968 Human Rights Campaign.* London: December 1967.
[6] Speech at Westminster College, Fulton, Mo., *Time* report, November 22, 1968.

Chapter 1

THE WORLD POPULATION EXPLOSION

ANYONE CONCERNED WITH THE DEVELOPING countries who has not at some time felt pessimistic during the past decade must be insensitive to the vast problems that poverty and population increase cause for these countries in their efforts to emerge from the half world of underdevelopment. Moreover, the developing countries are and will be bearing the brunt of the population expansion.

In order to view their problems in perspective, it is necessary to consider the population expansion in its world setting. A glance at the present population of the world and at reasonable projections for the future shows that the population expansion of this century is unprecedented and that it is affecting the countries least able to bear it.

The population of the world at the beginning of this century was estimated at just over 1.5 billion. By 1950 it was 2.5 billion and by 1961 it had reached 3 billion. By the end of 1969 it was over 3.55 billion.

United Nations projections in 1963 [1] estimated a total world population by the year 2000 at a minimum of 5.4 billion (on the assumption that fertility will drop more than it is expected to do), at a medium of 6.1 billion, and at a maximum of 7 billion (on the assumption that fertility will undergo a comparatively small decline). Since 1963 even the high projections have been increased. The high projections now predict a population of over 7 billion by A.D. 2000, possibly as much as 7.5 billion. On the whole, so far, actual population increase has tended to conform more to the high than the low expectation. It is therefore reasonable to project a doubling of world population in the remaining thirty-one years of this century.

The United Nations projections assumed declining mortality, declining fertility, and eventually declining rates of natural increase

[1] United Nations, *World Population Prospects, as Assessed in 1963.* New York: 1966.

in the less developed countries and hence for the world as a whole. Specifically, it was assumed that fertility would be reduced to half its original level within thirty years after decline began. High, medium, and low projections differ more in the dates at which the declines were assumed to begin than in the speeds of the declines. The medium estimates are intended to represent the future population trend that now appears most plausible in view of what is known of past experience and present circumstances in each region. The high and low variants are intended to represent upper and lower boundaries of a zone of greatest plausibility: they can be regarded as indications of the extent of error in the medium series that should not be considered a cause for surprise. The projections in the *World Population Prospects* remain basic, but as I have indicated, need to be revised upward on account of greater rates of increase since they were made.

Despite the inability of demographers to predict accurately the future long-term trends of fertility, mortality, or other relevant variables, experts agree about the need for projections of twenty years ahead. Such projections are a vital tool in the determination of economic and social policy. Moreover, many of the possibilities of error are significantly reduced for such a middle-term forecast, because, to take one example, the parents of the next generation are already born and can be counted with reasonable accuracy.

Among the major difficulties faced by specialists is uncertainty about the validity of existing data for many of the less developed countries of the world. However, a sufficient period of serious attempts at population statistics has elapsed to make predictions based on this data less hazardous than in the past, especially with regard to comparison of rates of population growth. A special problem in this respect arises from lack of satisfactory data available for China, which has more than one fifth of the world's population. While the figure of 583 million derived from a census in 1953 is generally accepted as a basis for projections, there is no accurate data on the sex and age distribution of the population, and levels of fertility and mortality are in doubt. As a result one expert has estimated a possible range of 1 billion to 2 billion in A.D. 2000, while United Nations assumptions result in a minimum of under 900 million and a maximum of over 1.4 billion.

The rapid growth of world population in this century is particularly striking when compared to the slow rates of the past. For example, it took the human race from the beginning of its existence until the year A.D. 1650 to reach the 500-million mark. By contrast, at present rates of expansion, it will take less than ten years to add another 500 million to the population of the world.

The explanation for the unprecedented modern population expansion is an involved one. Briefly, however, we can say it is because the checks on population growth have been overcome. During the time of man's span on the earth, population growth has until recently been slow and subject to repeated setbacks. Periods of increase were followed by decline. Nevertheless, the trend was upward in spite of periods of famine, pestilence, and war.

The decline in mortality that came with the advent of industrialization and advances in medical science meant that population soared in a way never before experienced, especially since 1900. The rise was even greater in the developing countries, which profited by the discoveries of modern science and began to achieve death control without a corresponding reduction in the birth rate. More effective death control in the developed countries was offset by a considerable fall in fertility due to birth control. At first this decline was not due mainly to artificial means, although later it was caused by sophisticated methods of family planning.

During the forty years from 1920 to 1960, it is estimated that the world population increased about 61 percent. The estimated increase was approximately one tenth in each decade from 1920 to 1950 and one fifth in the decade of the fifties.

Between 1950 and 1960, estimates are that the world received nearly half a billion more people—483 million—a number larger than the whole population of Europe in 1960 and approximately equal to the combined populations of Africa and Latin America. Europe was the only region not to share in the accelerated growth of that decade. Its rate of increase did not rise higher than the rates of the 1930's and the 1940's.

Latin America has had the highest rate of population growth in every decade since the 1920's, and Europe generally the lowest rate. The areas of fastest growth over the forty-year period from 1920 to 1960 included Latin America, with an estimated increase of 137 percent (more than doubling its population); South Asia, with 84 percent; and Oceania, with about 85 percent. An increase of 91 percent for Africa has not so much significance, since the figures are highly uncertain. The increase in East Asia (44 percent) is quite uncertain due to lack of hard evidence.

Even since 1950 very steep and unforeseen rises in the rate of population increase have occurred. In 1950 Julian Huxley warned about the dangers of population increase, estimating that the population of the world would be 3 billion by A.D. 2000.[2] Actually, the 3-billion mark was reached in 1961. In India the rate of population growth went from 1.3 percent in the 1953–57 period to the 2.7 percent it was estimated to be in 1969. And the same is true for most of the developing countries. In fact, the population explosion, and especially awareness of its implications for the rest of the century, has only become critical and crucial in the last ten or fifteen years.

The population of the world in 1969 was approximately 3.55 billion; its annual rate of natural increase is reckoned to be 1.9 percent. Therefore the population of the world is increasing at present by about 67 million per year—more than the total population of Great Britain. Every day there are 180,000 more mouths to feed. Every minute there are 125 more units added to the human sum; every second there are two more people on earth. It must be remembered that population increases in a way similar to compound interest. The population of the world, as stated above, was 3.55 billion in 1969. During that year it increased by about 67 million. The 1970 increase is therefore calculated on 3.618 billion, and so on each year.

If world population continues to increase at the present rate of 1.9 percent per year, the total population of the globe will be 25 billion by about A.D. 2065 and 50 billion by about A.D. 2110. This would cover the land surface of the six non-polar continents with a density of approximately 385 inhabitants per square kilometer, about the density of the Netherlands today. However, if this density were averaged out over all the habitable areas of the earth it would mean a much greater density than is at first apparent, since extensive arid lands and the permanent frost regions of Canada and Siberia would reduce the amount of land available for human occupation. Of course, improvements in those areas might have taken place by then. Still, 50 billion people does seem to be the limit of the world's population if people are to live at all "in comfort and convenience." [3]

In the long run, high birth rates and low death rates cannot con-

[2] "Population and Human Destiny," *World Review,* January 1950.
[3] The data given here are taken from Ackerman, Edward A., "Population and Natural Resources," United Nations, *Proceedings of the World Population Conference, 1965,* Vol. 1, *Summary Report,* pp. 260–261.

tinue without causing excessive rates of population growth that
are detrimental to the quality of human life. Unless one considers
mass migration to the planets or fatalistically thinks that nuclear
war will end the threat of ever-increasing populations, birth rates
must be reduced and brought closer to death rates so as to maintain an adequate population balance. Otherwise the old checks on
population increase—famine, disease, and competition for living
space and food and other resources—will begin to operate again.
Or to put it another way, as Robert McNamara, president of the
World Bank, has said:

What we must comprehend is this: the population problem *will* be
solved one way or the other. Our only fundamental option is whether it
is to be solved rationally and humanely—or irrationally and inhumanely.
Are we to solve it by famines? Are we to solve it by riot, by insurrection,
by the violence that desperately starving men can be driven to? Are we
to solve it by wars of expansion and aggression? Or are we to solve it rationally, humanely—in accord with man's dignity? [4]

The time will come when the maximum population the world
can support by food and other necessities, and especially space,
will be attained. Projections show that a continuation of the present growth rate of 1.9 percent over even ten or fifteen decades
would result in an increase in population that would be several
times the largest estimate of the maximum population that could
be supported by present knowledge and technology. Although such
treatment of global population problems is mathematical and academic, it shows that the population explosion cannot continue in-
definitely.

Long-term prospects are so alarming that they make speculation
beyond the present century profitless.[5] *Something will be done or
else something will happen* before an extreme situation is reached.

[4] Speech at Notre Dame University, Indiana, May 1, 1969.
[5] Cf. *Future Growth of World Population*, p. 21. United Nations Population Commission, 1958. In the preface of this report, there is a warning about "standing room" only within six hundred years' time on the earth
if present rates of growth continue. This mathematical projection has
often been repeated and tends to induce a panicky attitude which is not
particularly helpful. It is unrealistic also to expect action to be taken
with regard to a remote future. Rather, as I have already indicated, it is
important to concentrate on our present situation and the foreseeable future, which I would not extend beyond the present century.

Hence futuristic speculations are not given serious consideration in this book.

The main point that a study of global population problems brings out is the mathematical certainty that birth rates cannot remain high with low death rates for a long period, unless one contemplates mass migrations of populations amounting to billions to planets as yet undiscovered to be capable of supporting human life.

However, more important and more relevant to our study is whether present rates of birth plus declining death rates can be allowed to go on now and in the near future, especially in the developing countries, without causing serious problems and reasons for alarm.

In the developed countries of the West, Japan, Australia, and New Zealand, the total increase of population by the end of the century is projected to be about 500 million. In the less developed regions of the world it will be five times that figure, i.e., 2.5 billion in the year 2000. (Recent trends suggest an even higher figure.) By the end of this century, Asia will have as many inhabitants as the world has now, and 75 percent of the world's population will be in the lands now known as less developed.

In other words, for every 100 people in the developed countries in 1969 there will be 140 at the end of the century; even in North America, with its relatively high rate of population increase in the United States, there will only be about 160. But for every 100 people now living in the developing countries, there will be between 300 and 350 people.

Rates of future population growth or of "natural increase," which is the term generally used, are calculated on the difference between crude birth rates and death rates (ignoring migration, which on the whole is not a significant factor, though in certain areas it may be very important). Thus, if a country has an annual crude birth rate of 40 per 1,000 and a death rate of 20 per 1,000, its rate of population growth or natural increase will be 20 per 1,000 of its present population, or expressed as a percentage, 2 percent per year. For example, in Mexico, a high but relatively stable birth rate and a rapidly declining death rate produced an expanding population between 1930 and 1960. The rate of natural increase was 3.1 percent in 1960, whereas it was about 1.8 percent in 1930.

It should be stressed that the data given so far do not necessarily constitute accurate predictions. It is important to realize that these projections are mathematical manipulations of figures. They tell us what will happen, based on certain given facts, from a mathematical point of view. Predictions are an attempt to forecast what will actually happen by taking *everything* into consideration, including factors not open to mathematical calculation. Only the people who are alive in the year 2000 will know the actual population of the world and its various areas. Sensational breakthroughs in population-restriction policies could obviously affect the situation very much, and there are possibilities that such a breakthrough might occur. Nevertheless, at least for the next two decades, population projections will come very near to being accurate.

This survey of the population situation, however impressionistic, is adequate to show that we are facing an entirely unprecedented phenomenon. The rapidly increasing rate of growth is the main trouble, and it is this that impedes attempts to deal with the problems of population growth either by economic or agricultural advances and/or population-restriction policies. It is very important to realize the nature of the problem and to understand that the experiences and lessons of the past in developed countries are inadequate guides in today's new circumstances in developing countries.

Developing countries (sometimes known, less optimistically, as underdeveloped countries), are those with a low per capita income. From an economic point of view an underdeveloped country is essentially one with a very low standard of living for large numbers of the population, insufficient progress in well-being, and conditions unfavorable to development. In human terms this means that many of the people in these countries are poor, hungry, subject to disease, living in conditions unworthy of human beings, illiterate, and unemployed or underemployed.

The developed countries on the whole had their population expansion after, or at least concomitant with, their industrialization, and they had many decades to make their gradual adjustments. The population of the United Kingdom, for example, increased fivefold between 1800 and 1950. The industrial revolution and the agricultural revolution that preceded it allowed the increased population to be supported and fed. And there were vast temperate lands to siphon off the surplus population. Similarly, the United States population increased tenfold during the same period, partly by natural increase, partly by immigration from Europe. At the beginning and during the first half of this period the United States was a comparatively empty country, and the great fertile lands of the West and the Middle West were waiting to be opened up and to contribute to growing prosperity. Such a population increase was beneficial and indeed necessary.

The case of the developing countries in the postwar modern world is far different. In most of these countries population increase has occurred before an agricultural and technological revolution has enabled them to absorb it. Death rates have been lowered by modern medicine and hygiene, but birth rates have remained high. There have been no *easily developed* vast empty areas. The processes of modernizing agriculture and of industrialization are much more arduous ones, more time-consuming and more expensive, and yet they must occur if these countries are to develop as rapidly as they must in a fraction of the time that was allowed to the U.S.A. and the countries of Europe. For example, in Ceylon between 1940 and 1960 the death rate declined from 20 per 1,000 to 9.5 per 1,000, while the birth rate remained high—it actually increased slightly to 37 per 1,000. The rate of natural increase in 1940 was 35 minus 20, or 15 per 1,000. In 1960 it was 37 minus 9.5, or 27.5 per 1,000 —nearly double what it had been twenty years before.

The change in the rate of population increase from 1940 to 1960 in Ceylon meant that the time needed to double its population fell from about forty-six years in 1940 to about twenty-five years in 1960.

Nearly one hundred countries in the world with an average yearly per capita income of less than $200 are on the whole desperately in need of rapid economic growth. Yet population increase tends to prevent this or lessen it in two ways. First of all, actual economic growth achieved must always be calculated after subtracting the rate of increase of population. Thus, if a country is progressing economically at the annual rate of 3 percent (and some poorer countries achieve only this) and the rate of population growth is 3 percent, then actual economic growth is nil. Even the high but feasible rate of 6 percent for the developing countries suggested for the United Nations Second Development Decade of the seventies should be regarded as only 3.5 percent, or 3 percent, taking into account the fact that population growth of the developing countries will be running at a rate of 2.5 to 3 percent per year during that period.

Second, capital and other resources for investment, the condition of economic growth, have to be divided into two sets of investments—what Professor Alfred Sauvy, the famous French demographer, has called "economic" investments and "demographic" investments. These are distinct, though they overlap somewhat. Demographic investments are those necessary to maintain the level of living as it is at present; that is to say, they are investments whose sole purpose is to meet the growth of population. "Economic" investments are those that permit an improvement in the level of living of the population. Some fear that demographic investments may absorb the whole of the resources available for economic investment and that there will be little or nothing available for raising the standard of living.

At an annual increase rate of 3 percent a population doubles in just over 20 years and goes on doubling by compound interest, so to speak, while at the rate of 2 percent it takes 34.6 years to double. The cumulative "compound interest" effect can easily be understood, since the population on which the 2 percent or 3 percent is calculated itself increases each year.

As we shall often be referring to rates of population increase, it is useful to note the time it takes for a population to double at various rates of increase:

TABLE 1-1 [6]

Percent of population increase	Years needed for total population to double
1	69.3
1.5	46.2
2	34.6
2.5	27.6
3	23.1
4	17.3

To put it another way, one hundred years ago in England only twenty-two babies survived to adulthood out of a hundred; now

[6] This table is mathematically accurate and substantially useful. However, the more complicated calculations of Colin Clark in an as-yet unpublished book, *Men, Money and War*, need to be taken into account for a more sophisticated approach.

only eight *fail* to survive, and ninety out of a hundred survive through the reproductive years. If fertility had not declined in England, due, among other things, to family planning, England would have experienced a population explosion comparable to some of the developing countries at present. Although developing countries have not achieved such a low rate of infant mortality, they are approaching the lower rates of the developed countries, with a consequent boost to population increase.

In the past, the controversy between those who believed that population growth outstrips food supply by some "natural law" and those who optimistically relied on the almost limitless bounty of the earth played a large part in considerations of population questions and suggested solutions to population problems. There still is a considerable amount of tension, as I have indicated, between the more extreme adherents of the so-called pessimistic and optimistic schools, and the labels of Malthusian and neo-Malthusian [7] are still attached. Among a great number of population experts, however, the difference has come to be one largely of degree. Much higher rates of population increase than could have been anticipated have shown even the "optimists" that some kind of population-restriction policy is necessary, at least in some areas. The "panacea" of the birth-control approach to population policies is equally unrealistic, due to the much slower rate at which such policies take effect than was expected by the more enthusiastic. For example, the expenditure of $64 million in India's three Five Year Plans 1951–66 had hardly any impact on India's fertility problems; indeed the rate of natural increase at the end of the Third Five Year Plan (2.7 percent) was double the rate at the start.

Nevertheless, because these attitudes continue to have some influence and are still responsible for the extreme views of those who either threaten "birth control or starvation" or will not consider family limitation and even defiantly champion large families, it may be useful to sketch the two extreme positions.

These two positions in their simplest forms are answers to the question: Are the resources of the world adequate to cope with existing and projected world population? One answer, the Malthusian one, is given by the advocates of planned population equilib-

---

[7] After the Reverend T. R. Malthus, who in 1798 wrote the famous *Essay on the Principles of Population.*

rium. They see men heading for impending doom unless they drastically reduce their fertility, because the resources of the world are being used up and increasing populations will soon reach the limit of these resources. Aldous Huxley put this situation dramatically in his *Brave New World Revisited* when he said, referring to population increase in this century:

At the present rate, it will double in less than a century. And this fantastically rapid doubling of our numbers will be taking place on a planet whose most productive areas are already densely populated, whose soils are being eroded by the frantic efforts of bad farmers to raise more food, and where easily available mineral capital is being squandered with the reckless extravagance of a drunken sailor getting rid of his accumulated pay.[8]

In its more rational form the planned population equilibrium point of view takes the position that the world must plan not only for the regulation of resources but also regulate the number of people; that is, there must be a planned equilibrium between resources and people that takes into account both sides of the equation.

The other position might be described as one of technological optimism. Man, if properly organized, will not be faced with physical limitation in numbers for a long time to come, if ever. N. M. Zhavoronkov summed up this view very ably when he said that as long as the sun shone and people were capable of creative thinking, they had no need to fear the future.[9]

The fact that there has been bitter argument between the adherents of both these hypotheses in the past illustrates the difficulty that even specialists may have in arriving at the truth. The truth in this field is indeed a very complex matter. There is an element of veracity in both these positions, even at their extremes.

The argument may well seem now to be an academic one, since the developed countries are already far advanced in population limitation and half the developing countries are committed to population-restriction policies. Thus technological optimists will not have the chance to test their theories. On the other hand, projections based on present rates of increase of nearly 2 percent, the

[8] Huxley, Aldous, *Brave New World Revisited*, p. 17. London: Chatto & Windus, 1959.

[9] Zhavoronkov, N. M., "Chemistry and the Vital Resources of Mankind," *Proceedings of the World Population Conference*, Vol. 3.

bases of the pessimists' calculation, can easily be negated by a downward trend in fertility, such as has recently occurred in the United States.

The argument is academic also because the two positions are seldom defended in an absolute form. Few experts would regard population limitation as the only way to cope with the population-resources problem of the actual world today. And there are not many, even among the keenest advocates of the technological optimistic school, who would deny that in present world circumstances population-restriction policies are desirable in many cases. Even since the World Population Conference met in 1965, there has been a hardening of opinion in favor of some limitation of fertility of a voluntary nature, even where the resources, especially of food and technology, are held to be plentiful and to give the lie to the prophets of doom. A small example of this was provided at a Food and Agriculture Organization Conference I attended in Rome in mid-March 1968. Four speakers from the FAO, whose main concern was with food and who were by no means pessimistic about the ability of the world to feed its peoples, nevertheless all agreed that some amount of fertility limitation was desirable and necessary.

Perhaps I may be allowed a personal note here. In 1960 I wrote a book on population (already referred to) in which I expressed a moderately optimistic view. The period in between has produced developments that justified, I believe, my optimistic attitude, and I would not wish to substantially change it now. But the much higher rates of population increase that now obtain, and which may even go still higher for a time; the practical difficulties of developing countries in coping with all aspects of the problems of population increase; the fact that although rapid advance could, theoretically, take place it has not done so; the slowness with which people adapt to change—these and many other factors have convinced me that in certain areas of the world a population-restriction policy is urgently needed as a concomitant of positive efforts for agricultural and general economic advance. I would still place the main emphasis, as the rest of the book will show, on these positive measures, and I do not, I hope, overestimate the time needed for population policies to take effect. However, to rely on positive measures alone *now* seems to me completely unrealistic.

It is important also to concentrate on the short-term and middle-term prospects. Too often scary prophecies of *Standing Room Only* (the title of a recent book) distract from the urgency of the immediate situation. A prophecy made for six hundred years from now is an interesting mathematical projection. But most people are rightly concerned about the next sixteen or at most sixty years. If we cope as best we can with problems of world poverty complicated by the population explosion during the remainder of this century, we will have deserved well of posterity and will hardly be faulted for not allowing what may happen six hundred years hence to influence us unduly.

I shall deal in subsequent chapters with the food resources available and possibilities for increases in population, but one thing can be said at once. The view that there is no more land or hardly any more land available for food production and habitation is very far from the truth.

Chapter 2

FOOD AND THE WAR ON HUNGER

IN HIS STATE OF THE UNION MESSAGE DELIVered on January 10, 1967, President Johnson declared: "Next to the pursuit of peace, the greatest challenge to the human family is the race between food supply and population increase. That race tonight is being lost."

It must not be thought from this statement that provision for food is the only problem.

The *Report of the President's Committee on Population and Family Planning*, commissioned by President Johnson, made it clear that other factors of equal or perhaps even greater importance were involved:

The population problem is serious enough simply from the stand point of assuring a reasonably adequate supply of food for the anticipated increase in numbers. But it is far deeper than that since it affects health and nutrition, literacy and education, productive employment and living standards. In essence it is concerned, not with the quantity of human life, but with its quality. At the same time, solving the population problem will not solve everything. Reducing excessive rates of population growth will speed development in the poorer nations. But reductions in birth rates must be accompanied by positive programs of economic development.[1]

President Nixon, in his message to Congress on July 18, 1969, summed up the situation as follows:

It is in the developing nations of the world that population is growing most rapidly today. In these areas we often find rates of natural increase higher than any which have been experienced in all of human history. With their birth rates remaining high and with death rates dropping sharply, many countries of Latin America, Asia, and Africa now grow ten times as fast as they did a century ago. At present rates, many will dou-

[1] *Report of the President's Committee on Population and Family Planning*, p. 15. Washington, D.C.: November 1968.

ble and some may even triple their present populations before the year 2000. This fact is in large measure a consequence of rising health standards and economic progress throughout the world, improvements which allow more people to live longer and more of their children to survive to maturity.

As a result, many already impoverished nations are struggling under a handicap of intense population increase which the industrialized nations never had to bear. Even though most of these countries have made rapid progress in total economic growth—faster in percentage terms than many of the more industrialized nations—their far greater rates of population growth have made development in per capita terms very slow. Their standards of living are not rising quickly and the gap between life in the rich nations and life in the poor nations is not closing.

In spite of all the efforts of developing countries themselves, in spite of all the aid, in spite of all the efforts by international agencies, more people are actually hungry today, more people suffer from the concealed hunger of malnutrition, than ever before in history.

Why is this so? Is there any real possibility of winning the race between food and population? Or are we doomed, as the Paddock brothers and other prophets of gloom maintain, to inevitable famines and all the horrors of widespread lack of food? Is the modern world on the edge of famine? Will mass starvation occur in all population areas within fifty years?

There is no simple answer to any of these questions. The reasons why more people are hungry than ever before are complex and complicated. Whether we will escape the food shortages and famines that are prophesied, we honestly do not know. As Henri Bergson said in another context "the future of mankind remains uncertain because it is in our own hands." One answer, I believe, we can give: disaster is not inevitable; the future indeed rests in our own hands in this sphere, perhaps more than in many others. We have the means for the first time in history to wipe hunger, famine, malnutrition, off the face of the earth, *if* we choose to do so, *if* we get our priorities right, *if* the food problem and associated problems are given a high place in the scale of scientific and political values. So far, let us face it, this has not been done, and the reason is partly that neither in the developed or developing countries have enough people wished enough to do it.

The simple fact that so many are hungry and poor in our bountiful world should dominate our thinking and force us to accept the responsibilities of our choices. In May 1968, Pope Paul VI, in a speech to the Pontifical Academy of Sciences meeting, where scientists from all over Europe were gathered for a conference on organic materials and soil fertility, stated our duty quite bluntly:

It is perhaps unnecessary to point out that the most terrible calamities, capable of destroying all the inhabited earth, come from precisely the best-equipped laboratories of modern physical science. May you have the courage to renounce these things.

Rather, make the earth fertile, make it produce bread for all; fight against the sterility of desert zones, intensify farm production everywhere, make possible victory over hunger that still afflicts entire populations. This is your victory, your art, your mission, and your glory.

There is no doubt that if the war on hunger had been waged as singlemindedly as military adventures are undertaken and armaments are piled up, no one would now be prophesying famine. However, we live in a real world, and the victory against hunger does not and cannot depend on waiting for total disarmament.[2]

The war on want, unlike a military campaign, cannot be waged for a limited period of time. It is a war that will be with us for this generation, for this century. It will need more sustained effort, more generosity, more sacrifice, than has so far gone into the struggle. But we can win this war by expenditures that are very reasonable compared to costly military outlay and without the sacrifice of many of the freedoms and amenities of life. Several billion dollars more of aid, puny sums compared with the tens of billions spent on armaments, would suffice financially. Many more things are needed, it is true, but the weapons to win can be forged without insuperable difficulty. What seems to be lacking is the awareness of the need to win, and the will to win.

The words of the Pope were quoted to show the positive attitude that is necessary. It is also important to be completely convinced that it is possible to be victorious even without new advances in

[2] Nevertheless, even partial disarmament would release enough funds and resources to win the war against poverty. Cf. *Economic and Social Consequences of Disarmament*, United Nations, Economic and Social Council, 1962.

science and in spite of increasing populations. Ever since President Johnson issued his sober warning, grounds for hope have increased to such an extent that some experts, rather unwisely I think, are no longer stressing the danger of food shortages and regard the battle as almost won.

We must not fall into this opposite trap of ill-considered optimism. It is true that the world can feed its peoples. However, it is by no means certain that it will be done in time not only to prevent increasing populations from being exposed in some areas of the world to mass starvation, but to enable them to have diets adequate in quantity and quality for health and growth. But it is important and scientifically justifiable to approach these problems with a restrained optimism, or at least without that pessimism and despair that paralyzes efforts and thus brings on the very disasters that are prophesied.

The necessary determination to win the war on hunger is indeed at the heart of achieving victory, although we must recognize that even with the best will in the world there are great difficulties to be overcome. However, after listing these obstacles, Senator George McGovern in a speech to the United States Senate declared: ". . . in spite of the difficulties, a nation that can send a man to the moon can unlock the doors to food production and food distribution." [3]

To seek justification for this hopeful attitude it is necessary to examine as objectively as possible (1) the present extent of world hunger; (2) prospects of the situation for the future; (3) what can and must be done.

THE PRESENT EXTENT OF WORLD HUNGER Part of the pessimism about the food situation has come from an exaggeration of its extent. It used to be said that two out of three people go to bed hungry. That statement, taken with the rapid increase in the numbers of the hungry millions, gave the impression of a problem too enormous to even be tackled. However, figures based on FAO studies of 1957 and 1961, which have been widely accepted, suggest that between 350 million and 550 million of the 3.55 billion population of the world

[3] *Congressional Record*, September 23, 1965, Vol. 3, No. 176. The whole of this speech is well worth reading even though there have been developments since then.

do not get enough to eat—are *under*nourished. As many more again, indeed possibly as many as half the world's population, are *mal*nourished, do not get food of a quality to enable healthy living and especially healthy growth of children to take place. These figures are much more realistic and present a problem that is much more manageable.[4]

Some of the more pessimistic and alarmist estimates of hunger date back to the very bad years of 1965 and 1966. In these years, threats of extensive famine in India and in Kenya, due mainly to weather conditions, depleted stocks of surplus food, especially in the United States. Books such as *The Hungry Planet* and *Famine —1975* were written in this atmosphere. Even the excellent report of the President's Scientific Advisory Committee published in 1967 was influenced by this situation and spoke of depleted food stocks without sufficient emphasis on the circumstances that are hardly likely to be repeated.

The news in 1968 about world food production was much more hopeful. The United Nations has stated that 1967 was an exceptional year for world agriculture. There was a record grain crop in India, a 10 percent rise in Pakistan's farm production, and the largest rice crop in the Philippines' history.

Combined world agricultural production increased by about 3 percent in 1968. The increase for all developing countries combined (excluding fisheries and forestry) was some 2 percent and for food production alone about 3 percent—slightly ahead of the 2.6 percent average population growth rate in these countries, according to the FAO's yearly report, *The State of Food and Agriculture* (SOFA).

1968 was described globally as an average year. Progress was uneven, with Asia showing the largest increase, while according to preliminary figures, the Near East registered only a small increase and in Latin America the rate actually fell.

In the Far East food production increased by 5 percent, a rise of 3 percent per head, the largest since 1959. While good weather and enlarged areas helped raise production in many countries, the wider use of the newly developed high-yielding varieties of

---

[4] Conclusion of the FAO Reports of 1957 and 1961 by Dr. P. V. Sukhatme, accepted by the Third World Food Congress, Washington, 1963. For criticism even of these figures see Colin Clark, *Population Growth and Land Use*, p. 125. New York: Macmillan Company, 1967.

rice and wheat, and of modern inputs, contributed to this significant advance. This expansion in agricultural production was geographically widespread; important food-importing countries such as India, Indonesia, Malaysia, and Pakistan showed increases of 4 percent or more.

In my opinion, an accurate measurement of world hunger cannot yet be made. It should be remembered that even in regions where the average diet may be below the desirable level, there are many who eat quite well and who should not be included in the hungry millions. In many developing countries whose people are regarded as being short of food there is no evidence of hunger, still less of starvation, except in the urban slums or the rural areas of poverty. Not all poor or developing countries suffer from lack of food. West Cameroon, in West Africa, where I spent much of my life and which I have since revisited several times, is statistically one of the poorer of the less developed countries, but its people do not suffer from hunger, although some children suffer badly from malnutrition in the bush areas. Thus, some of the more dramatic statements about the extent of starvation that are given and repeated with the utmost assurance do lack adequate foundation.

However, to minimize exaggerations is not to minimize the very real problem of hunger. Even if only half the numbers given by Dr. P. V. Sukhatme in his FAO reports were true, this would indicate a very great volume of individual suffering, intolerable in terms of human values for the conscience of mankind. Perhaps the comments of Dr. B. R. Sen, former director-general of the FAO, are a more human and more valid way of indicating the plight of millions of our fellow men. Although hunger does not always accompany poverty, it is all too often a natural accompaniment, and therefore Dr. Sen's words are substantially true about hunger as well as poverty: "One does not have to seek the aid of statistics to discover the widespread poverty that exists in many parts of the world today. It is visible to the naked eye. One merely has to walk these parts of the world with one's eyes open." [5]

Senator George McGovern, the director of the United States Food for Peace program under President Kennedy, put it this way in an article called "We Are Losing the Race Against Hunger": [6]

[5] Sen, B. R., "Freedom from Hunger," *World Justice*, Vol. 1, No. 4, 1960, p. 423.
[6] *Look*, March 7, 1967.

In 1961, while studying food problems in Latin America for the late President Kennedy, I experienced my first direct encounter with hunger. I still visualize the scene inside a small hut in Brazil's stricken Northeast, where a young mother sat on the floor with her family at their noon meal. Two emaciated children lay ill, their heads resting in her lap. A younger child had died the previous day of smallpox complicated by the debilitating malnutrition plaguing the entire village.

"She is the symbol of the under-developed country", said a young Brazilian economist as we stared at the shapeless, prematurely aged mother.

In the following months, when I served as director of the U.S. Food for Peace program, I was to witness that scene countless times—in congested slums and benighted villages around the globe.

Hunger is not an occasional visitor but a constant companion to half of mankind.

Senator McGovern went on to say that the ever-present companions of malnutrition—lethargy, disease, and early death—generate a vicious circle of listless, ineffective humans, powerless to break out of their misery. Yet these people are capable of breeding more misery for later generations by irresponsible reproduction. The combination—a citizenry weakened by hunger and a mushrooming populace pressing ever harder against inadequate resources—is one of the chief barriers to development in the emerging nations. Students too lethargic to study, workers too weak to do a day's labor, mothers too burdened to care for their offspring—these are the most urgent concerns of a world striving for modernization. The Senator concluded: "If anyone doubts that hunger is not the most painful fact of life for these multitudes, let him experiment with a daily diet of a bowl of rice or a crust of bread."

The slums of Rio, or Recife, or Lima, or Santiago; the rural "barrios" of the Philippines or the crowded city slums of the East; parts of rural and urban Africa—these bring home the problem of hunger far more clearly and movingly than disputes about statistics and arguments about calories. As for India, in many of the 567,000 villages the difference between subsistence and hunger leaves little leeway for misfortune; and near-starvation is often the result of drought. In 1965 and 1966, it was only overseas aid on a grand scale that prevented famine greater than this century had yet witnessed. Even in 1968, the year of bumper harvests, 10 million school meals a day in South America, provided through the United

States Food for Peace program, were needed to prevent the under-nourishment that would have been the heritage of millions of children.

The number of deaths caused by hunger and malnutrition cannot be estimated with any accuracy because they frequently cause death indirectly by reducing resistance to infection. Especially in infancy, many deaths that are ascribed to dysentery, parasitic conditions, and infectious diseases of all kinds really take place because the sufferer is weakened by hunger and malnutrition.

At present, then, there are tens of millions who lack adequate food. It is clear that very great efforts will be required to supply them with what they need. In addition, the number of people in want is growing fast; a good proportion of the 45–50 million increase per year that is the developing countries' share of the annual world population increase of nearly 70 million is born to hunger. This makes the outlook for the future even more serious.

Let us examine more closely the present position and the needs for the future. Basically, the world's food problem is not that there is not enough food in the world, but that some people have too much and some have too little. The problem then is mainly one of *uneven distribution* of the food supply among countries, within countries, and among families of different levels of income. It is hard to assess actual hunger in the world on the rough basis of calories and protein intake, for a number of variables (such as climate, body weight, body temperature, kind of work, etc.) must be taken into account. However, calorie intake can be taken as a rough guide for comparison if its limitations are realized and allowed for. In Britain, for example, during the war, it was found that people consuming less than 2,800 calories every day lost weight, suggesting an inadequate diet.

Bearing this figure in mind, let us examine world calorie levels. On the basis of available figures it appears that food supplies of countries representing only about 20 percent of the world's population exceed a calorie level of 2,800. On the other hand, the food supplies of countries representing no less than 60 percent of the world's population actually fall below 2,200, of which nearly half are below 2,000—a figure 800 calories less than that at which British adults and children started to lose weight during the war years. And, of course, these are average figures; many people have diets much below this.

Moreover, it is the tropical and subtropical lands that are mainly affected. All twenty-one countries that exceed the 2,800-calorie level are located in either Europe, North America, Oceania (Australia and New Zealand), or the Río de la Plata area. Of the fifty remaining countries for which figures are available, only eight are located in Europe; the remainder are in the underdeveloped regions of the Near East, the Far East, Latin America, and the tropical parts of Africa.

In South Asia and Latin America, surveys show that the poorest 25 percent of the people consume diets lacking in quantity (i.e., calories) and quality (i.e., protein and other requirements of a healthy balanced diet) to such an extent that they fall below the calculated nutritional requirements. These are the people who are hungry and live on the brink of actual starvation. It is in these groups also that extensive malnutrition is found, particularly among the most susceptible groups: infants and preschool children, pregnant women, and nursing mothers.[7]

The level of nutrition in the Far East is among the lowest known. The individual intake of calories in Southeast Asia is not even as much as two thirds of that in the more developed countries of Europe. In India the typical intake is less than half that in Australia, New Zealand, Argentina, and the United States. This situation is highlighted by a passage quoted in *The Challenge of Hunger*.[8]

One hundred million villagers have never had enough to eat. Investigators will tell you that the Indian people are undernourished. But that has been their condition for ten or twenty generations, since long before there were any investigators. The Indian's bone formation and his very shape have been modified, thinned and made weaker. Hence the disquieting grace of these slim figures with breadth neither of shoulders nor of hips. One would swear that the enormous eyes, admirable in themselves, have eaten up their faces.

Comparison of a typical urban diet in the United States with a typical diet of a rice-eating, working-class family in India shows how widely nutritional standards vary. The Indian consumes 1.23

[7] President's Science Advisory Committee, *Report on the World Food Problem*, May 1967, Vol. 1, pp. 11, 12.
[8] Drogat, Noel, *The Challenge of Hunger*, p. 32. London: Burns & Oates, 1962.

pounds of food a day, the American city dweller 4.66 pounds. Rice, the basis of the Indian diet, represents 85 percent of the daily food. Lacking an adequate supply of proteins, fats, and vitamins, the Indian worker is subject to many diseases due to malnutrition, is lowered in stamina, and has a shorter life expectancy. This condition reduces his energy and ability to work and thus to contribute in full to the economic development of his country. The American diet is remarkable for its diversity and is one of the best balanced in the world. It has resulted in building a strong and healthy people who have achieved the most remarkable economic development in the Western Hemisphere, in spite of the considerable pockets of poverty and hunger within the cities and depressed rural areas of the country.

This comparison points to the effects of hunger and the dearth of protein and other ingredients of a balanced diet on the quality of life of those human beings who do not get enough to eat.

Undernourishment not only has a physical effect on the body, shown in reduction of weight and physical activity, but it also causes behavioral symptoms such as lack of mental alertness and creative thinking, apathy, depression, and irritability—leading in extreme cases to increasing weakening of moral standards and social ties. The evidence of observers in famine conditions bears witness to the accuracy of the last statement.

Undernutrition is also a major cause of inability and lack of inclination to work. When Gandhi blamed the indolence of the Indian peasant for the poverty of his country, he was less than fair to his people, because he did not consider the underlying causes of this apathy. There is no reason to suppose that this is the natural and inevitable trait of people in tropical countries, when in reality it may be due largely to the fact that they are not as well fed and as healthy as people in temperate countries. These considerations also give point to the remark of an Indian to a European: "For us Asiatics the most important thing is not to be free but to eat regularly."

In most underdeveloped countries the inadequacies are not only in the quantity of food, but in its quality—leading to malnutrition as well as to undernutrition. In the developed countries the diet is commonly drawn from a wide variety of sources, and staple cereals and starchy roots do not constitute an abnormally high proportion of the total food intake. The reverse is true of the underdeveloped countries. Whereas the proportion of staple cereals and starchy roots in the North American diet is estimated to be only 25 percent, and in the British diet only 31 percent, in Latin America it is 54 percent, in Africa 66, in the Near East 71, and in the Far East over 73 percent. Conversely, while the proportion of animal products—milk, meat, eggs, and fish—in the typical North American diet reaches the exceptionally high figure of 40 percent and in the British diet can be as high as 27 percent, the figure for Europe as a whole is estimated at 21 percent, for Latin America 17, for Africa 11, for the Near East 9, and for the Far East 5 percent. These differences are reflected in the shortage of protein, and particularly of animal protein, in the diets of the underdeveloped countries. The figures for total protein (expressed in grams per head per day) fall from 92 in North America to 57 in the Far East, and the figures for animal protein fall still more strikingly from 66 in North America to only 7 in the Far East—a tenfold difference.[9] Owing to the lack of variety in the diets of the less-developed countries, and particularly to the shortage of animal products, such diets also tend to lack adequate quantities of vitamins and essential mineral constituents. This, in turn, leads to the incidence of specific deficiency diseases—diseases that are seldom encountered in the more developed countries.

Of these diseases, probably the most widespread in its incidence and the most damaging in its effects is that now known, from its original African name, as Kwashiorkor. This condition is found most frequently in children between weaning and about four to six years of age, that is, during the first few years after the child is transferred from a milk diet to a diet which, in underdeveloped countries, is likely to consist largely of cereals. During this period the protein requirements for growth are high but are not available; at the same time, the child is particularly vulnerable to various infections that themselves tend to precipitate Kwashiorkor. The typical symptoms of the acute condition are edema, wasting, and skin sores, accompanied by liver degeneration; unless promptly treated by the administration of supplementary protein, the child usually dies.

Acute cases of this nature, however, although very prevalent,

[9] Animal protein: Far East, 7 grams per day; Near East, 14 grams per day; Latin America, 24 grams per day; Europe, 38 grams per day; North America, 66 grams per day.

form only a small part of the total problem of protein deficiency in children. Less acute cases are widespread and may result not only in lasting though concealed damage, particularly to the liver, but may also exacerbate the effects of intermittent infections, such as measles or dysentery, with a resulting high mortality rate not found among better-fed populations. Recent studies indicate that Kwashiorkor's relationship with what has for convenience been termed pre-Kwashiorkor is that of an underseas mountain (the underlying condition), of which only the tip of its peak (the disease) protrudes above the surface. The widespread incidence of this condition is shown by the claim that there is probably no African child who has not suffered from such a deficiency at some period of its life, while there is accumulating evidence that the condition is also prevalent in many parts of Central and Latin America and in Asia and the Far East—indeed, in all those areas where food supply data indicate a shortage of animal protein.

Kwashiorkor, and its less acute companion, pre-Kwashiorkor, is by no means the only prevalent deficiency-disease attributable to malnutrition in underdeveloped countries. Avitaminosis A is a frequent cause of deficiency symptoms, notably of blindness associated with keratomalacia. Indeed, in many Eastern countries keratomalacia is stated to be at least as potent as smallpox and venereal diseases in destroying children's sight. Avitaminosis A is still prevalent in certain areas of Africa, Asia, and Latin America. Pellagra is still endemic among peoples subsisting largely on a wheat diet; it is found in areas of Africa and the Near East and, sporadically, in Latin America. Rickets, normally rare in tropical countries, exists nevertheless in Africa, in parts of Asia, and in the Near East. Finally, nutritional anemia, associated with iron deficiency, still constitutes a serious health hazard, especially among expectant mothers and young children, and is the principal factor affecting maternal mortality in a number of underdeveloped countries.[10]

Much of the infant mortality in the developing countries is the direct or indirect result of malnutrition or undernutrition even when children do not actually die of diseases caused by lack of food. In the United States, approximately 25 children out of every 1,000 births fail to survive to the age of one year, and most of the deaths result from prematurity or congenital defects. But in the

[10] British Association, *Hunger—Can It Be Averted?* London: August 1961.

poor countries of Asia, Africa, and Latin America, published infant mortality rates (and these may be higher in reality) range from 100 to nearly 200 per 1,000 live births. Kwashiorkor, as I have mentioned, is a great killer. Acute diarrhea can be a dangerous illness for even a well-nourished American baby; for the malnourished infants of the developing countries it is an appalling cause of mortality. Common childhood diseases are catastrophic in protein-deficient children. In 1960, for example, the fatality rate from ordinary measles was more than a hundred times greater in Chile than in the United States.

Considering these conditions it is not to be wondered at that married couples in developing countries desire a higher number of children than those in the developed nations. Even so, the average number of live births per woman in the developing countries is 30 percent greater than the desired number of children. The desire for heirs leads to large families; also, subsistence farming requires large families to work the holding and to be a safeguard against old age. Only one son may be needed for ritual or economic purposes, but it is common to want two sons to ensure against the death or incapacity of one. Couples must average four children to obtain two sons. It is only when a decrease in infant and child mortality comes about that acceptance of responsible parenthood can be really expected. As the major underlying cause of excessive childhood deaths in the developing nations is lack of nourishment, it follows that an increase in both quantity and quality of food in these countries is essential to achieving reduction of excessive population growth. Far from being a first step, it is possible that extensive family planning will only be really successful when a certain amount of progress has been made in wiping out undernourishment and malnutrition. This will be considered further in a later chapter.

The hunger in the world is not due, as we shall see, to lack of nature's bounty or of man's ingenuity. Agricultural production in the world is keeping pace on the whole with the dizzy rate of growth of population, and in a number of countries food production is rising even faster than population growth. On the other hand, statistics also show that Latin America, the Far East, and the Near East, which contain three fifths of the world's population, dispose of only one third of the world's agricultural production and are hardly keeping pace with the rise in their populations. Indeed, food production in some areas is lagging behind very much and the gap is increasing. Today, in fact, although there is more food in the world than ever before, most men do not eat better. In some cases they are worse off than they were before World War II.

The reason for this state of affairs is partly the fact that food production in most developing countries has not kept pace with population increase. On account of this, while there has indeed been an absolute increase in food production since the war, per capita food production—food productivity—has not risen greatly in the developing countries.

Several years ago, in Latin America, the population was increasing at the rate of 2.7 percent per year, while food production was increasing at the rate of 1.6 percent. Now the gap has been increased by an upward movement of population and a downward movement of food production.

Indeed, without food imports from developed countries, especially from the U.S.A., the plight of some developing countries in the mid-sixties would have been desperate indeed. For example, up to 1967 India had imported as much as 25 percent of its grain requirements. Countries such as Tunisia depend heavily on food imports of a concessionary nature. These facts indicate the imbalance of production and distribution to which reference has already been made.

When details of the United States Food for Peace or Food for Development programs are criticized, it is too often forgotten that the immense amounts of food made available have staved off famine, have lessened the impact of other emergencies involving food (such as wars creating hungry refugees), and at the present time are making, in a number of places, all the difference between moderate sufficiency and actual undernourishment.

If the developing countries were not so poor, this lack of growth of food productivity might not be too important. But these countries do not have the means to pay for large imports of food, except at the cost of other needed imports, as we shall see in more detail later. Moreover, as most of these countries still have, or are only just emerging from, subsistence food economies, agricultural progress is one of their most urgent needs as a basis to promote development in other sectors.

During the first half of the First Development Decade 1960–65, according to the FAO, food production in the developing countries increased by 6.7 percent, whereas population increased by 11.4 percent. In 1965–66, admittedly a bad year, 2 percent less food was grown in the developing countries, while their populations increased by about 45 million.

A report published by the OECD [11] sums up the food situation and refers it to general economic conditions. The report says that although the 1960's have been designated a Decade of Development, in the first seven years of this decade the following phenomena have coincided:

(1) Food production in the developing countries taken together has grown more slowly than the demand.

(2) The area of good new land that could easily be brought under cultivation in developing countries has been sharply reduced.

(3) The population of developing countries has been growing at an increased and unexpected rate.

(4) The surplus stocks of grain in North America have, roughly speaking, been exhausted mainly through exports to less developed areas.

(5) The development aid from the richer countries has, on the whole, not increased.

(6) The debt burden of many developing countries has been rising fast.[12]

Even if recently the trend has been toward greater production, and the area of good new land is higher than the report allows,

[11] Organization for Economic Cooperation and Development, set up under a convention signed in Paris on December 14, 1960, by the member countries of the Organization for European Economic Cooperation and by Canada and the United States. This convention provides that the OECD shall promote policies designed (1) to achieve the highest sustainable economic growth and employment and a rising standard of living in member countries, while maintaining financial stability, and thus to contribute to the development of the world economy; (2) to contribute to sound economic expansion in member as well as nonmember countries in the process of economic development; (3) to contribute to the expansion of world trade on a multilateral, nondiscriminatory basis in accordance with international obligations.

The members of OECD are Austria, Belgium, Canada, Denmark, France, the Federal Republic of Germany, Greece, Iceland, Ireland, Italy, Japan, Luxembourg, the Netherlands, Norway, Portugal, Spain, Sweden, Switzerland, Turkey, the United Kingdom, and the United States.

[12] Secretary-General, OECD, *The Food Problem of Developing Countries*, p. 10. Paris: Jan. 1968.

these factors do constitute a grave situation, a situation that needs to be remedied.

PROSPECTS FOR The President's *Report on the World Food*
THE FUTURE *Problem* covers the period 1965–85. It is
OF THE FOOD rather unrealistic to project beyond that
SITUATION date with regard to the formulation of pol-
icy. New sources of food may then be available due to sciences and techniques still in little more than the embryo stage, and this advance may put a different complexion on the whole problem.

We have seen what the world food situation is at present. During the next fifteen to twenty years the populations of underdeveloped countries can be expected to increase at a rate of 2.5 to 3 percent each year. It is obvious, then, that for the future much more food will be needed even to maintain present inadequate levels of nutrition.

The magnitude of caloric needs related to population increase in the near future may be gauged from Table 2-1 on page 35. The President's report comments on these figures as follows:

If the world population continues to increase at 1965 rates, 52 percent more calories will be required in 1985. This estimate is based on calories actually consumed and does not consider production, losses, quality, and wastage of food. If, as a result of family planning programs during 1965–85, the fertility rate falls by 30 percent, the caloric requirements will still be 43 percent higher by 1985.

These projections of *world* food requirements, however, fail to depict the plight of the developing countries. India, at her present population growth rate, will require 108 percent more calories by 1985; with a 30 percent reduction in fertility, the increased nutritional requirement will be 88 percent more than current needs. The corresponding figures for Pakistan's increased caloric needs in 1985, allowing for the same reduction in fertility, are 146 and 118 percent, and for Brazil 104 and 91 percent. These estimates portray two of the most crucial aspects of the relationship between growth and food needs:

(1) Population and food problems are most severe in the already poor, already diet-deficient countries, where food production is low

TABLE 2-1: Projection of Caloric Requirements for the World, India, Pakistan, Brazil [13]

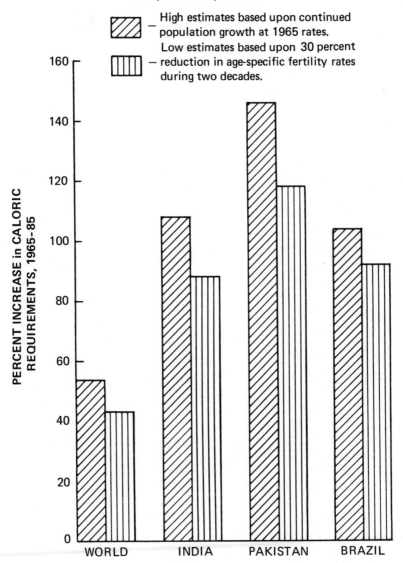

[13] Source: President's Committee, *World Food Problem*, Vol. 1, p. 13.

and population growth rates are high. In these developing nations, under the best of circumstances, food needs will at least double within the next two decades.

(2) The disproportionate additional need for food in the developing countries cannot be solved by successful programs of family planning alone during the next twenty years, although population control measures are inherently as important as increasing food production. The panel's [14] estimates show that the impact of successful family planning is cumulative and makes itself felt in the size of the next generation.

For example, the difference in high and low estimates (5.03 billion and 4.65 billion) for world population in 1985 is only 385 million, the latter figure assuming more successful family planning than at present expected. The difference is greater in later decades and amounts to 1.15 billion in the year 2000 (7.15 billion less 6.0 billion).[15]

According to the President's report, the continued worsening of the population-food situation during the years beyond 1965, which may even reach an economically or ecologically irreversible state of imbalance, makes it imperative to institute extensive programs of family planning now. But the food problem is not in the future; it is here now and must be solved in the next two decades. If it is solved during this time it can be solved for the years thereafter, providing family planning programs have the expected impact.

The panel was unanimous in supporting and urging, in the strongest terms, continuing and increasing emphasis upon research, technical assistance, and capital funding in family planning. "Only by such continuing emphasis and effort can the outpacing of food production by population growth be avoided as a problem that might continue well into the next century. The long lag period that necessarily precedes the main effect of programs of family planning adds to the urgency of the need for action now." [16]

It is perhaps unfortunate that such great emphasis is laid on family-planning projects, however important it is to get these effectively started and operating. In the President's report, the population control measures are given priority. Psychologically, this does

[14] The panel of experts of the President's Scientific Advisory Committee responsible for the report.

[15] Figures slightly different from those given in Chapter 1 of this book, due to slightly different bases of calculation.

[16] President's Committee, *World Food Problem*, Vol. 1, p. 14.

not seem to be a good thing. If food is short, surely the first thing to do is to produce more food. At all events, the old Malthusian proposition, "Birth control or starvation," and the idea that population control acts fast while agricultural improvement takes decades have been abandoned. It is now generally realized by all that to increase food production rapidly is possible, necessary, and urgent, while the significant impact of population regulatory measures will take time. This lag may be possibly not so long as the President's and OECD reports allow for: some experts, on the basis of certain limited successes and growing public interest, feel that rates of fertility may begin to drop within ten years instead of within twenty years after 1965. However, it seems safer to project on a higher rate of population increase than that of 1965, for in the developing countries increase can be expected to continue for some time to come. Kenya, for example, expects its rate of population growth to go higher, possibly touching 4 percent in a few years' time, before it starts to fall.

The simple example of a developing country like the Philippines highlights the problem of hunger. This country, with a population of 33 million increasing at about one million per year, has many advantages: a very good climate, fertile soil, suitable rainfall. It also has a larger number of educated and highly educated people than some developing countries (for example, in Africa), yet until 1968 it hardly produced enough rice for its present number of inhabitants, many of whom live in rural "barrios" or urban slums. Indeed, when I was there in February 1967, the country was importing 350,000 tons of rice. Its population, which has the high density for a developing country of 286 per square mile, is increasing at the rate of 3.4 percent per year. This means there will be double the number of people to feed by 1988. Yields can be more than doubled, especially with new varieties of rice but to do so will require great efforts, especially when political, social, and economic conditions are taken into account. For example, one tenth of one percent of the population owns 40 percent of the land. Supporting services, a precondition of food production for more than an individual farmer's own needs, are poor away from the capital and big towns. In Antique province in the Visayas in the central islands of the Philippines, I came across villages that, because of broken bridges, were virtually cut off, from a trading point of view, for nine months of the year. More intensive fishing with outboard motors along almost the whole coastal strip could be carried on if only adequate bridges existed over which the catch could be taken to market. One village had only twelve kilometers of road between two rapidly flowing rivers. Even in February, at the beginning of the dry season, our jeep crossed one of these rivers with water over its radiator, and the other river had to be forded at considerable risk. There are, or rather have been, bridges on this road, but of inferior workmanship, which are easily swept away. Reconstruction of broken bridges often depends on political vagaries rather than economic need. If there were a good all-season road from San José linking all these villages as far as Iloilo, the situation would be completely transformed. With better fishing catches from power-driven canoes, increased food production made possible by the "miracle" rice developed in Los Baños, and the introduction of fertilizers (water is no problem), the whole area could be made agriculturally self-sufficient and relatively prosperous.

FUTURE PRODUCTION AND FUTURE DEMAND Estimates of future demand and future production of food in the developing countries over the next fifteen or twenty years can be made only with a substantial degree of uncertainty. But such estimates are a necessary starting point for any discussions of policy issues.

In considering these and in considering the means necessary to cope with the near future, if famines are to be avoided, the four basic conclusions of the President's report should be borne in mind:

(1) The scale, severity, and duration of the world food problems are so great that a massive, long-range, innovative effort unprecedented in human history will be required to master them.

(2) The solution of the problems that will exist after about 1985 *demands* that programs of population control be initiated now. For the immediate future the food supply is critical.

(3) Food supply is directly related to agricultural development; agricultural development and overall economic development are in turn critically interdependent in a country lacking an adequate food supply.

(4) A strategy for attacking the world food problems will of necessity involve the entire foreign economic assistance effort of the United States in concert with other developed countries, voluntary organizations, institutions, and international organizations.[17]

The FAO has recently produced an Indicative World Food Plan for Agriculture which estimates that $112 billion would be the cumulative investment needed in agriculture of every type for the period 1963–1985.

The total costs of land and water development for the period 1962—1985 would be about $47 billion, three quarters being for water development. The total annual expenditure required to support crop production inputs would rise from the 1962 figure of $4.7 billion to $17.2 billion by 1985. The total value of certified seeds needed to meet requirements would be $900 million in 1985. The total value of fertilizer applied would rise from $664 million (1962) to $7.8 billion in 1985. To meet the total demand of 26 million nutrient tons of nitrogen and phosphate in the developing countries by 1985 would require an investment of approximately $12 billion.

The findings of the FAO's *Third World Food Survey*, completed in 1963, formulated food supply targets, both short term and long term, taking into account the UN's "medium" assumption of population growth and the need to eliminate undernutrition and provide a modest improvement in the nutritional quality of the diet. The short-term targets for 1980 call for an increase of 55 percent in cereals, 90 percent in pulses (seeds of vegetables such as beans and lentils), 80 percent in fruits and vegetables, 110 percent in animal foods, and 95 percent in fats and oils. The survey also indicated that these increases represent annual compound rates of increase of 3 percent in total food supplies and 3.7 percent in animal food supplies. These rates of increase have not, however, been achieved over comparable periods before, and increased population growth rates since they were computed mean that needs are now even greater.

As regards the long-term targets, that is, for the year 2000, total food supplies of the developing countries would have to be quad-

[17] President's Committee, *World Food Problem*, Vol. 1, p. 14.

rupled and animal food supplies increased fivefold. This would mean higher compound annual rates of increase after 1980, that is, 3.5 percent for total food supplies and 4.8 percent for animal food supplies. These increases are more or less in line with the targets of the Second Development Decade, which aim at an overall increase in the gross national product of the developing countries of 5 percent per year and a consequent yearly increase of 4 percent in food supplies. As I have already stated, this increased rate for food supplies has not been reached so far in any of the developing regions; in fact, the average annual rate of increase in food supplies during the last five years has not exceeded 2.5 percent.

In setting up the short-term food-supply targets, production possibilities were kept in mind, but it is questionable whether the large increases can in fact be achieved over a decade or so. These doubts may be even more justifiable in the case of the more distant targets. Doubts arise because the necessary effort to reach the targets may not be made. The financial resources required may not be forthcoming. A sustained effort to expand production may be lost in a feeling of despair.

Another factor in addition to need must be taken into account in assessing food production requirements. This is effective demand, in other words, what people can afford to buy. In poorer countries when income rises, much of the income is spent on food; this does not happen in the developed countries, where most people have sufficient food already. In a very poor country, demand may still fall short of what people need.

Taking the developing countries as a whole, it has been estimated that if total expenditure per person between 1965 and 1985 rises, the amount spent on food by each person will account for about half this rise.

There is no way of knowing exactly how much this will be. It depends on how rapidly national income rises in relation to population. If developing countries manage an economic growth rate of between 5 and 6 percent per year, between now and 1985, and at the same time have a population growth rate of 2.5 percent, food supplies will need to grow at nearly 4 percent a year to keep the economies of these countries in balance. This means that the total food supply in the less-developed countries must double in the twenty years from 1965 to 1985. This figure refers to economic demand, i.e., the amount that could be paid for out of income, not to nutritional needs, which especially for the poorer might have to be greater and therefore made up in some concessionary form.[18]

WHAT CAN AND MUST BE DONE The present prospects for increasing food production rapidly in the areas of greatest need are better than they *have ever been.* They are still not encouraging enough, however, for some areas do not as yet have all the conditions that brought about the enormous increase in agricultural productivity of the developed countries. The developed regions utilized modern technology, an educated rural population, a concerned government, economic incentives and fertilizer, pesticides, hybrid seed, and other innovations to increase the productivity of the land faster than the growth of population.

The effort to combat food scarcity in the less-developed countries in the next ten to fifteen years will probably still need to rely on imports of food, especially in times of crisis.

FOOD IMPORTS OF DEVELOPING COUNTRIES The inadequate growth of agricultural production in developing countries has not usually resulted in a permanent decline in actual food consumption. This gap between production and consumption has been made up by means of larger imports or, less often, smaller exports of food.

The food imports of the developing countries have approximately doubled in little more than a decade. This has had very serious consequences for their economies, since it has forced them to divert precious foreign exchange from importing the machinery and other capital goods they need for their development and industrial progress. And of the various ingredients needed for economic development, foreign exchange is one of the scarcest.

The foreign exchange resources of the developing countries have been cushioned against the full effect of the rise in their food imports as a result of food aid—that is, shipments of food, mainly cereals, under various special terms, including payment in local currency rather than in foreign exchange. Such aid has in recent years become a major feature of the international scene. The bulk

[18] Pawley, W. H., in speech to the "Pane per il Mondo" conference held in Rome under the auspices of the Vatican and the FAO, March 13, 1968.

of it has come from the vast stocks of cereals that accumulated during the 1950's, largely as a result of the agricultural surplus in North America. Much smaller but significant pioneer efforts to provide food aid on a multilateral basis have also been made jointly by the United Nations and FAO through the World Food Program.[19]

The present situation will necessitate a continuance of the United States' Food for Development program. The United States' food production must be increased, though perhaps it may be reduced in the late seventies or even earlier, if all developing countries manage to achieve a revolution in food production. A substantial contribution from other countries in a position to help will also be necessary. The World Food Program provides an opportunity for those who wish to give food aid on a multilateral basis. However, more technical guidance should be given to the receiving countries in building up port facilities, storage structures, and the entire system of food distribution. It seems probable that the existing Food for Peace program can be doubled within less than ten years if this buildup is preceded by improved distribution facilities in the developing countries.

This program, especially its element of concession (gifts, or loans on easy terms), must be regarded as a short- or middle-term emergency measure. For some developing countries, however, importing food on a commercial basis will always remain more profitable than growing it themselves. There is no reason why every country in the less-developed regions should be entirely self-sufficient agriculturally.

Still, the more fundamental front in the war against hunger is the rapid acceleration of food production in the less-developed regions. This will not be easy, but it may be easier than we think. Examples such as those of Pakistan and Mexico suggest a quicker tempo than the more pessimistic had expected, as we shall see.

Nevertheless, the longer-term problem of feeding the world cannot be solved without a considerable slowing down of population increase. It is, therefore, urgent to have family-planning programs —in keeping with the religious, moral, social, and cultural attitudes of the people concerned—in the developing countries *now*, so that their cumulative effect can make itself felt at least after 1985.

[19] Abercrombie, K. C., "The Present World Food Situation," speech at the "Pane per il Mondo" conference, March 13, 1968.

To recapitulate: In only a few regions of the world are there adequate food supplies. These are the United States and Canada, Australia and New Zealand, Western Europe, parts of Argentina, and parts of Southeast Asia. These regions have already utilized the means of increasing agricultural productivity, but only ten countries in the world today produce more food than they consume.

The food supply for the remaining four fifths of the world in Asia, Africa, Latin America, and the Middle East must be increased and must come primarily from the countries themselves. But this does not necessarily mean an immediate lessening of food aid from developed countries. Indeed, imports may be even more necessary in the near future so as to give the less-developed countries the time they need to increase their agricultural productivity.

Hunger and malnutrition cannot be finally overcome until poverty is overcome. At the same time, agricultural production itself has a major role to play in the economic development on which the gradual elimination of poverty depends. Lagging agricultural production in the developing countries has not only affected their food supplies. Because of the dominant role of agriculture in their economies, it has also had a detrimental effect on their overall development and their industrialization.

Chapter 3

INCREASING THE WORLD FOOD SUPPLY

THE VARIOUS MEANS OF INCREASING THE world's food supply and especially of increasing food production in the developing countries may be listed briefly. They include the following: (1) Increase in the amount of land under cultivation; (2) Improvement in conventional methods of production on land actually in cultivation; (3) Longer-term possibilities and unconventional sources of food; (4) Policies needed especially in the developed countries.

INCREASE IN THE AMOUNT OF LAND IN CULTIVATION

During the years since the war the less-developed countries have increased their food production at a rate of approximately 2.5 percent per year, probably the most rapid growth rate in history. The rise in food production was obtained mainly by bringing new land into cultivation. Yet, partly due to the population increase, the per capita amount of food available did not increase.

Here we must make a clear distinction between food production and food productivity. Food *production* means the absolute amount of food produced. Suppose, for example, a country produces a million tons of rice in one year and the next year produces 1.1 million tons. This is an increase in food *production* of 10 percent. Food *productivity* means the amount of food produced per head of those engaged in food production. Suppose one year a country produces a million tons of rice and the next year produces 1.1 million tons, *without* an increase in acreage of cultivated land or an increase in the number of people engaged in agriculture: this would be an increase in food *productivity* of 10 percent.

Bringing more land under cultivation, i.e., concentrating on more food production rather than on more food productivity, has meant an increase in the food available, and it has been indeed an important means, in the developing countries in recent years, of helping to feed the hungry millions. Where there was a good supply of easily available extra land it has often been the quickest, easiest, and cheapest way of obtaining more food. What are the prospects for the future in this regard?

First of all, it must be said that those who believe that the earth's land resources have nearly all been exploited, that there is no more cultivable land available, are not correct, as may be seen from Table 3-1 on the next page.

This table shows that with known methods and without further capital investment the arable land of the earth could nearly be doubled; with capital investment it could be quadrupled, and with new methods of cultivation already available and considerable capital investment, it could be increased more than sixfold.

Plenty of land could be brought into cultivation, some of it without too great an effort and expense. This is especially the case with regard to Africa and Latin America. Dr. Charles E. Kellogg, a great American authority on soil problems, has demonstrated that if we brought into use only 20 percent of the unused area in the tropical zone we would add over one billion acres, or 40 percent of the total, to the world's cultivable land.[1] It is still disputed whether there is a possibility of cultivating the vast areas of humid tropical forest around the equator in these continents. If more research were undertaken into the problems of tropical agriculture, however, it would seem that tropical food crops (on which little research has so far been expended) could at least approach the success of cash crops such as cocoa and sugar and other tropical products on which a great deal of research has been done so that crop yields have been greatly increased.

Of the potentially arable land in the world, about 850 million acres, or 11 percent of the total, would require irrigation to produce even one crop. In the remaining nearly 7 billion acres, at least one crop could be grown without irrigation, and over a considerable region multiple cropping would be possible. Without irrigation, multiple cropping could increase the gross cropped area (the cultivated area times the number of crops) to 9.8 billion acres annually, about 2 billion acres more than the present total arable land and about three times the presently "cultivated" land. The gross cropped area could be increased by an additional 6.5 billion

[1] Cf. McCormack, A., *People, Space, Food*, p. 118 (London: Sheed & Ward, 1960), in which I go into the question more thoroughly, with references.

TABLE 3-1 [2]

Total land area of earth, excluding Antarctica (in thousands of millions of hectares)	Arable land	Meadows and pas- tureland	Forest areas	Desert areas, unsuit- able land, built-up areas, 1961–1962	Arable land can be increased to the following totals (in thousands of millions of hectares)		
					With existing methods of cultivation and no capital investment	With capital investment	With new methods of cultivation and sub- stantial capital investment
	(In thousands of millions of hectares)						
13.6	1.43	2.58	4.10	5.42	2.67	5.49	9.33

[2] Source: Malin, K. M., *Food Resources of the Earth*, Vol. 3, p. 386, *Proceedings of the World Population Conference.*

acres if irrigation water could be made available for double or triple cropping. The maximum gross cropped area on the earth then would be 16.3 billion acres.

All potentially arable land is also potential grazing land, and all that is not too dry can also be used for economically productive forestry. An additional 28 percent of the land area of the earth has some grazing potential, even though it is not potentially arable. Without high-level technology, however, it is estimated that the total potential annual production of this grazing land is only about 24 million tons of live animal weight per year, a relatively small proportion of present livestock production.

Dr. George Harrar, president of the Rockefeller Foundation, stated in 1968:

I personally haven't the remotest doubt that if we could mobilize our technology, our manpower, our efforts, provide the back-up and accelerators that are necessary, we can gradually "invade" the tropics, convert the better agricultural areas initially to usefulness in the service of mankind either in the production of plant materials or the production of animal materials. It would be no problem, in my judgment, to double or triple world food supplies in terms of the potential which exists. The problem is not in terms of potential. People just haven't really been able to bring together the consortium of effort which is necessary.[3]

The Amazon basin could account for a great increase in the cultivable land of the earth. In Argentina only 20 percent of the cultivable area is cultivated; in Brazil the proportion is only 11 percent and in Colombia only 9 percent. These cultivable areas are well watered and only partially utilized due to bad communications and insufficient population. Uruguay could have its cultivable area vastly extended. Sometimes, in countries like Chile, the fact that marginal and hillside land is being farmed seems to indicate that the limits of the land have been reached, but this is not so. Actually this is more a social and political problem than an agricultural one. In the fertile plains, land is in the hands of large landowners who do not utilize it adequately.

The soil map the FAO is producing will give a much better idea of the land potential of the world. This is already turning out

[3] *On Agriculture, Science, and the Developing World*, p. 7. Ford Foundation, Office of Reports, 320 East 43rd Street, New York.

to be much greater than the pessimistic might imagine. Luis Bromao, responsible for this soil survey in Latin America, maintains that the Mato Grosso and other places in Brazil with highly fertile soil have great potential. In these areas the problem is underpopulation rather than overpopulation. There is only one inhabitant per square kilometer in Mato Grosso, Brazil's largest state, where the soil potential is tremendous. Bromao added that Brazil's population of 80 million (he was speaking in 1965), with relation to its land, is equivalent to France having a population of 5 million people instead of its present 50 million.[4]

There are great possibilities in Africa, assuming adequate research and investment, as Table 3-2 shows.[4a]

TABLE 3-2: Former French Equatorial Africa,
Cameroon, and Togoland, Breakdown
of Land Use

Classification of area	Number of acres
Desert and Wasteland	500,000,000
Shifting Cultivation	175,000,000
Additional Land for Grazing	75,000,000
Not utilized at all	1,150,000,000
Total	1,900,000,000

This is taking only one area. The highland areas of the whole of East and West Africa could produce very much more food than they do at present, and massive investment is not always needed. An example of a small project from my own experience illustrates this. In the Nandi Hills area of Kenya, with the help of $10,000 that I managed to obtain to buy a tractor and attachments, an area of 300 acres of "bush" was cleared, and yields of twenty bags of corn per acre (compared to the local average of four or five bags) were obtained within one year of the money being made available. In this case land reclamation was combined with the introduction of better seeds and fertilizer. I have experience of similar success stories not only in Africa but throughout the world.

It is true that large-scale reclamation often involves large invest-

[4] In a private conversation in Rome, Nov. 1965.
[4a] Source: Zimmerman, A., *Overpopulation,* p. 172. Washington, D.C.: Catholic University, 1957.

ment, and it may well be judged that it is more economic to use other methods of food production. But the fact that opportunities exist for extending the area of cultivation should offset a certain amount of pessimism, especially as concerns the longer term. Perhaps, now that men have landed on the moon, by investing billions of dollars and using a huge reservoir of scientific brainpower, it would not seem too extravagant to turn to the development of some of the earth's possibilities for feeding its peoples; the relative cost would be very much less.

The area of potentially arable land on the earth is much larger than anyone has previously supposed—at least 24 percent of the total ice-free area according to conservative estimates, and very much more according to Malin's optimum estimate—and considerably more than twice the land that has been cultivated at some time during the last few decades. It is more than three times the area actually harvested in any given year. More than half the potentially arable land, over 4 billion acres, lies in the tropics. Thirty percent of the tropical arable land is in the humid tropics; 36 percent in the subhumid tropics, where a season of abundant rainfall alternates with a relatively dry season; and 34 percent in the semi-arid or arid tropics.

Outside the tropics there are large areas of potentially arable land in temperate parts of North America and in Australia.

In contrast to the principal areas of potentially arable land, most of the presently cultivated land is in the cool-temperate zone.

The largest areas of potentially arable land lie in Africa and South America, which, outside the relatively small continents of Europe and Australia, have the smallest cultivated areas.

The potential for increasing net cultivated area is very small in Europe and many parts of Asia and relatively small in the Soviet Union.

In Asia, if we subtract the potentially arable land area in which water is so short that one four-month growing season is impossible, there is no great excess of potentially arable land over that actually cultivated.

In South America and Africa, there is room for optimism about the potential land and water resources. The limiting factors in agricultural development are not natural resources, but economic, institutional, and social problems.

The overcrowded land situation in Asia and the vast areas of potentially arable land in Africa, South America, and Australia would suggest the possibility of very large scale intercontinental migration. In the past there have been very successful examples of Japanese migration to South America. Such migrations could be comparable to those that characterized the nineteenth century. Nowadays there would be immense political difficulties, but the idea is surely worthy of consideration.

Human migrations within different countries will almost certainly be required in the crowded agricultural lands of Asia. There is hardly any scope to use more agricultural labor in these countries. It will be quite difficult to apply modern technology to raise agricultural production without moving large numbers of people off the land into the cities. For this, as well as other reasons, agricultural development must be accompanied by general economic improvement and particularly by large-scale urbanization.

Summing up, we could say that the Amazon and Congo basins together contain nearly a billion acres of potentially arable soils, with an abundant rainfall and little or no dry season. About the same area of potentially arable soils exists in peripheral belts around these basins with a dry season of six months or less. There are sizable acreages of potentially arable uncultivated soils in the humid tropics of Sumatra, on some other Pacific Islands, and in Australia.

Thus, we have close to 2 billion well-watered acres that today are largely unused (except locally for shifting cultivation), with deep friable soils on smooth terrain that would be easy to till. The principal soils in these vast areas are unfortunately low in fertility for crop plants, especially in South America, where fertility is so low that it is not known how to bring them to a sustained high level of productivity. But it seems reasonable to assume that, through research, ways can be found to make the infertile but otherwise favorable tropical soils acceptably productive. It was through research that the infertile sandy soils of Florida and, for that matter, many other soils in the southeastern United States, were made productive. Fifty years ago they were as low in fertility as many of the soils of the humid tropics.

The available evidence, especially from the impressive research in Central Africa, supports the prospect that the humid tropics have a tremendous potential for food production. The Belgians, for example, before suspending their research in the Congo, had developed an oil palm which when properly grown yielded about 4,000 kilograms of palm kernels per hectare, whereas the ordinary palm yielded approximately 500 kilograms per hectare. In the humid Amazon Valley, peppers have been grown successfully by several colonies of Japanese immigrants for at least twenty years. These peppers were grown on soils that are low in fertility by temperate-zone standards. If peppers can be grown successfully, cannot several other crops be grown?

Potentially arable land unused today for crop production is not limited to the tropical and subtropical areas of the world. In the United States and Canada the soils on at least several hundred million unused acres are suitable for cropping, and there are additional millions in southern South America and Australia. Moreover, with breeding of food plants that will mature in shorter and shorter periods, and a persistent search for the best combination of cultural practices, cropping could be pushed farther north than it is today, and many more millions of acres would thereby become potentially arable.

On a worldwide basis, therefore, soils capable, under good management, of producing food are not yet in short supply. They may not be in short supply for a long time. But there is the difficulty that large acreages of such soils are found away from areas where population densities are high. These areas lack the supporting services essential for successful, sustained agriculture.

Even within many Latin American countries, unused potentially arable soils are scarce in some localities while substantial areas of potentially arable soils still remain unused in other regions. But the principal shortage of arable land relative to population size and growth rate is in Asia. Here multiple cropping and increases in yields must be the principal means for increasing food production to meet human needs. This will require irrigation development and improved water management as well as vigorous and sustained application of all other factors of agricultural production. The capital and operative costs will be high, and the required levels of technology and skill will need to be greatly raised.[5]

Table 3-3 is a breakdown of the land available on each continent.

[5] President's Committee, *World Food Problem*, Vol. 3, pp. 407–410.

TABLE 3-3: Present Population and Cultivated Land on Each
Continent, Compared with Potentially Arable Land [6]

Continent	Population in 1965 (millions of persons) (1)	Area in billions of acres			Acres of culti-vated [a] land per person (5)	Ratio of cultivated to poten-tially arable land (%) (6)
		Total (2)	Poten-tially arable (3)	Culti-vated (4)		
Africa	310	7.46	1.81	.39	1.3	22
Asia	1,855	6.76	1.55	1.28	.7	83
Australia and New Zealand	14	2.03	.38	.04	2.9	12
Europe	445	1.18	.43	.38	.9	88
North America	255	5.21	1.15	.59	2.3	51
South America	197	4.33	1.68	.19	1.0	11
U.S.S.R.	234	5.52	.88	.56	2.4	64
Total	3,310	32.49	7.88	3.43	1.0	44

[a] Cultivated area is called by FAO "arable land and land under permanent crops." It includes land under crops, temporary fallow, temporary meadows; land for mowing or pasture; market and kitchen gardens; fruit trees, vines, shrubs, and rubber plantations. Within this definition there is said to be a wide variation among reporting countries. The land actually harvested during any particular year is about one half to two thirds of the total cultivated land.

INCREASING YIELDS ON LAND AT PRESENT UNDER CULTIVATION In the less-developed countries, between 60 and 80 percent of the people derive their livelihood from subsistence farming. This is the type of farming that produces only for the family, including the extended family, or for local needs. Subsistence farming, which is not only a method of agriculture, but also a way of life, is no longer adequate in the modern world. It cannot cope with population pressures or allow agriculture to play the role it must do in the economies of the developing countries. Agriculture must now not only produce food for rapidly increasing populations but must provide a margin for commercial use to start a process of capital formation. The initial impulse to increased economic pro-

[6] *Ibid.*, Vol. 2, p. 434.

duction and improved general welfare must come from the agricultural section.

This means that subsistence agriculture must be modernized, though we need not think of modernization in terms of the American or British pattern. But it must be accepted that a certain basic Westernization must take place if the developing countries are going to feed their peoples. By adopting one aspect of Western civilization—modern medical and public health technology—these countries have already put themselves on the way to a devastating population explosion. It is not possible to adopt Western ways piecemeal and expect unmitigated good to come of it. This does not mean that underdeveloped societies must adopt Western dress or political systems or food or religious practices. It does mean that they must make the transition, within a framework suitable to themselves, to modern means of farming. Essentially, this modernization involves creating the conditions that will make individual farmers wish to produce for markets some distance from their farming areas—and these conditions are increased yields plus the ability to market them.

The cornerstone of economic progress of any nation is the development of its natural resources and manpower. In the United States the great development in agriculture, which has released a very large percentage of the population for industrial work, has been a condition of development. However much one may deprecate urban overcrowding, the reason for the flight to the towns in the United States is a healthy one. People have left, and do leave, farm life precisely because farming has been so highly organized. It has been perfected technologically so that very great production can be achieved with a comparatively small amount of manpower. It will be decades before the developing nations have caught up or even approached this state of affairs. It may be doubted whether they should try to do so in exactly the same pattern as the Western world. Nevertheless they *must* concentrate on agricultural resources as a foundation for building self-sustaining, productive national economies. Whatever psychic satisfactions the old ways bring, they are scarcely defensible if they serve as obstacles to restoring the balance between food and people.[7]

For example, in Latin America—especially South America—

[7] Cf. Revelle, Roger, quoted in "Too Many Born?" by Milton Viorst, *Horizon*, 1968.

there is a fundamental lack of balance between agriculture and the development of cities. South America is a comparatively empty continent apart from these cities. The neglected agricultural sector is exposed to population pressures with which it is unable to cope. Farming is so bad in many agricultural areas, and landholding so inequitable, that people flock to the cities, not, as in the United States, because improved methods have increased agricultural productivity, but because the state of farming is such that it is not able to support them. They feel they have a better chance of livelihood in the cities. The first and most healthy reaction to this situation, in which population is increasing at the rate of 3 percent and food productivity at a much lower rate, if at all, should surely not be to give priority to birth-control campaigns—though I believe they are necessary—but to make urgently needed improvements in agriculture. Considering the low state of agriculture in so many regions, a rate of agricultural increase of 4 percent should be regarded as perfectly normal and feasible and the target to be aimed at, though tremendous efforts will be necessary to achieve it.

Conversely, the growth of the entire national economy will be essential in the future to increase the agricultural productivity. This will depend critically on the farmers' ability to purchase fertilizers, tools, and high-yielding seeds and to provide pest controls and irrigation. To be able to purchase the required materials farmers will need to sell a major portion of their harvest, which means there must be increasingly prosperous customers who can buy farm products. Because farmers in a subsistence economy are so close to the margin of survival, it is a formidable and complex task to persuade them to accept new techniques of modern agriculture. They are understandably wary of assuming new risks; moreover, they often do not have the capital or the available resources to invest in the modern inputs to increase the output of their land.

Food output per acre, rather static throughout most of history, began to increase rapidly in some of the more advanced countries in recent decades. All the increases in food production over the past quarter of a century in North America, Western Europe, and Japan have come from increasing the productivity of land already under cultivation. The area under cultivation has actually declined. For example, in the United States in 1963, 75 percent more corn was produced on 27 percent less cultivated land than in 1938.

Achieving dramatic gains in land productivity requires a massive investment of capital and the widespread adoption of new technology. A similar effort must now be made in the less-developed nations if these nations are to feed their people. The most important single factor influencing this rate of investment is food prices, more particularly the relationship between the price farmers actually receive for their food products and the cost of modern inputs such as fertilizer.

For the developing countries, a similar increase in productivity will also involve better use of the foodstuffs that are produced—through a reduction of waste and spoilage and through better basic services, which will make such increased production feasible and profitable. The main ways of improving food supplies may be listed under the following headings:

(1) Increased output of food crops
    (a) By use of better seeds and improved plant breeding.
    (b) By use of water.
    (c) By use of fertilizer.
    (d) By simple mechanization.
(2) Preventing wastage.
(3) Increased food from livestock.
(4) Conditions for increased food production—agricultural supports.
(5) Increased food from the sea.

The urgent need for this increased food production in the less-developed countries can be judged easily from Table 3-4 on page 56, which shows how the position of the less-developed countries with regard to grain has been reversed over the last twenty years.

Nearly half of man's dietary protein comes from cereal grains, and in the developing countries cereals provide 80 percent of the calories. Obviously any method of providing more cereal or improving the protein quality of cereals will have a direct impact on the nearly 2 billion people who today get their calories and protein mainly from cereal grains.

In addition, food resources could be vastly increased by achieving higher crop yields. The differences between high and low yields in various countries is very great, as shown in Table 3-5 on page 56.

TABLE 3-4 [8]

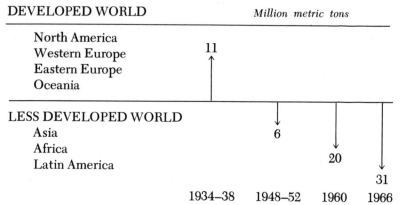

DEVELOPED WORLD   *Million metric tons*

North America
Western Europe   11
Eastern Europe
Oceania

LESS DEVELOPED WORLD
Asia   6
Africa
Latin America   20
                                            31
              1934–38   1948–52   1960   1966

TABLE 3-5 [9]

Yield in centners[a] per hectare

Crop	Average for all capitalist countries	High	Low
Wheat	10.7	42.7 (Denmark)	3.2 (Burma)
Rye	11.1	29.2 (Netherlands)	3.1 (Australia)
Barley	12.9	40.6 (Netherlands)	2.3 (Tunisia)
Oats	12.4	33.3 (Denmark)	4.1 (Portugal)
Rice	18.4	57.4 (Spain)	6.3 (Puerto Rico)

[a]A centner is 50 kilograms.

Higher yields in basic food crops would also allow land to be spared for diversifying the diet through production of milk, fruits, and vegetables. Moreover, higher yields in basic food crops would lower the cost of food while giving a fair profit to the farmer; such yields would thus ease the burden of food costs for the mass of the population who have to spend the greater part of their income in

[8] Source: *Changes in World Grain Stocks*, p. 606. U.S. Dept. of Agriculture.
[9] Source: Malin, K. M., *Proceedings of the World Population Conference*, Vol. 3, p. 386. New York: United Nations, 1967.

trying to satisfy their hunger. It would also give the less-developed countries a better competitive position in the export of processed and manufactured products.

How to achieve this productivity? The means are conventional and well tried, but they need special application to the less-developed countries: better seeds, fertilizer, adequate water supplies, better farm management (including simple mechanization), the use of insecticides and pesticides—and the research, technical assistance, and financial means to implement all these things.

USE OF BETTER SEEDS AND IMPROVED PLANT BREEDING At last there are considerable grounds for hope of a very great increase in food production in the developing countries, due to patient research and experimentation that has led to improved plant breeding. We are on the threshold of a breakthrough, of a "green revolution" of immense potential value to the food supply and general economic development of the developing countries. In recent years, especially the last three or four, new varieties of wheat and rice have been under successful trial, especially in India and Pakistan, but also in many Asian countries from Turkey to the Philippines, as well as in Colombia, Venezuela, Ecuador, Peru, and East and West Africa.

These improved wheat varieties—dwarf, hardy, resistant to "rust" disease—were developed in Mexico. This is a success story, showing what a developing country can do to help itself and other developing countries.

In 1940 Mexican farming was in a bad state. Yields of wheat and corn were low, mainly due to low-yielding, poor seed varieties and losses due to pests, disease, and bad farm management. Mexico was importing one third of its grain requirements. Enlightened government policy, aided by FAO advisers and the work of specialists of the Rockefeller Foundation, begun in 1941, completely changed the agricultural situation. By 1956 Mexico was self-supporting in wheat, and the grain gap was closed by 1958. Today Mexico can grow all the corn it needs on less land than it needed before, even though its population has almost doubled since 1943. One of the main factors was the development and perfecting of a hybrid wheat made possible by the research of American and Mexican agricultural experts, sponsored by the foundation that was institutionalized as the National Institute of Agricultural Research in 1960. The training program of the Institute is one of its most valuable features, and graduates from the Institute have been the main means of making effective use of the new varieties in other countries.

The new rice varieties originally came from Taiwan and, especially IR.8, the so-called miracle rice, were developed in the International Rice Institute at Los Baños about thirty miles from Manila in the Philippines. This center of research was set up by the Rockefeller and Ford foundations in 1961 to serve the rice-bowl area of Southeast Asia. The intense focus on the problems of rice production, in cooperation with experts from Taiwan, Thailand, India, Pakistan, and also Indonesia, Ceylon, and Malaysia, resulted in even more rapid and sensational success than in the case of Mexican wheat. The new varieties of rice yield five to seven times the national average of most countries and are hardier than the old types. Indeed, when I was there in February 1967, I was told that in the ideal conditions of the Institute's testing grounds the new varieties had actually produced 450 bags per hectare per year, as compared to the Philippines' average of 38 bags per hectare per year. These new varieties of wheat and rice have proved themselves in the countries in which they have been tried far more quickly than could have been expected, after trials and adaptation to local conditions. There has been, during this time, a similar improvement in plant breeding with regard to maize, millet, and sorghum. "Taken as a whole, this represents an agricultural revolution comparable with hybrid maize in the U.S.A., where the average yield has been raised from one and a half to over four tons per hectare. It is, however, an agricultural revolution of still greater significance to the world than that of hybrid corn in the United States." This is the considered opinion of Dr. W. H. Pawley, the director of the FAO World Indicative Plan for Agriculture.[10]

Figures from the U.S. Department of Agriculture show the unprecedented rapidity with which the new varieties have spread in relation to the total acreage planted in Asia. Table 3-6 gives figures for the perfected high-yielding varieties of wheat, rice, and to some extent corn-grain and sorghum, for the years from 1964.

[10] Expressed at the "Pane per Il Mondo" conference, Rome, March 13, 1968.

TABLE 3-6

Years	Acres
1964–65	200 (trial demonstration plots)
1965–66	23,000
1966–67	3 million
1967–68	20 million
1968–69	30–40 million (estimated)

This is a phenomenal rate of increase by any standards.[11]

These new varieties are not improved varieties in the traditional sense. They are not just 10 percent or 20 percent better than the old varieties. They are twice as good. This is one reason why their use is multiplying so rapidly. They are also largely independent of seasons, that is, they can be planted at any suitable time of the year. This makes multiple cropping feasible in a way that was not possible before. The result is that individual farmers are not replacing a low-yielding variety with a high-yielding one but are replacing one crop of a low-yielding variety with two crops (or more in some cases) of a high-yielding variety.

Dr. Addeke Boerma, director-general of the FAO, referred to this "green revolution" in a speech in April 1968. He said the world had trembled on the brink of a serious food disaster but "changing human attitudes combined with other developments" now permitted "a cautious optimism for the future." This optimism might not have been justified in 1967, Dr. Boerma said. In fact, one more bad harvest would have meant very serious trouble indeed. World wheat stocks had been stripped to danger level. But in 1968, India was looking forward to a bumper crop and wheat stocks were gradually rising in a healthy trend. The need now was for international policies on the holding of adequate reserves in both exporting and importing countries.

Dr. Boerma also said that new varieties of seeds were transforming traditional subsistence agriculture to the point where the peasant "has suddenly found he can make money and there's no staying him."

[11] Cf. Brown, Lester, U.S. Dept. of Agriculture, in *Congressional Record*, July 19, 1968, p. H5162, to whom I am indebted for some of the material which follows.

One of the most important effects of this revolution in agriculture has been to outdate and even dispel the pessimism about the possibilities of winning the race between food and population—pessimism that until recently had been widespread. A typical example of this unwarranted pessimism is in *Famine—1975:*

One cannot expect hybrid wheats to be widely used until the 1970's and they probably will have only a token impact outside North America by 1975 . . . . All evidence shows there is no possibility that sufficient new technology will be developed through research in time to avert widespread famine.[12]

Today there is no practical alternative to obtaining food by farming the land under cultivation. Nor do we have a practical way to increase production from the land in time to avert the famines and resultant civil unrest of the 70's.[13]

Pakistan was listed in this book, published in 1967, as one of the countries likely to be "hit by mass starvation in five to ten years' time." [14] In actual fact Pakistan hopes, before 1971, not only to be self-supporting with regard to grain but to be able to export. Pakistan in 1968 had a wheat crop, due to new varieties and good weather, that was one third to one half larger than its previous record. And even East Pakistan, much poorer than West Pakistan, is making successful attempts to increase its rice production.

The example of Pakistan illustrates how much the picture has changed in the space of several years.

Ceylon has profited by the new rice varieties to such an extent that there is a veritable boom in the paddy fields. The harvest rose by 20 percent in 1967. The prime minister, Dudley Senanayake, announced in October 1968 that the target for 1969 surpassed the original target fixed for 1970, which planned to make Ceylon 75 percent self-sufficient in rice. And he looked forward to the time when Ceylon would become a rice-exporting country. This result has not been due to the introduction of new rice strains only, but also to a whole series of agricultural reforms carried out by Mr. Senanayake. These reforms, over a number of years, have placed emphasis on domestic production by reclaiming land for paddies

[12] Paddock, William and Paul, *Famine—1975*, p. 78.
[13] *Ibid.*, p. 97.
[14] *Ibid.*, p. 60.

and also by providing price support to the rice growers. Agricultural growth has been part of, indeed the foundation of, general economic progress, in which the wise use of aid has played its part.

India, the epitome of a country with a food problem, in 1968 harvested a wheat crop 30 percent above the previous record. The Philippines, which had a stagnant agriculture for ten or fifteen years, suddenly began to move and in 1968 was self-sufficient in rice for the first time since 1903, in spite of its exploding population.

The agricultural revolution, so difficult to visualize, as it was beginning to take place while people's minds were obsessed by the food crisis in Asia in 1965 and 1966, has affected most countries in Asia to a certain extent, this group of countries (excluding China and Japan) containing about one billion people.

The reasons for this sensational change are many. Undoubtedly the new varieties are the major cause, but their use itself points to other causes. The new varieties need much heavier inputs of fertilizer, more water, and much better farm management, and these imply a greater concern for agriculture than in the past.

Another principal cause has been the importance given to agriculture, itself a result of the realization of the need to combat hunger in view of increasing populations. The Freedom from Hunger Campaign, started in 1960 by the FAO under Director-General B. R. Sen, put greater stress on agriculture in aid programs, for example those of the World Bank and AID, the U.S. Agency for International Development (which must get considerable credit for the Pakistan "miracle"). Above all, the growing realization of the governments of the developing countries themselves of the importance of food production has created the conditions for breakthrough. Agriculture is no longer the Cinderella of government departments.

The new wheat program of India is being directed from the prime minister's office. In 1967 the budget for agriculture was one third greater than in the preceding year. India is now using the equivalent of about one fifth of its foreign exchange earnings to import fertilizer. In the case of Pakistan the amount of fertilizer used up to the end of 1967 was several times the amount used in 1960, and the amount is due to double again before the end of 1970. Fertilizer imports in 1968 in Turkey vied with imports of petroleum, traditionally the leading import product. This gives an idea of the importance that Turkish policy is now giving to agriculture when there is real hope for vastly increased yields through the new varieties of grain, which require far more fertilizer than the older varieties.

All this would not have been possible without aid from abroad —in the case of Pakistan, largely American and World Bank aid. Foreign aid has made possible the construction of dams, highways, farm-to-market roads, and irrigation projects, which are the essential support for rapid agricultural advance. AID and other American agencies have trained more than four thousand agriculturalists from Asia in the past several years. In Asia, indigenous experts, together with the extension officers and technicians who are directing the agricultural revolution, especially in Pakistan, are an important factor.

Another factor has been the attention by governments to the need for adequate price incentives for the farmer. In the past there was a tendency to regard the price to the consumer as all-important and to want to keep it as low as possible, sometimes for political reasons. Although that tendency persists—and within reason it is not a bad tendency to want cheap food for the poor people who need it—there is much more awareness that farmers need a good return for their work and investment in the form of fair prices.

There is, therefore, reason for restrained optimism; there is no room for complacency. Many hard conditions must be fulfilled if the victory is not to be short-lived. What has so far been achieved must spread widely and reach right down to the grassroots level in all the countries that need an agricultural revolution. At the same time as there was great increase in grain supplies in Pakistan in 1968 and 1969, there were famine riots, because the advantages were mainly being absorbed by a comparative few, the richer farmers.

The new varieties require improvements in cultural techniques compared with traditional methods. These have to be demonstrated and adopted by farmers before the best results can be obtained. There are signs that such cultural changes are taking place in a country like Pakistan—which has a strong government, an efficient administrative service, and a high concentration of effort in the agricultural sector—but many developing countries do not have these advantages, and practical problems may be considerable.

A personal experience showed me at first hand how formidable these problems can be. After a visit to Los Baños in February 1967, where I saw different varieties of the "miracle" rice being grown in ideal conditions and had discussions with local experts on the practical problems of getting the seeds accepted by the farmers, I went to the very fertile but economically backward agricultural areas in the center of the Philippines—the province of Antique, on Panay Island in the Visayas group. I traveled along the coastal strip between the South China Sea and the mountains, for about seventy miles, from San José to Pandan. There was a great need for fertilizer, but the people did not have the money to buy it, and borrowing put them in the hands of the moneylenders. It took nearly two years to try to arrange a workable scheme for making fertilizer available to certain local cooperatives, despite prompt financial aid from an English Catholic aid agency (CAFOD). Although "miracle" rice is put at the disposal of the farmers on very good terms, there is a problem of availability and transport, and most of the area is still not using the new hybrid. Even when it is introduced, there will be difficulty in keeping the strain pure unless all the farmers of a given district start to use it together.

Five main things need to be done to consolidate the agricultural revolution and ensure that it spreads.

First, as has already been mentioned, a very great increase in the use of fertilizer and availability of water are needed. Dr. Pawley of the FAO has estimated that in the years immediately ahead India and Pakistan would need to increase their consumption of fertilizer at the fantastic rate of 33 percent per year. Second, insecticides and pesticides must be used on a scale quite beyond that to which farmers have ever been accustomed. Third, there must be a continuing breeding program in order to have new varieties available every few years, with a parallel research effort in other disciplines such as pathology, physiology, and agronomy. Fourth, a major effort is necessary to multiply and distribute the seed of the new varieties and to maintain its purity. Fifth, advisory services must be concentrated on teaching farmers the required techniques. All this will call for a large-scale effort in the organization, staffing, and financing of government services, particularly in respect to programs for plant protection, plant breeding, and seed.

These are the main things that need to be done on the *technical* side to turn the promise of greatly increased food production into reality. These technical programs will have to be accompanied by parallel action in such fields as the provision of credit, advisory services to farmers, and marketing, transportation, and storage. It has been natural to concentrate on food production. But if the production bottleneck is broken, other problems arise. In times of shortage and famine, to produce more food is the obvious goal, but there is the danger that success may bring about a sudden fall in prices, especially if the market side has not been taken care of. The government has, therefore, to plan very carefully to ensure that farmers do not suffer from their success and become disillusioned, as actually happened in the Philippines in 1968, when the government was not able or willing to pay the promised subsidized price for the rice produced in abundance by new methods.

To handle all these problems simultaneously will make great demands on administration, organization, and trained manpower. It will also require heavy investments and substantial expenditure of foreign exchange. In the initial stages of such an agricultural revolution developing countries are likely to need help from the developed countries, although they may no longer need so much help in the form of food. But as I have indicated, even the need for food imports will not disappear overnight: for example, only 20 percent of India's land is at present suitable for the new varieties.[15]

It is for these reasons that the optimism justified by technical success must be tempered with caution until we can see how the difficulties involved in the adoption on a wide scale of the new cereal varieties can be overcome. Perhaps we should put this more positively. If the developing countries wish to be free from the menace of hunger and famine, if they wish to win—at least in the short term—the race between food and population, they *must* adopt, as a matter of top priority, the measures necessary to realize the possibilities of freedom from food-shortage that science has put within their grasp. And the developed countries must seize this opportunity to support them with whatever financial aid and technical assistance is necessary. But the developing countries must do their share. It is in this spirit that the sober words of Dr. Pawley must be taken.

In brief, one may sum up the situation as follows: Asia is ripe for a technological revolution in agriculture and that revolution has commenced. In Africa and Latin America, while there are great oppor-

[15] Pointed out by Dr. Pawley, "Pane per il Mondo" speech.

tunities for improvement in techniques, the political, social, institutional, and ecological problems remain serious hindrances to the modernization of farming methods. Except for the ecology, *these are problems which the people of these regions must solve for themselves.*[16]

These considerations are not intended to minimize the importance of the breakthrough achieved through the new varieties of wheat and rice. I think it would be difficult to overestimate its importance, but by itself it will not bring about an agricultural revolution everywhere. However, the success of countries like Pakistan shows how, when all factors are mobilized by an enlightened and stable government in a country at peace, sensational results can be obtained. There is no doubt we have been given a very powerful weapon in the war against hunger.[17]

THE USE OF WATER   IRRIGATION AND RECLAMATION Not only in Asia, but in all parts of the world, water is the key to increased agricultural production. In the opinion of Professor W. A. Lewis, the factor that would make the greatest single contribution toward increased food output is better control of water.

Irrigation goes back to the third millennium B.C. in Egypt. By the second millennium, in the reign of Rameses II, who died in 1322 B.C., an extensive pattern of reservoirs and canals had been developed. During the time of the Roman Empire an extensive irrigation system, still visible in Roman ruins, made parts of North Africa, now arid, one of the granaries of the empire. A thousand years ago canals crisscrossed from the Tigris to the Euphrates, making what is now modern Iraq a lush wheat-growing country estimated to have supported 20 million people.

The need for rapid progress in irrigation did not occur until the nineteenth century, when the irrigation area in the world increased from 20 million to 100 million acres, largely due to the work of British engineers in India and Egypt. By 1951 the area had doubled; by the mid-sixties estimates showed that more than 420 million acres were under irrigation—China, India, and Pakistan accounting for approximately two thirds of this total.

As has already been said, the high-yielding varieties of cereals

[16] *Ibid.*
[17] *Ibid.*

require much more moisture than their predecessors. Both India and Pakistan are planning extremely heavy investment in irrigation in order to be able to grow these types of wheat and rice on a larger proportion of their land.

By themselves, better seeds, water, and fertilizer are not of very much use. It is the combination that is important. These factors are being treated separately merely for the sake of clarity, not to suggest that they can be utilized in isolation. It is obvious that water has been a vital factor in agricultural progress. The new varieties have merely given it an added importance. The need for more fertilizer has increased the importance of water because additional production through fertilizer is largely dependent on a plentiful water supply. Water can enable arid land, even deserts, to be brought into production, or can increase the yield of food on land that is producing less than its maximum potential.

Even without the reclamation of new land, for example, by clearing jungle or forest, irrigation could vastly increase the area and yield of cultivable land. An FAO report in the late 1950's pointed out that in the basin of the Ganges and Brahmaputra rivers, where there are 130 million people, the cultivated area could be doubled if full use were made of the water that is now allowed to flow away unutilized.

In former times, some of the areas that today are deserts were major sources of grain. There is nothing in principle to prevent history from being reversed. The earth is not like a mine which, when it is worked out, is useless. We have means at our disposal that could make the arid lands and deserts flourish once again. The formerly cultivated lands along the Tigris, the Indus, the Euphrates, even the Sahara itself, could be made to produce food. If in the times of Haroun-al-Raschid, Mesopotamia (namely Iraq) was more fertile than it is today, surely this is an incentive to use our superior modern equipment to make these arid lands flourish again.

It is surely not Utopian to think along these lines. According to scientists who have studied the pictures found on the walls of caves in the deep Sahara, this desert was fertile and well populated as late as 4000 B.C. With water it could be made to flourish again. If oil and minerals make it economic, water is found and made available through deep wells. Similarly, water resources could be made available for agriculture. An artificial oasis was created at Zelfana in the northeast Sahara by means of a well 4,000 feet deep. There is believed to be a vast underground lake stretching from the Atlas Mountains far into the Sahara. One of the most remarkable underground water supplies known is a river 6 miles wide that flows under the Nile in strata 300 to 900 feet down, from Luxor to the Nile delta, for a distance of about 560 miles. A wealthy Egyptian made spectacular use of this river. He acquired a large area of desert for his private use. He bored two wells down to the hidden river and installed powerful pumps. He then plowed manure into the sand of the desert, and also used artificial fertilizer. The result was that around his villa, in the heart of the arid wastes, are green lawns with fountains playing; the orchards and vineyards produce oranges, lemons, and good grapes; he has fields of clover that support a herd of Jersey cows; he gets bumper crops of grain and vegetables.

Lord Ritchie Calder, who some years ago devoted part of his life to the study of making deserts fertile, wrote in the conclusion of the second edition of his book *Men Against the Desert,* in 1958: "In the years between I have become less simple-minded about deserts, but I am still simple-hearted. I do not believe, I *know* that given purposeful men as settlers and given the achievements of modern science, the desert can be made to blossom as the rose." [18]

An interesting possibility is that photographs taken from spaceships may make it possible to locate underground sources of water supply and may save the trouble and expense of boring for water without being sure of getting it.

There is no need to labor the point about making the deserts fertile. In the United States there are golf courses of tournament status and ranches in the middle of desert country. It is clear, then, that there are great possibilities, given the will and know-how, to improve agricultural production through irrigation and reclamation.

DESALINIZATION

In recent years the processes of producing pure water from salt or brackish water—desalinization—have made great progress. When they become a feasible economic proposition there will be opportunity to reclaim much of the world's in-

[18] Calder, Ritchie, *Men Against the Desert,* 2nd ed., p. 202. London: Allen & Unwin, 1958.

sufficiently watered land. Until recently this seemed rather a remote possibility, but now there are plants working in different parts of the world. In any case, this challenge should surely not daunt the scientists of the Space Age. After 1957, when the first *Sputnik* orbited the earth, space science progressed rapidly, culminating in 1969 with man's landing on the moon. Yet twenty years previously space travel had seemed one of the wildest dreams of science fiction, providing material for the more fantastic comic strips. To make the deserts fertile is a very down-to-earth scientific venture, and not nearly so costly as space adventures. Peter Podyashchikh, the Russian delegate to the thirteenth United Nations Population Commission meeting in Geneva in 1967, remarked that the Sahara could be made fertile again by an expenditure equal to the amount spent in one month by the combatants in World War II.

And it is not lack of money or knowhow [19] that is preventing the implementing of the grand plan based on desalinization of water which was proposed in 1967 for the Middle East. This proposal, as formulated by Admiral Lewis Strauss, chairman of the Atomic Energy Commission under President Eisenhower, calls for the creation of a large corporation to build giant nuclear desalinization and power-generating plants on the shore of the Mediterranean and the Gulf of Aqaba. The first of the plants would be designed to produce 450 million gallons of fresh water a day. This would be far larger than anything that has so far been attempted, but it would not present any special difficulty. It represents a simple scaling-up of an existing technology that has already been proved.

The electric power obtained would be used to pump water to desert areas that had never produced food before, and the availability of plentiful power would attract industry to the areas near the plant.

Admiral Strauss claims that the water could be produced for less than 15 cents a gallon. If this is so, it would be economically practical for use in both industry and agriculture in arid countries.

In addition, the Strauss proposal claims advantages more immediate than the eventual production of water and power. The building of the plants, the construction of reservoirs and pipelines, would demand enormous supplies of labor. The Arab refugee pop-

[19] Nor was it lack of money or knowhow that thwarted the famous Lowdermilk plan for the same area nearly a generation ago.

ulation could supply this. And once construction was completed, the workers could be settled on the newly irrigated lands. The cost of the plan would be $200 million. Strauss suggests that the United States should put up half of this (the remainder would be obtained on the world security markets). International agencies, like the World Bank, might also contribute. Obviously such a plan would meet huge political difficulties and would depend on a Middle East settlement. But to a nonpolitical outsider, it seems a better way of coping with the refugee problem than fighting about it— especially when enough money has already been spent on arms to keep every pitiable refugee in luxury for the rest of his life.

Attempts to assess the possible benefits of further conventional irrigation in the world are largely speculative. Since World War II hundreds of million of dollars have been invested in irrigation projects. Some of these have been highly disappointing, if not outright failures, because lands or water were unsuitable. At other times water made available by a big dam or other project was the only factor in agricultural development and there was no attempt to see that the water was made available at grass-roots levels through canals and ditches linked to the main project. We have now learned that each irrigation project, to have a chance of success, must be based on a fairly intensive study of local land and water and should involve careful planning for providing necessary inputs to production besides water.

This also shows that problems of water management and the interaction of water with other factors of production must be given special emphasis. Whenever irrigation removes the moisture ceiling on crop yield, other management practices such as fertilization, liming, use of improved varieties, and insect and disease control, become more critical. Failure to follow through with all required practices can easily offset the advantages of irrigation.

Most major irrigation projects are concerned with only a small part of the total picture. Such projects are normally limited to storage dams, canals, ditches, and in some cases tube wells. Everyone involved in project planning, project authorization, and project operation should recognize the vital necessity of providing adequately not only for water but for all the inputs and processes that are required if an irrigation scheme is to make a major contribution to increased agricultural productivity. Only in this way can the high cost of such projects be really justified.

Training of personnel and providing of organizational capability for planning and implementation of projects within the developing nations are vital. It is likely that these requirements may be more difficult to provide than the capital for construction, but they are not impossible.

While large amounts of investment capital are urgently needed for irrigation projects in the developing countries, the needs for hydrologic and engineering data and for highly trained specialists who can analyze and plan such projects are even more pressing. The training and organization of these specialists should be an important component of technical assistance from developed to developing countries.

It is difficult to give global estimates of land potential through water use, but the following gives some idea of this.

TABLE 3-7: India-Pakistan, Irrigation Potential [20]

WATER AND LAND

	Million acres
Total land area	1,043
Total arable area	480
Land in irrigable classes except V2	314
Land in class V2	141
Ultimate irrigation potential	230
Presently irrigated	90

	Million acre-feet per year
Annual runoff of major rivers	1,233
Present water use	224
Eventual water use	596

The India-Pakistan land area (with a total land mass of 1,043 billion acres) is of special interest, because about one fifth of the world's population lives on it. This land area is subjected to extreme variation in rainfall, ranging from a few inches in the north and west to more than 100 inches in Assam and Bengal and along the west coast of the peninsula. Almost invariably there is both a

[20] Source: President's Committee, *World Food Problem*, Vol. 2, p. 445.

wet and dry season, with from 60 to 95 percent of the precipitation falling during the summer monsoon between June and September.

The five large rivers of the subcontinent—the Brahmaputra, Ganges, Indus, Godavari, and Kistna—produce an estimated 1,233 million acres annually (through runoff).

India reports 337 million acres actually cultivated in 1962–63, with 63.5 million acres irrigated—an increase from 29 million acres in 1895 and 51.5 million acres in 1951. Table 3-7 gives the situation briefly and highlights the potential.

IRRIGATION POTENTIAL IN SOUTHWESTERN ASIA

This region includes Afghanistan, Cyprus, Iran, Iraq, Israel, Jordan, Lebanon, Syria, Turkey, and the Arabian Peninsula, with a total of 1,704 million acres and a population of about 107 million people. Estimates of total "cultivated" and presently irrigated area are available for all the countries except those on the Arabian Peninsula.

There is considerable irrigation in Yemen, probably accounting for at least half that on the Arabian Peninsula. In those countries of the Arabian Peninsula for which there are estimates of irrigation potential, nearly half the total area is cultivated, covering 154 million acres; irrigated lands cover 28 million acres; irrigation potential is 71 million acres. These countries would account for the largest part of the irrigation in the region. Considering that some of the irrigation presently practiced is quite sporadic and that the potential of the Euphrates-Tigris valley is probably less than that planned by Syria, Iran, and Turkey—the three countries concerned—perhaps estimates of 40 million acres and 80 million acres for present and potential irrigation in the region would be reasonable.

IRRIGATION POTENTIAL IN SOUTHEAST ASIA, SOUTH AMERICA, AND AFRICA

The examples cited of India-Pakistan and of Southwest Asia, climatic classifications, and the surface water supply (as indicated by the runoff from large rivers) provide a basis for making rough estimates of the possibilities for irrigation development in other areas. While the estimates of the two case studies may be somewhat optimistic, they do not appear impossible. Israel, for example, has developed an extremely efficient irrigation system and proposes to utilize 95 percent of surface and ground water within the decade.

Irrigation is necessary or desirable in most of India, Pakistan, and southern South America; the same is probably true for most of Southwest Asia, about one fourth of tropical Africa, and only about 2 percent of tropical South America. On a worldwide basis irrigation has been necessary to grow a single crop on about 0.85 billion acres and a gross cropped area of 6.52 billion acres could be obtained by irrigation. Of course, any projection of irrigation potential without detailed survey information is speculative, and estimates should be regarded as gross projections.

GROUND WATER

In general, ground-water reservoirs are integral with the continuous river system and are in dynamic balance with precipitation, evaporation, and drainage to the sea. Even so, the amount in storage is relatively large. The volume of ground water stored at depths of less than half a mile is estimated to be three thousand times as large as that contained in all surface rivers. For example, the vast underground reservoirs of the Sahara have been tapped in places and have proved that the deserts can indeed be made to flourish. An artificial oasis was created at Zelfana in the northeastern Sahara by sinking a well 4,000 feet deep, as described earlier.

Table 3-8, on pages 73 and 74, gives an idea of the water potential in Asia, Africa, and South America.

Ground-water development, as in West Pakistan, may also make extensive electrification feasible also, with consequent additional benefits to agriculture and industry. In West Pakistan the cost of well development and electrification in the area that was formerly Punjab and Bahawalpur was $41 per acre; capital costs of drainage, fertilizer, pest control, and educational facilities raised this to $81 per acre.

It is probable that extensive ground-water supplies exist within those heavily populated areas of the subarid world where surface supplies have already been exploited or where their rapid development is inhibited by the magnitude of the task or by international complications—for example, in the Ganges basin, other Indian subcontinental coastal basins, and in Southeast Asia. *An intensive*

TABLE 3-8: Estimate of Irrigation Potential in Parts of Asia, Africa, and South America [21]

Region	Major river basins and annual runoff (million acre-feet per year)	Arable area (10^6 acres)	Arable area in irrigable climate zones (10^6 acres)	Potential irrigation (10^6 acres)
India (810 million acres)	Indus, Brahmaputra, Ganges, Godaveri, Kistna: 1,233	403	(266) (116)	187
Pakistan (234 million acres)	Indus, Brahmaputra, Ganges: 1,127	86	(48) (25)	43
Southwest Asia (1,704 million acres)	Tigris, Euphrates: 50			80
Continental Southeast Asia (511 million acres)	Irrawaddy, Mekong, Salween: 690	. . .	(102)	25
Brazil (2,102 million acres)	Amazon, San Francisco, Paraná: 2,679	966	10	10
Tropical South America less Brazil (945 million acres)	Orinoco, Magdalena: 549	312	14	10

[21] Source: President's Committee, World Food Problem, Vol. 2, p. 447.

TABLE 3-8 (continued):

Region	Major river basins and annual runoff (million acre-feet per year)	Arable area (10^6 acres)	Arable area in irrigable climate zones (10^6 acres)	Potential irrigation (10^6 acres)
Middle South America (372 million acres)	Paraná: 378	125	24	10
Southern South America (913 million acres)	Paraná, Uruguay, Bueno, Valderia, Bío-Bío, Negro: 574	266	246	125
Tropical Africa (2,359 million acres)	Congo, Niger, Zambesi: 1,520	967	250	150
Total	7,673	3,225	1,101	640

effort should be made to identify potential areas of available ground water, particularly in these areas of the world, and to assess their economic potentials.

Ground-water development should be planned together with development of surface water. The use of underground reservoirs by artificial recharge methods saves the cost of expensive surface reservoir development and avoids evaporation losses.

Development of ground-water reserves *could* provide the quickest, easiest, and least expensive means to improve water supplies and develop food supplies in large areas of the world. Overdraft or "mining" of such water supplies in the earlier stages of comprehensive development can provide the economic impetus on which later, more comprehensive development might be founded, but there must be foreseeable replacement from surface supplies. *Emphasis should be placed on initiating development in those areas,*

*or in nearby heavily populated regions, where ground-water re-
sources are reasonably available.*

A Critical Prototype for Ground-Water Development

Priority consideration should be given to
attempting to implement a critical-size agricultural development
prototype in northern India based on ground water. Recent success
in West Pakistan in utilizing ground water, which can be developed relatively quickly and inexpensively as a means for rapidly
increasing food production, provides the basic guidelines for such
an attempt. The probability of the existence of relatively large
ground-water supplies and the relatively high level of education
and commerce suggest northern India, possibly Uttar Pradesh or
Punjab, as the most favorable spot—probably in the whole world
—to conduct such an effort. Based on the Pakistan experience, the
area chosen should be of the order of one million acres.

Introduction of relatively low-cost power for pumping into the
development area will be essential; hence, one of the important
considerations will be electrification, including availability of fuel
resources or, possibly, nuclear energy. Success would require a definite commitment on the part of both the Indian central government and the particular state. There is a great deal of talent in
India, and foreign technical assistance, while essential, might be
kept relatively low. Based on the Pakistan experiences, capital investment would be of the order of $100 million for the first proto-
type.

Once confidence in the success of such an effort is established,
additional areas could be developed and a fairly large area of
northeast India and possibly East Pakistan might become involved.
Success in the development of agriculture, water resources, and
electrification, and the use of nuclear energy sources, if available,
could generate effort toward a coordinated plan for the development of the surface supplies of the Ganges-Brahmaputra basin before excessive ground-water mining occurs.

Costs of Irrigation Development

Comprehensive cost data from Southwest
Asia is scarce. Two projects in Iraq, not including storage, provided diversion and canal facilities for $127 per acre (Greater Mus-

saib) and $217 per acre (Kirkuk). Recent costs of developing land for sugar-beet production in Iran and Iraq have been reported at $1,230 per acre and $975 per acre respectively. The cost of developing sugar-refining facilities was about $1,000 per acre. For a recent project in Greece, costs, including farm systems, are reported at $362 per acre, and if sprinkling is used, $590 per acre. Annual costs are $38 and $68 per acre respectively. Cost data from modern projects in other similar areas of the world indicates that complete development at costs of less than $400 per acre is unlikely; thus an increase of 40 million irrigated acres would cost about *$16 billion.*

In arid Iraq it appears that about 2.4 percent of the total land area is now irrigated, but this could be raised to nearly 5 percent, about one fourth of which would be supplied by the Tigris and Euphrates if their flows were utilized to the maximum possible extent.

India reports that the 19 million acres placed under irrigation under the three Five Year Plans beginning in 1951–52 cost 13,100 million rupees ($146 per acre). The estimated cost of irrigating 13.8 million acres now planned is 5,800 million rupees ($89 per acre). In 1956 costs for the 2-million acre Nagajunasagar project were estimated at $151 per acre net. Costs for the Rajasthan project are estimated by the Central Water and Power Commission at $134 per acre net. These costs include only reservoirs and distribution canals. Costs for well development and electrification were estimated at $41 per acre in former Punjab and Bahawalpur, West Pakistan. Capital costs for fertilizer, drainage, and pest control, as well as education, research, and management, raised these to $81 per acre; comparable costs were $100 per acre to $110 per acre in the Sind. The estimated cost of coastal flood protection works in East Pakistan is given by AID sources as $84 per acre for a 2.4 million acre project.

Including lateral distribution works and other investments, costs in India may well exceed $250 per acre for irrigation development. In many areas of the world costs are commonly higher than this, but the Indian projects are large in size. Assuming $250 to $300 per acre, the capital investment costs for additional irrigation on the subcontinent would be $35 to $40 billion.

On the Indian subcontinent 47 percent of the land is classified as arable, and 22 percent as potentially irrigable. At present 8.5 percent is irrigated. Present water use is about 18 percent of major river flow, and this would be increased eventually to 48 percent.

The value of wells can be judged from what happened in Bihar and in West Pakistan. The state of Bihar in India was one of the hardest hit of the famine areas of 1965 and 1966 (bad harvest years caused by drought). One result of the famine was an intensive well-drilling campaign. In Bihar hundreds of wells have been installed since 1966; in Pakistan 6,000 to 8,000 tube wells have been installed in recent years.

The record crops of India and Pakistan in 1967 were due not only to favorable weather conditions, but to measures taken as a result of the shock that the famine conditions of 1965–66 (mercifully alleviated by imported food) caused.

The cost of irrigation and water management is high, especially on a large scale. The example of well-drilling in Bihar shows how small schemes, which are relatively inexpensive, can help very considerably—but big schemes are vital where genuinely necessary. The largest project in recent years has been the Indus basin scheme in West Pakistan. It began in 1960 and includes the Mangla Dam—one of the largest earth dams in the world—six barrages, and nearly 400 miles of large canals, with a total value of about $1 billion. Three of these canals will each carry ten times as much as the average flow of the Thames.

The work is ahead of schedule; two thirds has already been commissioned and the remainder is due for completion in 1970. In a further stage the contract for another dam, at Tarbela, on the Indus River, has just been awarded at an estimated value of $450 million.

The scheme is the result of the 1960 Indus Water Treaty between India and Pakistan, by which the waters of the three eastern rivers—Ravi, Beas, and Sutlej, tributaries of the Indus—were allocated to India, which will be able to use them for increased irrigation. The waters of the three western rivers—Indus, Jhelum, and Chenab—are for the use of Pakistan, the boundary having been drawn across the Indus system when the two countries were partitioned in 1947.

British engineers have been responsible for the design of a large part of these Indus works, as well as the overall supervision of the scheme on behalf of the World Bank. In addition, the design and supervision of irrigation schemes in twelve other countries is under the direction of British consulting engineers and accounts for about one fifth of the total volume of their overseas work.

It has been estimated that by the year 2000 the acreage of land under irrigation to meet the needs of the world population should be increased by 80 percent. This is a vast undertaking, but perfectly possible if the potential indicated is utilized.

THE USE OF FERTILIZERS Where adequate water is available the best return on investment and efforts for food production, as has been continually stressed, comes through the better farming methods that include better seeds and fertilizer. Fertilizer accounts for most of the capital costs, apart from water, needed to improve crop production; the capital investment in new varieties of seeds is reckoned at only about $300 million compared to the $17 billion which is the total required by 1985 for manufacturing and distribution of fertilizer. The need to increase the use of plant nutrition can be shown from the figures of such use for the years 1966 and 1967. Out of a world total of almost 30 million tons of plant nutrients applied as fertilizers nearly 27 million tons were used in industrial countries and only 3 million tons in developing areas. Until fairly recently, due to some bad mistakes, such as applying fertilizer at the wrong time and without proper soil surveys to rice, crops were spoiled instead of being improved, and there was, in some quarters, a rather skeptical attitude to the use of fertilizer in tropical and semitropical lands, especially those with high rainfall. However, as a result of many thousands of fertilizer trials carried out in developing areas, man's knowledge has increased immeasurably, and with it the possibility that now even farmers only just emerging from the subsistence level can "plough with hope." [22-23]

There is no reason in principle, though obviously there will be many differences in practice, why fertilizers in the developing countries, in the second half of the century, cannot fulfill the same role as they did in the food revolution of the developed countries in the first half of the century.

Estimates by the United States Department of Agriculture indi-

[22-23] The title of a book by Donald Faris written in 1958, which even then proposed a moderately optimistic view, although the advantages we now have were barely thought of.

cate that 35 to 40 percent of the increased agricultural production in the country during recent years is directly attributable to increased use of fertilizer. In developing countries, where soils are less fertile, the use of fertilizers is even more important, since food production can be increased very little without them. However, fertilizers alone, without use of improved crop varieties, insect and plant disease control, and other improved cultural practices, can

FIGURE 3-9 [24]

Yield-Value Index vs. Fertilizer Use — 1961-63

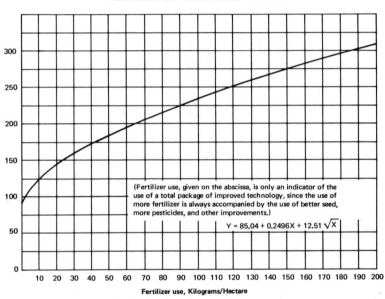

(Fertilizer use, given on the abscissa, is only an indicator of the use of a total package of improved technology, since the use of more fertilizer is always accompanied by the use of better seed, more pesticides, and other improvements.)

$$Y = 85.04 + 0.2496X + 12.51 \sqrt{X}$$

Fertilizer use, Kilograms/Hectare

have only minimal effect in increasing production. An FAO graph based on figures from forty-one developed and developing countries (Figure 3-9) shows the effect of fertilizer on yields. The technical equation is complicated and need not concern us but the general picture is very clear. Using more fertilizer increased yields remarkably, so much so that the maximum input resulted in a threefold crop increase, i.e., three times more food was available.

World fertilizer consumption (excluding mainland China) during the fiscal year 1965–66 was estimated to be about 17.6 million met-

[24] Source: President's Committee, *World Food Problem*, Vol. 3, p. 97.

ric tons of nitrogen, 14.5 million metric tons of soluble phosphate (P_2O_5), and 12.1 million metric tons of potash (K_2O). Eighty-six percent of the world's consumption is in the more developed countries, containing 39 percent of the world's total population, and only 14 percent is in the less developed areas that contain 61 percent of the population. Paradoxically the least use is in those countries suffering most from the population explosion and food deficits.

TABLE 3-10: Additional Requirements of Developing Nations for Required Increase in Plant Nutrient Use [25]

Year	Additional plant nutrient requirements (in tons)	Capital needed (billion $)	Additional farmer credit (billion $)	Additional skilled personnel (thousands)
1970	5,000	2.5	1.20	15
1975	13,000	6.5	2.10	39
1980	22,000	11.0	3.10	66
1985	34,000	17.0	4.40	102

In fertilizer production the lack of balance is even greater, since the world's production of fertilizer is still mainly in the industrialized nations. For example, about one third of the current capacity for fertilizer production is in the United States. Although the excess capacity of the developed countries can be used to provide fertilizers for the developing countries, these countries usually prefer to build their own plants and to import only the essential raw materials. If fertilizers are imported, they represent a heavy drain upon the limited funds available for foreign exchange.

The overall needs for additional fertilizer by the developing nations to avert famine and feed rapidly increasing populations are quite vast. Even a cursory glance at the projections of the experts of needs and capital shows up the very large quantities and capital requirements for facilities to produce this fertilizer. In projecting the fertilizer needs, it is assumed that increased fertilizer will be accompanied by increased use of other key inputs such as improved seeds, pesticides, machinery, and other cultural practices. Estimates are also made of the credit and skilled manpower re-

[25] Source: President's Committee, *World Food Problem*, Vol. 3, p. 115.

quirements, and the adequacy of basic raw materials needed to produce the fertilizers is evaluated.

It must not be forgotten that the production and distribution of fertilizer needs skilled personnel. Extension officers with simple soil-testing kits for advising farmers are also essential.

Table 3-10 gives a summary of the size of the problem with regard to supplies and costs.

Projections for future use of fertilizer probably need to be considerably increased in view of the greater use of the new varieties. These projections were made without complete realization of the possibilities of the extensive success and spread of the new varieties of seeds.

SIMPLE MECHANIZATION Power has played a large part in the agricultural revolution of the developed countries. Mechanization adapted to the needs and circumstances of developing countries can do the same for

TABLE 3-11: Power Available for
Agricultural Field Production 1964–65
(Arable Land and Land Under Permanent Crops) [26]

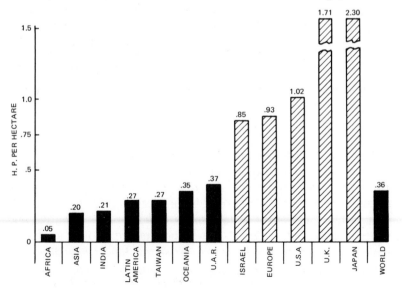

[26] Source: *World Food Problem*, Vol. 3, Fig. 1, p. 177.

them. Tables 3-11 and 3-12 give in clear contrast the positions of developed and developing countries.

Improved methods of plowing involving the use of small tractors, leveling equipment, and other innovations can have a very significant impact. In the part of the Philippines to which I have earlier referred, very slow water bullocks till the paddy fields to

TABLE 3-12: Available Horsepower per Hectare of Arable Land and Land Under Permanent Crops [27]

	Africa	Asia	India	Latin America	Taiwan	Oceania
Tractor [a]	.03	.02	.008	.18	.080	.33
Garden tractor [b]	—	.03	—	—	.063	.006
Animal	.01	.10	.145	.07	.063	.011
Human	.01	.05	.056	.02	.113	.001
Total	.05	.20	.21	.27	.27	.35

	U.A.R.	Israel	Europe	U.S.A.	U.K.	Japan	World
Tractor [a]	.181	.815	.81	1.0	1.57	.004	.266
Garden tractor [b]	—	.007	.02	.014	.03	2.060	.024
Animal	.065	.010	.08	—	.02	.088	.044
Human	.12	.016	.02	.002	.09	.148	.024
Total	.37	.85	.93	1.02	1.71	2.30	.36

[a] Defined by FAO as wheel and crawler tractors developing over 8 H.P. and used in agriculture.

[b] Defined by FAO as tractors developing under 8 H.P. and/or weighing under 850 kgs. and used in agriculture.

prepare the soil for rice but often enough they do not complete the work in time, even for quite small holdings. The use of simple steel plows and other farm machinery that is obsolete for more sophisticated farmers in the West could be of great assistance. Simple hydraulic rams and small water pumps could replace primitive and wasteful means of irrigation. Small tractors can also be used, as I have noted with regard to Kenya, for simple land reclamation and

[27] Source: World Food Problem, Vol. 3, Table I, p. 178; calculations based largely on values taken from FAO, 1965 Production Yearbook.

clearing of the "bush." Such unsophisticated means fit in well with the idea of using plentiful available labor, i.e., labor-intensive farming, in the spirit of what has been called the intermediate technology approach.

The use of more power than that supplied by man alone or by oxen and bullocks is a further weapon in the subsistence farmers' armory for change and greater production. Even without the use of tractors and mechanical tillers, animal power can be greatly enhanced by better mechanical aids such as a modern seed drill with fertilizer drawn by animals; this is estimated to increase yields by 12.5 percent and reduce the hours for seeding by 40 percent. The use of tractors and such vehicles has to be supported by a good servicing and repair network. There may be uses for more elaborate machinery in certain areas. For example, in India, under the Colombo Plan, tens of millions of acres of land were made suitable for cultivation by heavy machinery that destroyed deep-seated weeds. In addition, a certain type of combine harvester is very useful for rice harvesting. But there is, on the whole, no opportunity, nor is it desirable, to use heavy machinery of the type made familiar by mechanized farming in the U.S.A. or Canada, because the terrain in developing countries is often not suitable and labor-intensive schemes are more practical when labor supply is plentiful and capital is scarce. A secondhand obsolete European or American drill would generally be of much more use than a new combine harvester.

I have laid emphasis on the simple forms of power and mechanization because there has been, in the past, a tendency to push Western technology that on the whole is far too sophisticated for countries in the intermediate stage.

More and more it is coming to be realized that an intermediate technology is needed for the developing countries. This would be a technology adapted to the actual situations of countries at various stages in their emergence, rather than a wholesale imitation of the highly sophisticated technology of the West with its capital-intensive, huge developments.

This does not mean a second-rate or secondhand technology. The true point is that these countries need to select, from the entire world reservoir of scientific and technological ideas, including the very latest, those best suited to their structures, resources, and needs, especially their abundance of manpower.

This intermediate technology will also give the possibility for even the poorest to participate in their own development. For what is needed in the developing countries is not only food production and economic progress but the development of the whole man—the human dignity that comes from true involvement in one's own development. These ideas and the philosophy behind them have been developed by the Intermediate Technology Group, which began in England but is spreading in the developed and developing world and may well be one of the most significant developments in the United Nations Second Development Decade (1971–81).[28]

To sum up, more machinery is badly needed—not as a labor-saving device but to increase productivity. At the present time, machine power available to the farmers of Asia, Africa, and Latin America averages only a fraction of the more than one horsepower per hectare utilized by the farmers of Europe and the United States. This lack of power makes it difficult to prepare seedbeds efficiently and in time, and to place seed and fertilizer accurately, both of which can contribute markedly to improved yields and to the economical utilization of these inputs. Although there are one or two exceptions, an analysis of yields in various countries indicates that a power level approaching 0.5 horsepower per hectare is needed for an efficient agriculture. It is estimated that $500 million will need to be invested by the end of this century in plants for the production of farm machinery in the developing countries. The total capital investment, including components that can best be imported, will approximate $2 billion.

PREVENTING WASTAGE So far, we have been considering the production of more food. But much of the food that is actually produced at present does not find its way into the mouths of the hungry. Human beings have to compete with pests for their food. Rats, insects, and other pests ravage food crops that could feed millions of people. Statistics show what a serious drain on food production they are. Even in the United States, with good modern storage, it is reckoned that about 7 million metric tons of grain yearly are lost in storage due to rats, while insects account for 8 to 16 million tons per year. Throughout

[28] The Intermediate Technology Group, 9 King Street, London, W.C. 2, has further information and literature.

the world, the FAO estimates that 33 million tons of essential food-stuffs are lost yearly from these causes. That is enough to feed the whole of the United States for a year. Or, on a world scale, "one out of fourteen persons in the world is liable to die of starvation for the lack of the food which these pests eat." [29] *On a world scale, field pests consume at least eight times as much food as would be necessary to provide rations for an annual increase in world population of 70 million.*

It is clear, then, that one of the greatest enemies of increased food supply in the developing countries is the depredations by pests of both growing and stored crops. Pesticides to destroy insects, fungi, and weeds, as well as rats, mice, and other small rodents responsible for crop losses must be used in much greater quantities. At present only 120,000 metric tons are used in the developing world, excluding mainland China.

If food production is to be doubled, 700,000 metric tons of pesticides will be required. To provide this quantity of pesticides will require a total of $1.2 billion in capital for manufacturing plants and $670 million for formulation and distribution facilities by 1985. Most pesticides should be manufactured in the developed nations where skilled manpower, utilities, and raw materials are easily available, but trade and monetary restrictions and excessive nationalism may be limiting factors.

Better storage facilities and marketing facilities for harvested grain are also needed. In India, for example, remarkable crop savings have resulted from vastly improved storage of crops in prefabricated aluminum bins set in a masonry base. At present food storage often consists of nothing more protective than piling the crop on the ground with matting thrown over it. Half the crop can be lost in this way to insects and rodents. The humidity of the tropics can take an enormous toll of badly stored food.[30]

INCREASED FOOD FROM LIVESTOCK One of the problems of the world food situation is to increase supplies of protein to prevent the hidden hunger of malnutrition. Foods of animal origin supply not only

[29] Calder, Ritchie, *Common Sense About a Starving World*, p. 136. London: Victor Gollancz, Ltd., 1962.
[30] Cf. Llewellyn, B., *The Poor World*, p. 122. London: Zenith Books, 1961.

protein and vitamins but fat and minerals also. The FAO has shown that there is no real shortage of animal protein in the world as a whole. However, supplies in the developing countries amount to only 9 grams per person a day as compared to 44 grams a day in developed countries. Short-term FAO targets for the developing countries aim at 15 grams, and long-term targets are 21 grams.

TABLE 3-13 [31]

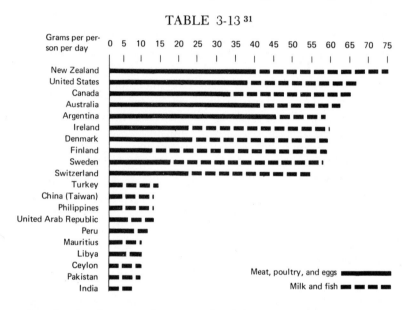

Land animals can make a considerable contribution to the world food supply, although they sometimes eat or destroy food that people would otherwise eat. Livestock, however, can live on substances that cannot be eaten by man, such as forage crops, garbage, byproducts of food processing, and even chemicals.

According to FAO data, world production of milk, eggs, and meat increased during the decade 1953 to 1963, particularly in the developing countries, where with few exceptions this increase was as rapid as the increase in population.

However, although 60 percent of the world's 6 billion livestock and 6 billion domesticated fowls are raised in the developing countries, these regions produce less than 30 percent of the world's meat, milk, and eggs. One example of the difference in productivity is that nearly 200 million cows in India yield only 750 lbs. of milk per cow on the average per year. In the U.S.A. the average yield is 5,000 lbs. for ordinary dairy farmers and 8,000 for those who belong to dairy herd improvement associations. This low productivity of the developing countries is largely due to failure to utilize scientific principles of disease control and animal husbandry.

There is a great need in the developing countries for disease and animal pest control. According to the FAO, a 50 percent reduction of losses from animal diseases in the developing countries, which is a realistic goal, would result in a 25 percent increase in available protein. Prospects for controlling most of the major livestock diseases are very good, provided agriculturists and political leaders decide to invest the necessary effort and money.

Better feeding and livestock management could also improve production of animal protein. Substantial proportions of the agricultural land of Asia, Africa, and Latin America are grazing lands. The productivity of these lands would be increased enormously by the use of improved techniques of pasture and range management. On a recent tour of Uganda I saw the possibilities of a well-managed ranching scheme in the Masaka-Fort Portal area near the Congo border, and I was able to discuss this with the vice-president of Uganda, Mr. Babiiha. Significantly, he had chosen the Veterinary Department as his own ministry and was vigorously pursuing the scheme with the help of a grant from England of one million pounds and a highly trained staff, which had been built up over the thirty-year period that he himself had been connected with the department as a trained veterinary officer.

The improvement in breeding of pigs and hens can be on quite a small basis. I remember seeing the work of a missionary among the land Dyaks in eastern Malaysia, about thirty miles from Kuching, who had a very successful poultry and pig scheme. He provided eggs and better breeds of pigs and hens for the local "kampongs" and was also training local boys in better methods of small-livestock management. He was on the way to bringing about a small revolution in the area the mission served.

The possibilities, then, for future increase of animal protein production in Latin America, Africa, the Near East, and Southeast Asia are very good. The problem is more complex in India and

Pakistan, but even in these countries substantial increases are possible. The development of animal programs in developing countries could be accelerated considerably if this objective were given priority in planning.[32]

Wild animals could probably make a considerable contribution to food supplies, especially in Africa, which is richly endowed with wild-animal species. They contribute to human diets at present and offer a great potential for the future. Under certain natural conditions the wild animals produce more meat than livestock species. More research is needed in this field. More attempts to domesticate new species that are better adapted to tropical conditions than existing species of livestock should also be made. Such animals include wild game such as zebra, wildebeest, impala, and others. Some of these, notably the eland, can even be domesticated, and—as Ritchie Calder said at the Massachusetts Institute of Technology symposium on "The Future of Life Sciences in 1965"—"the hippopotamus is a large hunk of edible pork." Game ranching has already been started in Southern Rhodesia, South Africa, and eastern and western Africa.

CONDITIONS FOR INCREASED FOOD PRODUCTION

AGRICULTURAL SUPPORTS

With the consideration of the problem of farming credit and other conditions of successful agricultural change, we come to the much wider question of the external conditions in which food production can increase and agricultural progress be made. Agriculture cannot prosper in a vacuum. A whole range of supports from the general conditions and the policy of a country is needed. In fact, food supply, agriculture, and general economic development are and must be closely interrelated. In other words, if the world's supply of food is to increase there must be general economic progress in the developing nations and not just a change in farming itself. Many types of investment throughout each national economy are required to create the demand for food and to make possible the production of inputs essential to farming.

As the President's report says:

[32] President's Committee, *World Food Problem*, Vol. 1, p. 90.

Stated differently, current justifiable concern about food supplies does not constitute a crisis that should cause us to put general economic, social, and political development aside to make way for a crash food production program. The need for more food should cause a re-examination of programs for general economic development, in order that both the magnitude and the characteristics of policies and programs be consistent with food needs arising from current malnutrition and rapidly increasing numbers of people to be fed. The discussion to follow examines the nature of inter-relationships between food supplies, agriculture, and economic development.[33]

The world needs more food, but increased supplies will only be forthcoming, even in the developing countries themselves, in response to an increased demand for food by those who have the money to buy it. It is true that for humanitarian reasons food aid may be made available to those who need it but have not the means to create an economic demand for it. But this is not the point here. The point I am making is that farming, in developed and developing countries, is a business, not a charitable enterprise —a business whose role includes the production of food and which involves costs that someone has to pay. Either the prices paid for farm products by consumers must be high enough to make it profitable for farmers to increase production or some third party must pay these costs.

One of the most difficult problems encountered in meeting the world's needs for more food arises from the fact that in most of the countries where this need is most urgent a high percentage of the labor force is engaged in farming. This situation is likely to change slowly, even where the most strenuous efforts are made to industrialize and to increase off-farm employment opportunities. Yet it is off-farm employment, either domestic or foreign, that creates the extra market for farm products.

A second important dimension of the problem of increasing the world's supply of food is the necessity of capital investments of almost staggering proportions. Some of these investments are needed on farms. Even more are needed elsewhere in each sector of the economy, partly to make greater agricultural production possible and partly to increase nonagricultural production. The latter is important because the people of each country want products in addition to food and because the increased economic demand for food created by nonagricultural production calls for more farm production.

These investments are needed on a continuing basis, year after year. Thus, part of the task of increasing food production is management of each total economy in such a way that investments are kept at the highest possible level and allocated most advantageously among the various sectors of the economy.

For the reasons given above, overall economic development in each country is essential to increasing the world's supply of food. The demand generated by total economic development, if appropriate measures are taken, may call forth increased domestic food production from regions within the countries that have substantial agricultural potential. If a country does not have such agricultural potential, the demand for food generated by its economic development will stimulate production in other countries and its income from nonfarm production can pay for food imports.

Food production is not a separate industry but an integral part of an agriculture that produces other materials also. In many instances the most profitable combination of enterprises for a single farm business is one that produces both food and nonfood products. In other circumstances the production of food and the production of industrial raw materials such as fibers, rubber, or oils must compete for the use of the same land resources.

Two points deserve emphasis here. First, that stimulating greater food production must take the form of stimulating general agricultural development because of the complementary relationships between food and nonfood products on each of many farms. Second, increasing the farm production of nonfood products frequently plays an important role in general economic development. Under such circumstances, it is often a mistake to force a shift to food crops.[34]

It is not possible here to go into too much detail about marketing and transport facilities, and to single out one particular factor might give it undue emphasis. Nevertheless, the importance of the infrastructure of roads, bridges, railways, and marketing and transport facilities needs to be given due weight because often these things are neglected and it is often difficult to get either govern-

[34] *Ibid.*, Vol. 1, pp. 59–60.

ment or private finance for them. It is little use getting the farmer to produce beyond his own needs if he has to carry the extra grain on his head or by some other primitive means over bad or virtually nonexistent roads. I have already illustrated that from the Philippines. In Antique, on the coast road—quite a good road—it was

FIGURE 3-14: Major Factors in Agricultural Production [35]

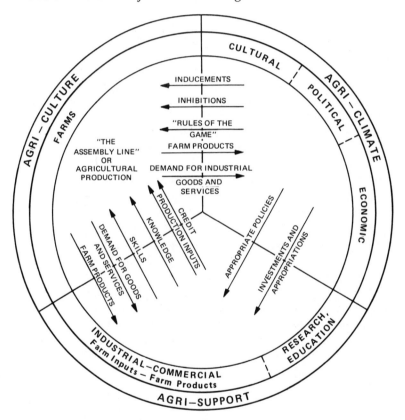

hardly any use encouraging the people beyond twenty miles from the capital, San José, to grow more food, because for nine months of the year it was almost impossible to transport it. Here is an example of positive disincentive to produce more food. It is no wonder that the people there are desperately poor.

[35] *Ibid.*, Vol. 3, p. 61.

The President's report has a summary of the whole complex of
elements required if agriculture is to play its true part. It puts
them under three headings: (1) Agri-*culture;* (2) Agri-*support;* (3)
Agri-*climate.* The terms are almost self-explanatory, but what they
comprise in detail may be seen in Figure 3-14.

It is not possible to go into all the conditions of improving farming. One of the most important, however, is the provision of farm
credits.

FARM CREDIT

It is estimated that the annual cost to farm-
ers of improved inputs such as fertilizers, seeds, pesticides, and
machinery will amount to approximately $4 billion by 1985. This
is a huge amount; however, immediate annual needs are at present but a fraction of this, and if agriculture continues to improve
and general economic progress in the developing countries keeps
pace, this need not be an impossible figure, especially if aid from
the developed countries is adequate from 1970 to 1985.

However, it is obvious that it will be necessary to provide for
farm credit on a scale many times greater than it is today.

All these inputs are well beyond the financial means of the average farmer in developing countries, and yet they are the essential
conditions for significant change in agriculture. The poor farmer
has, in addition to a low income that necessitates a system of farming credit, very little margin for speculation. He must be encouraged by the assurance of compensation for possible loss incurred in
the process of change. Above all, he must be shown concretely that
the potential gain is worth the real risks. Land tenure systems,
therefore, must be altered so that the benefit of the changes will
come to the farmer rather than to the landlord. Government pricing policies should not favor the industrial worker at the expense
of the farm producer, although there is often a great political temptation to do so; even in some developed countries this has been the
great bane of farming. It is estimated, for example, that if proper
farming returns were assured even to the British farmer, possibly
£200 million of the foreign exchange used in importing food could
be saved.

In the developing countries farmers need greater incentives to
use new materials, including better prices for their products, as a

means to more inputs. For example, a bushel of rice will pay for four times as much fertilizer in the United States as it will in Egypt, and more than twice as much as it will in Thailand or in India. The Mexican government has arranged a good pricing policy for agricultural products. This is a major reason for the growing promise of the Mexican agricultural development program.

To induce farmers to change, the potential prospects of increased return must be reasonably high. If, as the result of his improvements, a farmer is only going to gain 5 to 10 percent, it is not worth all his trouble and risk. A gain of at least 50 to 100 percent is needed. Adoption of deep wells for supplementary irrigation in West Pakistan is an example. In five years nearly 32,000 private tube wells were installed in the cotton and rice regions of the former Punjab at a cost of $1,000 to $2,500 each on farms no larger than twenty-five acres. In other words, a private investment of $50 million was made by traditional farmers without government subsidy. The reason for this was that the wells paid for themselves in two years. If the payoff is large enough, farmers will change, and will change far more rapidly than the academic social scientists thought possible. We now have living models of rapid change when the above factors were present, and this is far more valuable than any amount of theorizing on the difficulties of bringing about change.

In addition to farm credit and adequate remuneration, the farmer needs to be instructed in the proper and economic use of better seeds, fertilizer, pesticides, and so on. The best way to achieve this in many parts of the developing world is not by means of top-level government instruction or pamphlets and leaflets the farmer cannot read. The primary need is for a network of agricultural extension officers who can be the principal agent of change on the spot by their personal instruction and guidance. One might well argue that the work of extension officers and training institutes was as much responsible for the food production revolution in West Pakistan as the investment in big irrigation schemes, necessary as these were.

The relationship between agriculture and the total economy is one that is equally important. In the past, agriculture was the Cinderella of the economy. Cabinet-level positions in agriculture were often given to less able men, and the parts of budgets devoted to agriculture were meager. As we shall see, this state of affairs is being remedied, but agriculture needs to take its rightful place everywhere.

Most discussions on agriculture give the impression that it is important mainly in the beginning of development, that its role is primarily to make industrialization possible at the expense of its own early welfare and eventual decline. This interpretation is grossly misleading.

Agriculture remains virtually the only way known to produce human food in quantity. Food never loses its importance, and today, due to rapid population increase, it is a matter of urgent concern. This food does not have to be produced by a relatively primitive and disadvantaged sector of an economy. Instead, agriculture can and should be as highly dynamic and efficient as most other types of production. At the present time in the United States productivity per worker is increasing more than twice as fast in agriculture as it is elsewhere in the economy. Agriculture need not give way to more productive types of industry; the productivities of the farm and nonfarm sectors of an economy are mutually dependent.

Moreover, in a world of international trade any one nation need not grow food in order to have enough to eat, but it must be *productive* and therefore able to purchase the foods it needs but does not produce. What is needed is an international division of labor. This would mean that some of the developing nations might concentrate much more on manufactured or semimanufactured goods than on food production. This would require considerable adaptation on the part of the richer trading nations, but it is an essential part of a just and realistic reform of the world's economic structure.

Because of the greater economic power and potential of the more advanced countries, this approach is far better than the violent confrontations and disruptions that may be the alternative. At this stage, the main thing that developing countries must establish is a modicum of peace and stability. Revolution of a violent kind is the enemy of real, steady economic progress except in very exceptional circumstances, and an international division of labor could be one of the main factors making for stability.

The importance of agriculture in many currently developing countries, in this context, flows not so much from the fact that agriculture produces food as from the fact that it represents the preponderant opportunity of most of the people of these countries to be productively employed. They have land, sunlight, draft animals, and agricultural skills. They can build on this basis, thereby contributing both to the world's supply of food and to their own purchasing power for necessities they do not themselves produce.

Agriculture must provide employment for a large share of the labor force. In the currently developing countries, the total number of persons dependent upon agriculture for a livelihood will not decline for many years to come. This results from current rapid rates of population increase and the high capital costs of creating nonfarm industrial employment. It will be extremely difficult and very costly in terms of investment to create urban industrial employment fast enough to absorb the annual net increase in the total labor force in most countries for many years. Agriculture, as the "residual employer," will likely be required to support increasing numbers of people, even when additional farm workers can add very little to agricultural output. Meanwhile, there are more than enough workers to staff new industries without any being released from agriculture. This is one of the unfortunate restraints within which agricultural development must be pursued today.

Enormous amounts of capital are needed for investment both inside and outside of agriculture if productivity is to rise. Part of this capital can be borrowed from abroad if the situation is favorable to foreign investors. An important but relatively small portion may be provided by capital grants from abroad. Most of it must come from current production within each country, and if production within a country is chiefly agricultural, the net flow of capital will have to be from agriculture to nonagricultural industry. However, the needs for investment within agriculture are great. Unlike the situation historically in certain developed economies, the situation in many countries today is such that it may be more productive to concentrate on investments within agriculture for the time being rather than to drain capital out of agriculture to finance nonagricultural industrialization. Each case is unique. Certainly each country that has substantial agricultural potential should try to assure that "agri-support" types of industry are given priority in whatever programs of industrialization it may inaugurate.

In summary, the role of agriculture in the economy of any country where there is agricultural potential must be seen as *coordi-*

nate, not *subordinate.* The interrelationships between agriculture and the total economy are presented in Figure 3-15.

From agriculture, the national economy needs food, industrial raw materials, and an economic demand for its nonagricultural industries supported by rising farm incomes. In many countries the

FIGURE 3-15: Major Interrelationships Between
Agriculture and the Total Economy [36]

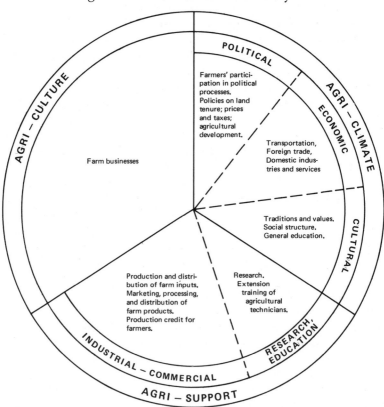

national economy needs foreign exchange to finance purchases of industrial equipment and finds its greatest opportunity to secure such foreign exchange through exports of farm products. The national economy must also depend on agriculture to employ a major part of its total labor force.

[36] Source: President's Committee, *World Food Problem,* Vol. 1, p. 76.

From the national economy, agriculture, if it is to advance, must have a research program that is constantly developing new technology to maintain and increase the potential for more abundant and efficient farm production. Agriculture must have easy access to farm supplies and equipment embodying this new technology, to markets for its products, to new knowledge and skills, and to the services of trained technicians of many types. The national economy must provide a favorable pattern of land tenure, price relationships, and tax policies to induce farm operators to increase production and industrialists to produce farm equipment.[37]

The farmers in a country should be well represented by politicians in legislative assemblies and the executive branch so that there is sufficient pressure to make such contributions from the national economy forthcoming.

INCREASED FOOD FROM THE SEA Land animals are a source of food that can at least be roughly estimated. The exact fishing potential of the ocean remains unknown. Indeed, fish farming as a serious industry is still in its infancy in most parts of the world. The Northern Hemisphere is 61 percent water and provides 98 percent of the world's fish supplies. The Southern Hemisphere is 81 percent water but it supplies only 2 percent of the fish. The fisheries of the world could yield far more food—and of a particularly valuable type—than they are doing at present. Only a few of the 20,000 to 25,000 species found in the oceans are currently being harvested and used by man. To obtain even part of the food potential available in the oceans will require, as in the case of other attacks on the food problem, a great deal of money for equipment and training. In addition, fishing areas other than the North Atlantic must be investigated and opened up. There is no doubt that the annual fishery haul can be greatly increased by catching new species and accepting them as regular parts of the human diet. Developing new methods could eventually change fishing from hunting and capturing to herding and cultivating, a change that happened with regard to land animals a few millennia ago.

Opinions differ on the extent to which the seas of the Northern Hemisphere can be fished more heavily. But the even vaster oceans of the Southern Hemisphere supply very few fish in relation to

37 *Ibid.,* Vol. 3, pp. 74 ff.

their potential, although many of the regions of rapid population growth are in, or fairly near, this area. In any case, there are other ways of utilizing current resources. Modern methods of refrigeration enable fish to be kept in good condition for some time, and the use of refrigeration in places where fishing is still carried on in primitive ways can stop the great wastage that occurs at present and greatly increase the amount and quality of this very nutritious food.

Many schemes to improve and develop marine fisheries are working in various parts of the world. Recently Israel doubled its catches of sea fish in two years. A new fish harbor is in use in Karachi, designed by FAO experts from the Netherlands. With the use of mechanized vessels, it has resulted in a large rise in yields. The rich fisheries of the Indian Ocean are only now beginning to be exploited; a large supply of fresh fish can now be obtained, not only for the inhabitants of Karachi, but for those of the interior as well. Processed and dried fish is now available over the whole of western Afghanistan, though formerly much of the population did not eat fish at all. The fishing industry of Ceylon was formerly dependent on unmechanized boats, and consequently incomplete advantage was taken of the rich fisheries surrounding its shores. Plans have gone ahead to modernize fishing craft and methods and —of equal importance—to improve marketing arrangements. Similar information comes from other lands. The use of diesel-powered or other mechanized vessels will mean that much more fishing can be undertaken in deep-sea waters, instead of in areas comparatively near land.

Fresh-water fisheries afford particularly promising scope for providing food and improving diets deficient in protein, because paddy fields can yield a rich harvest of fish if properly managed. But these possibilities are often neglected through ignorance or lack of effort. If all such resources were used to the full a very great rise in fish production could take place. In some parts of China, yields of fish are between 2,000 and 4,000 pounds an acre of pond per year; the methods used in India result in lower production, from 700 to 2,000 pounds per acre. The "paddy-cum-fish culture" practiced in many rice-growing lands can be made much more efficient by the introduction of the most suitable types of fish. Too much stress cannot be laid on the great possibilities of extending this resource.

In the 1930's, for instance, a certain African fish was introduced into Java. This fish hatches all the year round and so makes unnecessary the introduction of young fish into the rice fields after every harvest. Another advantage is that it lives on algae that otherwise foster malarious mosquitoes. This fish yields catches of 400 kilograms per hectare in ponds that were formerly neglected. It is not known how this species was brought to Java, but if haphazard introductions can give such happy results, more systematic attempts to breed the best fish and to extend knowledge of them—such as are being made by the FAO—give promise of spectacular effects. For example, very little use has been made of Thailand's inland waters for this purpose, and only a few fish ponds have been developed there. At the same time, there are many large areas of fresh water and many expanses of brackish water in mangrove swamps and mudflats where a considerable fishing industry could be developed, as has been done in China and Japan. The FAO is giving advice on possible lines of development.

PROSPECTS FOR THE FUTURE The First Development Decade did not have the statistical successes for some countries that were hoped for. As I pointed out, in the first half of the 1960's agricultural production in the developing countries rose by 6.7 percent while population rose by 11.4 percent. The disastrous setbacks of 1965 and 1966 further reduced the small gains that food production had made.

But as we have already seen, 1967 was a very good year and there was a world grain surplus in 1968–69. The future, with its promise of a "green revolution," is making nonsense of some of the gloomy forecasts of the past few years. In fact, the past is now an unreliable guide to the future. We are in a situation that is almost as unprecedented as the population expansion itself. The speed with which new varieties have been adopted also makes nonsense of the forebodings of those who say it takes years for new varieties to be transferred from one area to another with success.[38] As Professor Gustav Ranis, a distinguished authority on foreign aid and director of the Economic Growth Center of Yale University, says: "We have never seen anything like it: the progress from 200 acres

[38] Cf. *Famine—1975*, pp. 17 ff. This section is one of the main reasons for the segment of opinion that is prophesying famine by 1975.

to 20 million acres planted with new varieties in just four years. That this is happening all over Asia verges on the incredible." [39]

This agricultural revolution that is now underway will have these main effects:

First, it means a much more rapid rate of growth in food production in Asia, which could mean that by 1975 the rate of increase could be double what it was in the early and mid-fifties.

Second, not only will there be a much more rapid rate of growth in the farm sector, which constitutes a third to half of the economies of the developing countries, but this will contribute in itself to a more rapid rate of overall economic growth and a more rapid rate of growth than was expected in the nonfarm sector.

Third, if it continues, this "green revolution" may result in one of the most sustained rates of regional economic growth experienced in any region almost at any time.

Fourth, in world economic terms it may be perhaps the most significant development since the economic reconstruction of Europe after World War II.

Fifth, the progress being made toward the solution of a problem many regarded as insoluble will have an excellent psychological effect on the developing countries. It should give the leadership confidence in what the new technology, properly applied, can do to improve the welfare of their people.

Sixth, it will give the necessary breathing space for measures of population control to begin to have their effect, and it will take the element of panic out of consideration of the problem of rapidly increasing populations. It will not, of course, remove the need for fertility-control programs, but it will certainly ease the situation.

Seventh, the new varieties require a great deal more care and attention than the older varieties. They are utilizing labor that has in some instances been unemployed during the off-season and has been, in a more general case, underemployed. They are mobilizing capital in the rural areas of Asia in a way not thought possible a short time ago.

The past decade has also shown progress in other areas that is less tangible but possibly just as valuable. There has been a revolution in attitudes of governments in developing countries and in

---

[39] *Congressional Record*, July 19, 1968, p. H5158.

developed donor countries with regard to agriculture. In a number of countries and in a number of aid programs, it is getting the priority it deserves.

Research by the FAO and by the large foundations is beginning to pay off; the new varieties are only the more dramatic outcome of such research.

Moreover, there is a much greater awareness of the problem of hunger in the world, and this has been the most important achievement of the Freedom from Hunger Campaign, with its central year of 1963 during which the World Food Congress took place. It is now realized by public leaders, by men of goodwill everywhere, and by the rising elites in the developing countries that peace and war may well depend, partly at least, on the outcome of the race between population and resources. Communications media have played a big part and have contributed to the solidarity shown by the ongoing response that the Freedom from Hunger Campaign has evoked in the developed countries. It has strikingly shown that common people everywhere are ready to work together in the task of development.[40]

The very fact of the studies and publication of the President's *Report on the World Food Problem,* which has provided much of the information in this chapter, is an indication of the importance and scope of government interest and of the desire that this should be based on the advice of the best experts in the wide variety of fields covered.

The Food for Peace and Food for Development programs of the United States government, which have been and still will be of such great value, are examples, on a higher level, of international solidarity. How many lives have been saved; how many ill-nourished people, especially children, have been helped to avoid consequences of famine and national food shortages, it would be impossible to estimate, but the numbers must run into millions—an example of sharing abundance and knowhow without precedent in history.

In 1966 President Johnson called the United States to lead the world in a war against hunger, and Congressional approval of the

---

[40] Cf. the paper given by Charles Weitz, coordinator of the World Freedom from Hunger Campaign at the Oxford Committee for Famine Relief (OXFAM) Conference, July–August 1963.

Food for Peace Act was a magnificent response to this call. This act gave the means to raise home food production to meet the food needs abroad. Farmers were invited to cultivate half of the million acres made idle under government control programs to build up depleted food stocks. The food act highlighted self-help in the developing nations and endorsed population-control measures. The followup of this act has met with some criticism. Senator McGovern has said that "the most important war of our time—the war on hunger—is being waged without a chief of staff and without paying the troops—the U.S. food producers." The Senator compared this war with the war in Vietnam:

> In Vietnam, we are willing to pour a million dollars in ammunition into the jungle, if one VC sticks up his head. But hunger threatens to swallow civilization and we are hesitant to mount a solid counter-offensive.
> We are spending seven-tenths of one percent of our gross national product for food and development assistance. This is only one-sixth the cost of our military operations in Vietnam. And the irony is that by not facing up to this overriding challenge of our time, we may be allowing the creation of many Vietnams.[41]

It may be that in a few years' time the need to share American abundance abroad may diminish somewhat and much greater support of self-help measures abroad be needed, but in the short term it does seem that exports of food will be needed where developing countries cannot increase their food production fast enough and before new food production and population control measures have their effect. In the 1966 legislation the United States has given itself the power to perform this essential service, and the initial administrative difficulties referred to by Senator McGovern should not be too hard to overcome.

Instead of lessening commitment to the war against hunger, the recent hopeful developments should give it a greater impetus. Before, there were many who were influenced by pessimistic prophecies that famines are inevitable, no matter what action be taken. Now that it is clearer than ever before that victory is possible, all available forces should be mobilized to make this the century when hunger was wiped off the face of the earth. This would be an

[41] *Look*, March 7, 1967.

even greater achievement than landing a man on the moon at a cost of $24 billion, and after a decade of intense scientific effort.

FOOD FROM UNCONVEN- TIONAL SOURCES The statement made by Sir John Russell in 1954 that "there are techniques still in embryo which may completely dispel our present fears," which events are now proving correct, applies even more, I believe, to the present time, when science has made such amazing advances in so many fields. I have not mentioned these new sources of food before because I do not feel that in the short and medium term there will be great need for them and also because most of them, but not all, will take time to develop into large-scale economically and socially acceptable additions to the diet. For this reason they are also dealt with in a summary fashion. From a scientific point of view the story is a fascinating one and well worth studying in more detail than is possible here.[42]

In general, technological feasibility in developing food products from unconventional sources is not a limiting factor, since modern food technology can cope easily with most problems. The most critical and difficult aspects of introducing these products for large-scale use in the human diet are acceptability and marketing.

FISH PROTEIN

Fish protein concentrate (F.P.C.) is the high-protein powder food obtained from the whole fish. F.P.C. of high quality is now being made in small quantities. We have every reason to suppose that commercial quantities can be made. To make it available in such quantities would require immediate investment in plant and dock facilities, as well as in boats and in training programs for crews. The cost would be $6 billion to supply a million people with one year's daily twenty-gram supply containing 80 percent pure protein. Although much research remains to be done, F.P.C. could represent a stable source of high-quality protein that could be mixed with flour and other conventional foods. The value of this for treating malnutrition is clear.

[42] The President's report deals with these nonconventional foods in Vol. 2, pp. 355–371. Other sources of information are articles in technical journals and OECD, *The Food Problem of Developing Countries*, Paris: Jan. 1968.

FOOD YEAST
Considerable effort has been applied to research and developmental aspects of the supply of protein from less conventional sources, with highly promising results. The carbohydrate-rich byproducts of certain industries, such as the sugar and the wood pulp and paper industries, could be used to produce sizeable quantities of edible yeast. So far only minor quantities of food yeast are used as human food, mainly as a good source of certain vitamins (B-complex), rather than as a source of protein and calories.

PETROLEUM PROTEINS
A recent development is the production of proteins by yeasts growing on paraffinic hydrocarbons obtained by refining crude petroleum. Such products are currently being studied for wholesomeness and biological value. With the exception of food yeast, these so-called petroleum products seem to offer the best hope for a cheap and good source of protein.

ALGAE
Algae are increasingly attracting the interest of research workers in various countries. Pilot mass-culture of the genus *Chlorella* has provided extremely encouraging products in satisfactory yields.

LEAVES
Protein extracted from green leaves is a very promising potential source of food. A considerable amount of pioneering work has been done, but as in the case of algae, a number of problems remain to be solved before a low-cost product of good nutritional value and acceptable to the human palate can be produced.

LYSINE
Fortification of grain by the addition of lysine from oilseed proteins is also a promising possibility.[43] "Based on a reported (1966) U.S. production of 629 million bushels of soybeans, each additional per cent increase of production

---

[43] President's Committee, *World Food Problem*, Vol. 2, pp. 316 ff.

would yield 30.3 thousand metric tons of oil and 61.5 thousand metric tons of protein or enough protein to correct the lysine deficiency of 1.0 million metric tons of wheat." [44] Such an increase in the United States would probably require price support because yields per acre, and probably cash return to the farmer, would be below those of alternate crops such as corn.

The improvement of the protein quality by genetic means seems to offer even more promising possibilities. The application of modern genetics could achieve the equivalent of fortification with amino acids, thereby obviating the necessity of producing, purifying, mixing, and extra handling of foodstuffs. A superior quality of corn (opaque 2) has been under investigation. This has about the same protein quality as animal protein. "The potentialities of corn improved in protein quality by genetics are tremendous," is the verdict of the President's report.[45] Already grain fortified with additional protein is being used in Food for Peace shipments.

Nearly ten years ago, I referred to the experiments in the manufacture of protein from leaves or grass at Rothamsted Experimental Research Station in England under N. W. Pirie, carried out by means of a machine—a sort of "mechanical cow" but far more efficient.[46-47]

The process has now gone beyond the experimental stage, and the product has been used in field trials in Mysore with great success.

The latest version of the large-scale machine designed at Rothamsted is extremely versatile and will treat one ton per hour of wet foliage from a very wide variety of plants, yielding 66 to 80 pounds per hour of high-quality protein. This means that one such machine could supply the protein needs of 7,000 to 8,000 people. The cost of the machine is about $35,000.

The British Ministry of Overseas Development, in October 1968, authorized the following statement:

The Ministry of Overseas Development has expressed interest in helping to arrange a large-scale feeding trial to be mounted in a humid tropical area to furnish unchallengeable evidence of the value of the leaf protein extraction process at Rothamsted. The trial is to cover the strictly

[44] *Ibid.,* Vol. 2, p. 330.
[45] *Ibid.,* Vol. 2, p. 342.
[46-47] In *People, Space, Food,* p. 172.

nutritional aspects of the process—and here the Ministry hopes to be able to participate—and also the sociological and agronomic aspects which will include the acceptability of a new food additive and any social or economic problems associated with its production.

Further considerations will be the possible use of the leaf residue as a fodder or manure constituent, and of the surplus liquid for microbiological cultures.

The report on the Mysore research and trials shows the successful use of a similar machine with tropical vegetation.[48]

POLICIES FOR THE WAR ON HUNGER Perhaps the most important part of the *Report on the World Food Problem* of the President's Science Advisory Committee is taken up with recommendations as to how the techniques of increasing food production can be made available to and implemented by the developing countries. The report gives detailed and far-reaching suggestions as to how this should be done. There is no need here, however, to go into anything more detailed than the major policy decisions and the broad assessment of needs.[49] Perhaps it might be useful to preface this section with two points from the report. The first concerns the reasons why— at the time the report was written in 1967—food production seemed to be losing the race between food and population. The second is the statement why the United States should be concerned. These explanations are important, because to adopt the necessary policies, programs, and measures in free countries presumes a realization and a willingness to act not only on the part of governments but also on the part of people. There is a vast program of education needed not only to present the facts to people in the rich and poor countries, but to provide incentives to make people ready to act upon them.

To mount such a program is far from simple, precisely because the food problem itself and the population pressures which aggravate it are so large and complex that it is impossible to present it simply and dramatically and truthfully. There is no way of making

<hr />

[48] Report of Central Food Technological Research Institute, Mysore, October 1968, which gives an interesting and up-to-date technical bibliography.

[49] Cf. President's Committee, *World Food Problem*, Vol. 1, pp. 25–38, where the report's recommendations are summarized.

it—except occasionally—a "newsworthy" story. Two small incidents in my own experience brought this home vividly to me. On an American television program, which shall be nameless, I was asked by an interviewer, "Tell us in one sentence what the population explosion is all about and how to deal with it." My inability to do so obviously disappointed the interviewer and no doubt thousands of viewers. On another occasion, when I was discussing the possibility of an article on world hunger and poverty and Christian responsibility with the editor of an internationally famous religious periodical—a man very interested in arousing Christian commitment in this field—he said, "Of course world poverty and world hunger are not very interesting subjects." This has indeed been my experience during the past ten years. I can remember giving a lecture to students in an English university on "Freedom from Hunger." There were seven in the audience. However, a fortnight later I gave the same lecture in another university where the Students' Union had enterprisingly given it the title "Freedom from Hunger and Birth Control." The lecture was so crowded that students stood in the corridor to hear me.

The comments of the President's report are especially valuable as frankly recognizing the difficulties, which are not, however, unsurmountable, as growing interest in the U.S.A., Canada, England, and other European countries proves. Here is the summary of the factors that explain why the race between food and population was being lost and why it is so difficult to reverse the trend.

(1) The overall problem of the world's food supply is so large and so extremely complex that it is almost impossible for the casual, or even moderately concerned, observer to comprehend its true dimensions or to grasp its intricate interrelationships with the many other aspects of economic growth and development.

(2) Despite its true complexity, the problem at first glance seems deceptively straightforward and is, therefore, unusually susceptible to oversimplification. Because eating and even farming seem readily understandable to the average citizen in a developed country such as the United States, the temptation to act on the basis of superficial or incomplete information is almost irresistible. This leads to seizure of, and overemphasis upon, panaceas and piecemeal "solutions" that are inapplicable, ineffectual, or inadequate. The cumulative delays engendered by false starts and stopgap measures mask the requirement for broad and effective programs, tailored to the demands and dimensions of the overall problem.

(3) The details of the task involved in increasing food production to meet world needs have never been charted with the clarity and exactness that the available information will permit. The problem has been treated dramatically but incompletely—usually to incite short-term action for humanitarian reasons. A *wholehearted response* to an *incomplete proposal*, however, lulls the participants into an unjustified feeling of security that the problem is coming under control.

(4) Food shortage and rapid population growth are separate but interrelated problems. The solutions, likewise, are separate but related. The choice is not to solve one or the other; to solve both is an absolute necessity. The current tendency to think of food production and fertility control as alternative solutions to a common problem is dangerously misleading.

(5) The twin problems of food and population imbalance have one feature in common that adds immeasurably to the difficulties of achieving control. Their eventual solution is crucially dependent upon success in convincing millions of citizens in the developing nations to take *individual* action. Fertility control cannot be achieved by declarations of government policy or by executive decree, although adoption of a policy and the provision of information, instruction, and materials are obviously needed and helpful. Similarly, political declarations concerning agricultural productivity are ineffective unless individual farmers can be convinced to adopt the necessary improved practices. The provision of these personal incentives is a task encompassing a vast array of social, economic, and political considerations that differ between countries and within countries. Indeed, the very fabric of traditional societies must be rewoven if the situation is to change permanently.

(6) The eventual alleviation of world hunger will require many years. It is dependent on far-reaching social reforms and long-range programs of hard work, which offer no promises of quick and dramatic results of the type so helpful in maintaining enthusiasm for a concerted, difficult undertaking. The short-term results cannot be seen—as can a dedication of new buildings, a successful launching into space, or other spectacular, "newsworthy" events—to punctuate the year-in, year-out, toil.

(7) The problem of food production is but one part, albeit a very important part, of the enormous problem of economic development in the poor nations. As the years have passed, the great ex-

pectations that ushered in our foreign assistance programs, fresh on the heels of the heady successors of the Marshall Plan, have not been realized. Domestic political constraints have so eroded the programs and the agencies responsible for them, that there remains virtually no possibility of commitment to long-range, coordinated action, dedicated to the systematic solution of a series of interrelated problems, none of which can be solved in isolation from its fellows. The original emphasis upon technical assistance has been so diluted that it is almost correct to say that this form of aid, indispensable to the accomplishment of increases in food production, now receives little more than lip service. Despite chronic reiterations of the need to involve private industry in economic assistance, no significant progress in engaging this rich reservoir of resources and skills can be reported at this time.

The chief handicap faced by all is the impatience of the modern, fast-moving world—expressed in the desire of philanthropists (individuals, foundations, national, and international) for concrete evidence of good they are doing—expressed in the wish of the specialist, during a tour of one and a half or two years, to leave a permanent mark upon the culture that has been evolving for one and a half or two millennia.[50]

In presenting the report to the nation, President Johnson said in his message, "The world food problem is one of the foremost challenges of mankind today. The dimension of the challenge will define the dimension of our response and the means of that response. We must join with others in a massive effort to help the less fortunate of the earth to help themselves."

This is the appeal to the country most able to respond. But the reluctance to do so, shown by falling aid programs, is not only, or not primarily, due to lack of generosity and of interest on the part of the people of the United States alone. Many other factors come into play.

However, it seems clear that without a wholehearted commitment on the part of the United States, the necessary programs to take advantage of the improved possibilities of helping the hungry nations will hardly be mounted or be brought to a successful conclusion.

This makes it all the more necessary to have a clear idea why

[50] *Ibid.*, Vol. 1, p. 4.

the United States should be involved, in spite of setbacks, difficulties, and disillusionments, which should serve as an incentive to improve aid programs in cooperation with the developing countries, but not to a slackening of effort. The panel of the President's report gives the following three main reasons for the United States to be concerned with the plight of the hungry nations:

(1) *Humanitarian:* We should help the less fortunate simply because they need help and we are able to help them. The benefits of altruism are by no means unilateral. The challenge of a different task and the moral uplift that comes only from doing for others are needed to temper and balance the leisure and affluence of American life. The real successes of the Peace Corps center in the fundamentally inspired, collective aim that is exemplified in the late Albert Schweitzer's dictum, "It is only giving that stimulates."

(2) *Security:* Populations in the developing countries double in eighteen to twenty-seven years; fifty-five to eighty-eight years are required for populations to double in the developed countries. By the year 2000, if present rates of growth continue, there will be more than four times as many people in the developing countries as there are in the developed nations. To avoid a threat to the peace of the world, as well as to our own national security, we cannot afford to be too little and too late with our development assistance. The expectations of the poor are demanding fulfillment. It is to be hoped that some measure of their ambitions can be realized by peaceful means.

(3) *A better tomorrow for us, too:* This is a long-range goal, an economic reason for investment. An important way to expand our own economy in the future will be through further specialization and trade; both parties to a transaction benefit. Trading partners are likely to be peaceful protagonists.

In the view of the panel, if the United States is to deal seriously and productively with international development:

(1) The American public must be convinced that the efforts merit investment of their taxes and will be effective in meeting the overall problem.

(2) The American public must have confidence in the substance of the programs that are implemented and in the arm of the government responsible for administration of those programs.

(3) Funding and programs must be placed on a long-range basis, not budgeted and funded hand-to-mouth, from year to year.

Foreign economic assistance is doomed to frustration and failure if the responsible agency is forced to deal only with quick payoff projects and to show results tomorrow in order to survive the next budget cycle.[51]

After stating that they found the prospects for the future both sobering and alarming, the members of the panel give the following two choices as open to the United States:

(1) The first is for the United States to continue to provide technical and capital assistance and private investment to poor countries willing to make the self-help effort to achieve self-sustaining growth. Our foreign assistance program would then continue to be largely an American effort, with coordinating relationships with the United Nations organizations and other international institutions. While the course might lead to some improvement over the status quo, it would not suffice to meet the food problem, because for all of its own economic recourses, the United States cannot possibly accomplish the immense ask of alleviating the world food problem alone. *This course would be unsuccessful in halting or reversing the rapid deterioration of the population-food situation in the developing countries and the world would continue to lose ground.*

(2) *The other alternative is for the United States to take the lead in mounting a global effort,* in concert with other developed nations and with international organizations, that will bring to bear the technical skills and capital resources needed to reverse the downward course of the developing countries and to restore the chance of their people for a better life.

The panel then states: "We are unanimous in the belief that the *United States must assume leadership of the free world and all of its international institutions in a coordinated, long-range development strategy for raising the economic level of the poor nations, thereby meeting the threat of hunger, increasing the volume of world trade and economic activity, and contributing to the achievement of the goal of ultimate importance, a lasting peace.*"[52]

Such a decision by the United States could be of vital importance unless it is vitiated by isolationism at home or anti-American hostility abroad, often synthetically worked up. This is not to say that the isolationists are necessarily selfish or that American aid

[51] *Ibid.*, p. 24.
[52] *Ibid.*, Vol. 1, p. 23.

has not had many imperfections. But the crisis is too important for the provincialisms that are behind both attitudes.[53]

Policy decisions to ensure that the potential food production is achieved must spring from the analysis that the report has made. Effective demand, we have seen, is a critical factor. Policy with regard to food production cannot be divorced from overall economic development; the food situation is linked with the whole problem of world poverty and development. Ideally, economic growth and income must increase at a rate that enables consumers to buy the projected food requirements for a healthy life. Similarly, on the production or supply side, agricultural food production is linked with overall production. The production of food and crops requires manufactured inputs such as fertilizers, pesticides, and machinery, which must be imported or produced domestically. If they are imported, the overall economy must create sufficient exports or must rely on a net inflow of foreign assistance or private capital to pay for the imports. If these inputs are to be produced domestically or paid for by industrial exports, the nonagricultural sectors must expand at rates consistent with the need of the agricultural sectors. Similarly, various nonagricultural sectors are dependent on agricultural raw materials, and in some cases food products.

In addition, of course, social progress must be made from a humanitarian and also from a commonsense point of view. Therefore, as Pope John indicated in his encyclical *Mater et Magistra*, there must be harmonious development of agricultural production, the industrial sector, and the social progress of the people, who in the final analysis are the object and aim of all the progress. However, although this cycle cannot and should not be regarded from a purely economic point of view, nevertheless economic factors play a vital role.

Because of the interdependence that exists among food need, food demand, overall income, agricultural output, total output (gross national product—G.N.P.—or gross domestic product—G.D.P.), it is meaningless to consider a nation's demand and supply of foodstuffs independently from overall economic progress. It is important to stress this because there is a pendulum movement now swinging toward agricultural production. In the past—

[53] Cf. speech of Senator Edward Kennedy at Johns Hopkins University, Baltimore, May 2, 1967.

especially, for example, in India's Second Five Year Plan—too much emphasis was laid on the growth of industry, particularly heavy industry, to the neglect of agriculture. This process is now being reversed, but as I have said, it must be seen in the context of a general economic and social advance.

It is difficult to put a price tag for the whole world on the improvements that must be made in world agriculture to provide the increased food supply necessitated by the need to improve present diets and to cope with the rate of population increase. It is, indeed, rather undesirable to make such global projections when the real need is for projections at regional and country and even at district levels. However, there is considerable usefulness in getting an idea of the size of the problem in financial terms and therefore the size of the commitment of the developed and developing countries to this urgent task. It has been estimated that the required compound annual growth rates for the developing countries in aggregate will be:

Increase in food demand	3.0 percent
Increase in food production	2.7 percent
Increase in national income	4.5 percent

Only countries such as Mexico, Taiwan, and West Pakistan are achieving growth rates of the order deemed necessary.

Additional investments for acceleration of agricultural output in the developing countries as a whole have been estimated but not verified by detailed studies of individual countries. The direct capital requirement for fertilizers, seeds, mechanization, and pesticides for a 4 percent growth rate in agricultural output approximates annual aid in the early years of $300 million, increasing to almost $4 billion per year by 1985. This estimate does not include direct investments in land and water resources; nor does it include the necessary direct "infrastructure" investments: investments in power, transportation, marketing, and credit, and in food processing, storage, and distribution. It is estimated that *to achieve a 4 percent annual growth rate in food demand and supply, capital investments will have to increase from the present 15 percent of the gross national products of the developing countries to 19 percent.* This would mean the equivalent of a $12 billion increase in investment above the 1965 base. *To achieve such a feat will require capital and technical involvement of developed and developing coun-*

tries alike on a scale unparalleled in the peacetime history of mankind.[54]

It may be well here to add a comment with regard to the necessity for foreign aid. In the developed countries of the world, just when circumstances are ripe and conditions require that there should be a considerable increase in aid, there has been a slackening of effort.

There is at present an unfortunate "backlash" with regard to aid. It is supported on the one hand by those who are disillusioned by the lack of effectiveness of the efforts of the last twenty years to wipe out world poverty, or by the lack of "gratitude" of recipients; it is also supported by those who consider genuine needs at home. On the other hand, it is supported, equally unfortunately in my view, by some advanced economists who regard aid as a "myth," a capitalistic trick, or belated reparations for past injustice. Both these views stress the many failures or imperfections of aid and neglect the tremendous achievements made possible by it. If either attitude prevails, the urgently needed development of the coming decade will be hampered.

By all means, the giving and receiving of aid should be purified, better organized, and more effective. But to imagine that expenditure of the magnitude needed to ensure the chance of people in developing countries to live with human dignity within the foreseeable future can be secured without the financial support and personnel and technical knowhow of the developed countries is doctrinaire, dangerous, and even destructive. The quality of the aid in many cases can and must be improved, but the reduction rather than increase in its quantity might well be fatal for development efforts.

In spite of the conclusions of the President's report, in spite of the President's own declaration of war on hunger in 1966, there was a savage cut in foreign aid in 1968. If this mood continues, the above targets have no chance of being realized; the promise of the green revolution may be aborted; some, at least, of the more alarmist menaces foretold in books such as *Famine—1975* may be fulfilled. There are many arguments against more foreign aid, many obstacles to its efficient use, many justifications for simply not giving it during the time and in the quantity needed for it to

[54] President's Committee, *World Food Problem*, Vol. 1, p. 113.

be effective. But if the decade of rising expectations is followed by the decade of disappointed hopes, then we may well be facing disaster. And history has no time for alibis. Reasons and arguments are not acceptable as excuses for failing to read the signs of the times. Only the academic historian now studies the many good reasons why, for example, Napoleon lost the Battle of Waterloo. History coldly records that he did and thereby changed the whole history of Europe and the world.

Some developing countries have been showing an increasing restiveness at the idea that they should be recipients of aid over a long period, and some have even rather defiantly suggested that they can "go it alone." The facts and projections in the President's report make both attitudes unrealistic, and one of the first essentials for eradicating hunger is a change of attitude on the part of developed and developing countries alike. There should be very much greater stress on cooperation, because, as President Johnson has said, no one can be safe sitting on an island of plenty in a sea of misery.

This points to the main policy decision to be made, namely that the United States must regard assistance in a spirit of partnership to the developing countries as of first priority. To quote an eloquent passage of the report:

After nearly a year of study of the World Food Problem, the Panel is unanimous in the belief that the solution of the problem will be crucially dependent upon the actions taken by the United States within the immediate future. We further believe that to have any chance of averting widespread starvation, with all of its attendant misery and political upheavals, a new, long-term, global policy is required that will address directly and effectively the massive task of alleviating this central problem of today's world. If an assault on the World Food Problem is deemed an objective of first priority, the United States will have to assume leadership of the free world . . . .[55]

The urgent need for the United States to take the lead is nowhere better illustrated than in the attitude expressed in the so-called Jeanneney Report, a detailed review of France's foreign aid program:

[55] *Ibid.*, p. 115.

The conclusion reached by the only approach to the problem which appeared possible was that it will undoubtedly be impossible to satisfy the needs of the Third World for aid. This being so, it has been considered here that the only problem was to determine how much it was possible for France to offer.[56]

While it is understandable that France or almost any other of the world's developed nations might adopt this viewpoint, the panel expressed the belief that the American people, once fully informed of the magnitude of the problem, will choose to embark upon a course that promises the successful achievement of a better life for all. It is essential that decisions about long-range programs be taken with the best possible understanding of their immensity and difficulty.

The recommendations of the President's report stress the necessity for food aid and technical assistance, both of which "should be administered to stimulate agricultural and economic development and to improve the food producing capability of recipient nations."

The problem now shades into the more general one of world development through world economic cooperation. In this the other developed nations must play their full part. The United States' position with regard to agriculture is a special one, but no one country can or should be asked to tackle alone the problem of the progress of the developing countries.

CONCLUSION In this book, very much space—at the expense of what others might regard as even more important aspects of the population problem—has been given to population and food for a number of reasons.

First of all, because it is so fundamental. If this problem of feeding people is not solved, then it will not be of much use coping with other problems. Man must eat in order to live. And indeed, the solution of other problems will depend to a large extent on solving this one.

Second, because much of the pessimistic writing on the subject has concentrated on this aspect. The pessimists have prophesied famine and widespread hunger, and they have gone into such de-

[56] *French Aid,* a translation of the Jeanneney Report, *Le Politique de Coopération avec les Pays en Voies de Développement,* 1963. London: Overseas Development Institute, 1964.

tail about how and why this will take place that it seemed necessary to treat this aspect thoroughly and as much as possible from official sources, and even in the very words of these sources.

Third, because the recent developments in this field have been so important—indeed, revolutionary.

Fourth, because the subject is a dramatic one in comparison with other aspects of development, such as economic growth, and helps to focus attention on the whole problem of development.

Finally, because some of the ways of coping with it are especially the concern of the United States, and because the United States has such a fine record in this field and is obviously the one to take the lead in the war against hunger.

There are several reasons why, not being an American, I have concentrated so much on American sources in this section—because this book is intended for American readers; because of the United States' position in this field, symbolized by the Food for Peace program; because United States foundations and research have been responsible (often in cooperation with the FAO) for major breakthroughs in this field; and because the President's report is the most thorough and authoritative assessment produced by any government.

Chapter 4

POPULATION GROWTH AND ECONOMIC DEVELOPMENT

WITH THE EASING OF THE MOST ACUTE worries about the food situation, other problems and their relation to rapid population growth are coming to the fore—for example, the danger of large-scale unemployment and increase of the poverty belt and urban slums in the rapidly growing cities and large towns of the developing world.

Significant improvement of economic conditions generally is rendered most unlikely by a high rate of population growth. In this sense, the population problem is not primarily a food problem but a general development problem. Although at current income levels in the developing countries food is a dominant item in expenditure, nothing is gained by suggesting that the economic significance of population growth is specifically related to food when the whole prospect of economic and social development is in jeopardy.

As Goran Ohlin points out:

The gravest prospect to be feared in the under-developed countries does not seem to be a failure to provide for continued food supply at present levels. One must face the more probable and equally far-reaching problem that excessive population growth will make the hopes of diminishing international inequalities futile, will be a hindrance to the economic growth which would rob the food situation of its menace and keep whole countries in economic backwardness.[1]

Hunger, indeed, is only one of the evils summed up by the unemotional word "underdevelopment." The misery and degradation of poverty include many more human problems: lack of medical services, of basic education, of adequate housing and clothing. They involve the inability to put into practice the simple rules of hygiene that would be a defense against mass disease. They cause and are caused by industrial underdevelopment; lack of employ-

[1] Ohlin, Goran, *Population Control and Economic Development*, p. 51. Paris: OECD, 1967.

ment or concealed unemployment; lack of capital and savings to break through the vicious circle of poverty breeding poverty and turn it into a constructive spiral leading to self-sustained growth; lack of opportunities for improvement, even the absence of desire to improve, caused by years of malnutrition and disease, bringing in their train apathy and despair. Rapid population increase does not cause all these conditions but it complicates and compounds them and makes them vastly more difficult to remedy.

This is the situation in the developing countries, whose people are multiplying twice or three times as fast as the more affluent populations. The denizens of these slums indeed are often multiplying at a far higher rate than the national population rate of increase would suggest. For example, in Venezuela the rate of increase is high at 3.6 percent. But this national average, as I have indicated, covers the moderate rate of about 1.5 to 2 percent of the richer people and the extremely high rate of 4.5 to 5 percent or more of the slum-dwellers, whose shanties perch on the hills overlooking Caracas—the first things one sees as one enters that beautiful and affluent city.

However, the relationship between rapidly increasing population figures and economic underdevelopment is not so clear as that between food and population increase. It is obvious that the more people there are to eat a meal, the less there will be for each unless additional food is obtained. But historically population increase has often been a condition of and a stimulant to economic growth. It is not self-evident that a high rate of natural increase is an obstacle to a significant improvement of economic conditions.

A further reservation might be introduced. Even if it is admitted that population increase does limit economic growth at present and will do so in the foreseeable future, is it more limiting than other factors? And will the cost of a program to reduce population increase give better results than the cost of removing other factors that are obstacles to development? As Simon Kuznets has put it:

If our discussion is to serve as a guide to policy consideration it must examine critically the impacts on economic growth of demographic trends relative to other possible obstacles to economic growth, scrutinize the costs of various policies compared with their returns in reducing inhibitive effects on economic growth, and consider the likely differences among countries in the relative weight of demographic trends as growth obstacles, and the no less likely differences in the relative costs of alternative policy lines and action. So long as attention to these important aspects of policy choice does not serve as an excuse for inaction, in itself a policy commitment, there is much to be gained from an attempt to consider them specifically for given countries and given times rather than resorting to a general dogma that either views population growth as the overwhelming threat or takes for granted man's capacity to provide for growing population at satisfactorily increasing levels of per capita product.[2]

On the whole, however, I think two conclusions can be established, even though they are subject to exceptions in special cases. First, that the lessons of history with regard to economic growth do not apply with regard to the unprecedented population pressures of the second half of the twentieth century; second, that population pressures now constitute such a threat to economic growth that regulatory population policies need to be undertaken as a condition of such growth together with action against other obstacles to development. This naturally leads to the consideration of other aspects of the desirability of such population policies in the context, for example, of the quality of human life, especially of family life; the provision of better housing, better education, better medical attention.

Generalizations are difficult in this field of economic growth and underline the need for population problems to be considered continent by continent, region by region, country by country, area by area, even district by district. For example, the impression is sometimes given that a large population or a high population density inevitably means poverty. This generalization is easily proved false by a glance at Table 4-1, which shows countries with very low and very high population densities. Some of those with the highest population densities are among the most prosperous countries in the world.

Looking at population pressures from the historical point of view, no one single pattern emerges. The erudite historical sweep of Colin Clark's analysis in his *Population Growth and Land Use* [3] implicitly contains many warnings concerning rash generalizations. He ranges over the millennia of humanity's adjustments to the slow

[2] Kuznets, Simon, "Demographic Aspects of Economic Growth," statement of the moderator, *Proceedings, World Population Conference,* Vol. 1, p. 314. New York: United Nations, 1967.
[3] New York: The Macmillan Company, 1967.

shifts in food technology, reaching back to the hunting economy. The net rate of increase among primitive men in the hunting period was very slow. There were not anywhere "more men than game" from the beginning of the world until about 7000 B.C., the date of the first known agricultural settlement. Indeed, in paleolithic France, it is estimated the ratio was one man to fifty-five square kilometers (the present population density of France is ninety people to one square kilometer).

It was when the population had reached about 15,000 (i.e., a

TABLE 4-1 [4]

	Popula-tion	Rate of increase	Area in sq. km.	Density per sq. km.
Examples of Some Low Population Densities				
Africa				
Cameroons	753,358	Not computed	475,442	11
Central African Republic	1,227,400	2.3	612,000	2
Congo (Brazzaville)	581,600	1.5	342,000	2
Kenya	8,636,263	3.5	322,463	11
Uganda	6,536,616	2.5	236,037	30
South America				
Bolivia	2,704,165	1.4	1,098,581	3
Chile	7,374,115	2.3	741,767	11
Colombia	11,548,172	2.2	1,138,338	13
Australia	10,508,186	2.1	7,695,094	1
New Zealand	2,414,984	2.2	268,676	9
Examples of Some High Population Densities				
Japan	93,418,501	0.9	369,661	259
England	46,104,548	0.8	151,120	309
West Germany	53,977,418	1.3	247,973	224
Belgium	9,189,741	0.5	30,513	304
Holland	11,461,964	1.4	33,612	356
India	435,511,606	2.3	3,046,232	151

[4] Source: United Nations, *Demographic Year Book*, 1965.

density of one man to ten square kilometers) that England could
be regarded as overpopulated for hunting and fishing man. Agriculture eventually had to be adopted because the increasing pressure of population left no alternative.

Coming nearer to our own times, when white settlers arrived in
the U.S.A. and Canada (about 12 million square kilometers, deducting tundra and desert), the area had a population of one million, i.e., one man to twelve square kilometers. At that density population was pressing on subsistence for a hunting and fishing
community.[5] Agriculture meant that a very much greater population could be sustained, and industrialization increased the population-carrying capacity of the land so that with a population two
hundred times as great for the U.S.A. alone, the land still could
hardly be regarded as overpopulated with a density of fifty-three
per square kilometer.

In England, the Reverend Thomas Robert Malthus in 1798 propounded his famous theory, which has already been referred to,
that populations tend to expand until they reach the limit of subsistence: population tends to increase in geometrical progression,
while agricultural production only increases in arithmetical progression. This statement is still quoted—though not so often in this
decade as in the last—as if it were a law of nature, although no
evidence was ever produced for it, most contemporaries did not accept it, and subsequent events proved it false.

When Malthus wrote in 1798 the population of Britain was approaching 10 million, ánd judging by what he knew about contemporary agricultural methods, he did not see how a larger number
of people could be fed. But during his long lifetime he also seemed
to be unaware of the agricultural, commercial, and industrial revolution going on around him, which enabled Britain not only to
produce manufactured exports to purchase food elsewhere, but also
to increase agricultural production within the country.

However, in 1817, in a later edition of his book, he himself admitted the beneficial effect of population growth, that many areas
of the world were underpopulated, and that "were it possible for
men to limit the number of their children by a wish the natural in-

[5] The above material has been taken from Colin Clark, *op. cit.*, especially pp. 59–122, where the whole subject is treated with an impressive
array of scholarly erudition which makes fascinating reading.

dolence of mankind would be greatly increased and the population of countries would never reach its proper or natural extent." [6]

In fact, as I have already said, it seems impossible to detect any significant stable relationship between population growth and economic backwardness over longer or shorter periods.

Indeed, the opposite of the above statement seemed to hold good in the crucial period between the Industrial Revolution and World War I. Comparing the growth of the industrial countries with that of the rest of the world during that period, population growth seems to have been a cause or at least a concomitant of great growth and prosperity. Between 1800 and 1950, both England, the leader of the Industrial Revolution, and the United States greatly increased their populations. In the case of England there was a fivefold increase; in the case of the United States there was a tenfold increase. Yet this was the time of England's greatest prosperity (at least until the beginning of World War II), and the economic growth rate of the U.S.A. was so considerable as to form the basis of the economic supremacy it has achieved in the second half of this century.

Indeed, it could be argued that population growth largely accounted for the Industrial Revolution. Population growth had a stimulating effect in a number of ways: it encouraged investment and employment; it made the labor force more flexible and mobile; and perhaps it pushed people out of their natural torpor in the effort to defend the standard they enjoyed, which was threatened by increasing population. As one writer remarks, "The qualities of imagination and organization developed in these tasks of *maintaining* standards of living in face of population pressures are very similar to those that are needed to *increase* per capita incomes." [7]

The long historical experience of population growth, then, suggests that no single role can be ascribed to this factor. At times it has been linked to the cultivation of new territories, the founding of cities, and the spread of civilization in the larger sense. At other times inexorable population increase has been the source of distress and crisis when, for one reason or another, the capacity of absorption or expansion was inadequate to provide for the orderly in-

[6] Cf. Clark, *Population Growth*, p. 60.
[7] Hirschman, Albert C., *The Strategy of Economic Development*, p. 177. New Haven: Yale University Press, 1958.

clusion of ever-larger generations into the community or for their migration into areas with greater opportunities. It is possible that sudden changes in the rates of population growth, which put great burdens of adjustment on economic and social institutions, are more important than the mere fact of population increase. This would seem to be the case at present with regard to many developing countries.

In European history, failures to absorb a growing population expressed themselves in pauperization of the rural population and roving migration, the very aimlessness of which proved it to be the response to push rather than pull. This occurred when rates of population growth were very low—a good deal less than one percent in the sixteenth century, never above 1.5 percent in the nineteenth century. On the other hand, in North America and other areas of recent European settlement nineteenth-century development was associated with much higher rates of growth than that. Nevertheless, the demand for labor was so great that it has been suggested that American technological change was stimulated by labor scarcity and the slow expansion of the labor force.[8]

There is also the case of population growth artificially induced for military purposes. It is very difficult to judge whether the population growth in Germany and in Japan in the thirties caused war, or whether this growth was artificially induced for military purposes. On the other hand, the population decline of France, which was regarded as one of the contributory causes of the defeat of France in 1940, led to population growth being regarded in the postwar years as desirable for other than economic causes. By and large, the growth of population in the past must, to a large extent, have been a response to economic advance in a broad sense. Instances of "population pressure" undoubtedly occurred, but the broad sweep of growth is more easily interpreted as a consequence of the opening up of new territories and industries.

There are, however, features that make the case of the developing countries very different now from that of the developed countries then, and therefore make their present situation less amenable to historical parallels. First of all, the rate of economic growth and population growth in the developed countries was spread over a

---

[8] The above analysis is from Ohlin, who quotes, among others, Kuznets' statement to the World Population Conference, already referred to.

considerable period of fifty to a hundred years or even longer. Second, it started from a base of considerable preparation for such a development. Third, it was sparked by inventions that gave a very great advantage to the developed countries. Fourth, and this is especially important, it was not subject to the pressure of a world economy in which a considerable portion of the community had already developed and was increasing its economic growth, while the countries in process of development were held back. Fifth, it took place in an environment where education was already highly developed and was increasingly, if gradually, being made available to the great masses of the people.

The great problem of the developing countries is that for their very survival in a world economy, and in order to be able to take any suitable place in it, they have had to develop and have still to develop very rapidly from a very low economic base, with an extremely rapid and unprecedented population growth complicating the process. The situation of the developing countries today, then, differs most sharply from the earlier history of the industrial world. The swift and sustained decline in mortality in the underdeveloped countries of recent years is of a magnitude that has no earlier counterpart. It has occurred for the most part in a different phase of the development process. This is why the fact that rapid population growth has often in the past been associated with rising prosperity seems fairly irrelevant today.

The lessons of history are inadequate guides in the present situation. Nevertheless, the tendency is for developing countries to look to the model of developed countries during the industrial expansion of the latter, when population pressures certainly had a beneficial influence with regard to economic growth in whatever way this influence is interpreted. But it is dangerous to think that history will repeat itself if we consider the conditions and technology of the Space Age, the scale of urbanization, and the absolute numbers of world population, the rapidly increasing rates of increase, so different from the past, and also if we take into account mankind's vastly improved potential for "inventing the future." Dr. Jorge Eliézer Ruiz, director of the Population Bureau's Latin American office in Bogotá, puts the picture for *present-day* Latin America as follows after describing the effects of rapid population increase on housing, morals, and public health.

No economist, finally, would seriously attempt to ignore the fact that it is impossible to achieve the economic surplus necessary for the take-off towards development in societies where the new beings which enter life continually use up this surplus, so painfully obtained, for their own physical survival.[9]

It was for these reasons also that the OECD report, even though it gives a rapid review of the course of economic growth over the last few centuries, with its lack of decisive indications of a general correlation between population and poverty and population and riches, states unequivocally:

The stress and strain caused by rapid population increase in the developing world is so tangible that there are few, and least of all the planners and economists of these countries, who doubt that *per capita* incomes would be increased faster if fertility and growth rates were lower— indeed in some cases they might otherwise not increase at all.[10]

Before going on to consider that statement, I would like to suggest that to keep the effects of the population explosion in perspective, it must be stressed that rapid population growth is only one of the causes or complications of the poverty of the less-developed countries.

It is important to realize that even in present circumstances the population expansion is not the only or the chief cause of underdevelopment. Even in India, with its net extra population of nearly 14 million persons per year, there are many other causes of hunger, malnutrition, and lack of sufficiently rapid development.

Indeed, most developing countries are hampered by factors that have little relation to population growth: backward agriculture, low industrial activity (or the contrary error of overinsistence on premature expansion of heavy industry), currency depreciation, instability of primary commodity prices, lack of adequate markets, unwise international trade and monetary policies, outmoded social and political structures, political corruption, political instability, doctrinaire political theories, expensive military adventures. To rely on population control while neglecting to deal with these causes would be as ill-advised as to concentrate only on them and to omit, where necessary, regulatory population policies.

[9] *Population Bulletin*, Vol. 24, No. 1, February 1968, p. 9.
[10] Ohlin, *Population Control*, p. 53.

Bearing this in mind, and bearing in mind also the danger of over-stressing the effect of population pressures on capital formation and economic growth, nevertheless in most developing countries today rapid rates of population growth do have a retarding effect on economic growth. As we pointed out in Chapter 1, population increase lowers the net rate of economic growth. If a country's population is increasing at the rate of 2.5–3 percent and its economic growth rate is as high as 5 percent, growth rate in reality is 2–2.5 percent, not nearly so impressive a figure.

In the past decade population growth was partly responsible for the slow increase in per capita income almost universally experienced in the developing countries. It did not constitute the main factor, but it aggravated the other factors by precisely the amount of increase that there was.

It may be useful here to sketch the main features of development. Development in the economically less developed countries is much more than simple *economic* development, though this is obviously a crucial factor, one that is indispensable to any more general growth. But it is important to remember that for the developing countries, development affects every aspect of the life of the nation and of the people. Social, political, and cultural changes all form part of the development process. They influence it and are influenced by it. Figures with regard to economic growth cannot give any adequate idea of the transformation and change that are taking place on a wider plane than the merely economic. Even with regard to the economic aspect of change, figures about income and production—income and production indices measuring economic growth—do not always give full credit to the progress achieved. The efforts that the developing countries need to make to promote their economic growth are not necessarily shown in the growth of income or production in relatively short periods of time. They are guidelines but not accurate measurements.

This is especially the case when one goes beyond the purely economic. The developing countries must first achieve a basic transformation of their economies in order to enter into the modern world's economy. This involves more than economic changes, and it often requires considerable investment. It requires building up a new social order as well as a new economic order and the physical basis for economic growth. It is difficult to assess or to justify such investments in noneconomic factors directly by pointing to visible growth, for example, of the national income. But such change is the precondition for making future direct investment more productive and stable.

These ideas must be borne in mind as we turn to the experiences of the developing world with regard to economic development in the 1960's and try to assess the progress they have made.

The target of the United Nations First Development Decade, the decade of the sixties, called "the decade of rising expectations," was an annual growth rate of 5 percent in the developing countries. It is well known that the Development Decade has been a disappointment, partly because population pressures, greater than expected, reduced real growth rates. Still the average annual growth rate was nearly on target at 4.9 percent for the first six years. This compared with 4.7 percent per year during the previous decade. The success of countries like Ceylon, Kenya, and Pakistan may well mean that the target of 5 percent has been reached. But averages are deceptive. They conceal in this case wide variations: some countries have done very well, possibly due to special favorable circumstances, such as oil revenue or the fact that they were already among the richer of the less-developed countries. Other countries have fared badly possibly because they started from a very low economic base or had disastrous military experiences.

Among the major regions, the fastest growth in the 1960's, more than 7 percent per year, has been in Southern Europe and the Middle East. These regions also experienced considerable acceleration in their growth rates in the 1960's compared with the average of the 1950's (in the 1950's, the growth rate in both these regions was 5.6 percent). East Asia achieved average growth of 4.9 percent in the period 1960–66, which was somewhat lower than the growth rate achieved in the 1950's (5.2 percent). Korea, Malaysia, Taiwan, and Thailand achieved growth rates that were much above the average, but the regional average was reduced by sluggish growth in Indonesia.[11] Latin America sustained overall growth of 4.7 percent in the 1960's. Increases in the gross national product for the region

[11] The slowdown in the regional growth rates due to setbacks in the growth of individual countries is only an interesting statistical observation; it does not imply that, as a result of slow growth in one or two countries, other countries in these regions grew less quickly than they otherwise would have.

as a whole were held back by the relatively slow expansion of Argentina and Brazil. As a result, despite the acceleration of economic growth in Chile, Colombia, Peru, and the countries of Central America, the annual average growth rate for the region as a whole was lower in the 1960's than the average of the 1950's.

The slowest-growing regions in the 1960's, as in the 50's, have been Africa and South Asia. Gross Domestic Product (sometimes called Gross National Product or G.N.P.) [12] in these regions increased at average annual rates of 3.3 percent and 3.4 percent, respectively—somewhat less than in the previous decade. The decline in the average for Africa resulted largely from special circumstances in Algeria, where the Gross Domestic Product actually declined, and in the Republic of the Congo. Nigeria too, after a promising start, has suffered economically from its terrible war. The slow growth of India, averaging less than 3 percent per year, chiefly accounted for the sluggishness of the indices of South Asia's expansion in the 1960's.

In per capita terms, growth of developing countries has been even slower. Their rate of population growth accelerated to 2.5 percent yearly from 1960 to 1966, compared with 2.2 percent in the 1950's. Correspondingly, their average per capita economic growth in the 1960's was reduced to 2.3 percent. All the major developing regions have experienced rates of population growth of more than 2 percent in the last decade, except Southern Europe, where the growth rate has been 1.4 percent per year. If Southern Europe is excluded, the average per capita income growth in the developing countries in the 1960's is considerably reduced; it amounts to somewhat more than 1.5 percent. The fastest growth in population in the 60's, following the pattern observed in the 50's, has been in the Middle East (2.9 percent) and Latin America (2.7 percent). There are also considerable variations among countries: for example, Argentina, Barbados, Bolivia, Chad, Greece, Tunisia, and Yugoslavia had relatively low rates of population growth (1.6 percent per year or below), while a considerably larger number of countries, such as Colombia, the Dominican Republic, Ecuador, Guatemala, Honduras, Iraq, Israel, Libya, Nicaragua, Niger, Malaysia, the Philippines, Peru, Somaliland, Thailand, and Venezuela, had rates of population growth between 3 and 4 percent yearly. Two countries

[12] Gross National Product generally exceeds National Income by 10 to 20 percent.

—China (mainland) and India—between them accounted for well over one third of the world's total population. Six countries of the developing regions—India, Pakistan, Indonesia, Brazil, Mexico, and Nigeria—which together contain 28 percent of the world's population, had relatively high rates of increase varying from 3.4 percent (Mexico) to 2 percent (Nigeria). Between 1960 and 1966 the population of Asia increased by 200 million—enough to repopulate the entire United States or the Soviet Union.

While the arithmetic of this relationship between economic growth and population is perfectly clear, unfortunately the economics of it is not, and attempts at generalizations in this respect are often misleading. The available data indicates varying correlations between rates of population growth and rates of economic growth in different countries. Countries like Korea and Thailand, which have experienced high rates of growth, have also had rapid increases in their population. In the case of India, on the other hand, a high rate of population growth has served to increase poverty.[13]

The important point, as we have seen already, is that what happens to economic growth does not depend on the size and growth of population in themselves but on whether productive use can be made of rising population. Where there are plentiful natural resources to be brought into use, or where productive capacity and efficiency are increasing rapidly and the population is so sparse that a sufficiently large-scale economy remains to be realized, a larger population may be no drawback but actually a positive advantage in terms of the average standard of life. Australia and Canada are important examples of this. Some of the African countries, now sparsely populated, may potentially be able to gain rather than lose from larger populations. But for most countries— India is a leading example—the existing numbers may already be too large, at least for the foreseeable future, since there already exists a very large potential labor force that needs to be equipped for production. It is in the inability of most developing countries to use their increasing manpower productively that the economic dis-

[13] For most of the material in this sketch of development, I am indebted to the special paper prepared by Irving Friedman for the Beirut Conference on World Cooperation for Development held in Lebanon, April 21–27, 1968, cosponsored by the World Council of Churches and the Pontifical Justice and Peace Commission.

advantages of their population growth lie. Population control for many of these countries seems a necessity—not only on economic grounds but also on grounds of health, human relations, and indeed as the very basis of civilized life. In judging the efforts of these countries, however, it is important to remember that it usually takes many years before birth rates can be substantially reduced; also, the current increase in population is largely a reflection of the tremendous progress that has been made in cutting down death rates and in improving health care—in itself a fruit of economic development—and this increase in population is likely to continue.[14]

Sometimes health services are blamed, especially by economists, for being responsible for the population explosion, by reducing death rates, which has nullified economic efforts to increase per capita income. One could turn this objection the other way and say what a pity it is that the agriculturalists and economists did not produce advances in agricultural and economic growth to match medical advances. In any case it is generally accepted that the right kind of health services, those of a comprehensive type, are an asset to the ordered growth of the population and of the economy.

Gunnar Myrdal expresses a consensus when he says "rapid and accelerating population increase in South Asia is retarding economic advance and holds the threat of economic stagnation or deterioration sooner or later depending on the conditions in each country."[15] There is a general agreement that this formulation holds good for the developing world as a whole,[16] though circumstances vary so much, because although there are reservations, these generally do not apply to the developing countries (unless, as in the cases of Korea and Taiwan there are special circumstances such as abundant aid and technical assistance), especially where the rapidity of population increase is taken into account.

In order to develop, a country needs savings, capital formation, and investment. Rapid population growth is a retarding factor in this process in the circumstances in which the developing countries

[14] *World Population Conference*, Vol. 1, p. 304.

[15] *Asian Drama*, 3 vols., p. 1463. New York: Pantheon Press (Random House), 1968.

[16] Cf. *World Population Conference*, Vol. 1, pp. 297–300. In this section the complexity of the problem is indicated and refinements are made for which there is not space here.

now find themselves. Population increase may not be the main obstacle—it is certainly not the only obstacle—but it is often an obstacle and an important one.

Coale and Hoover have worked out models in their classic *Population Growth and Economic Development*,[17] illustrating the advantage in terms of per capita income to be gained by a decline in fertility, as opposed to a constant level of fertility.

They take two identical imaginary populations of 1,000 each, with a rate of population increase of 3 percent and a life expectancy of fifty-three years, rising after a period of thirty years to an expectancy of seventy years—a model typical of a developing country. They assume in one case that fertility will remain unchanged and in the other case that fertility will decline until it is halved, after twenty-five years.

The two populations after sixty years will differ in size by nearly 4,000: the first, with unchanged fertility, will be 8,297, and the second will be 3,420. There will also be a change in the age distribution, for in the second case there will be fewer people in the age group of zero to fourteen years, with far more in the age group of fifteen to sixty-four years.

If everything else remains constant, there will be an increase in per capita income due to reduction in fertility alone in the low-fertility population. In this particular projection the total output in thirty years would be 11 percent higher than in the case of sustained fertility, and this would be divided among a population 26 percent smaller.

This is an extremely simplified version of the Hoover-Coale model, which itself makes assumptions to simplify the case, and it has been criticized for omissions: for example, no account is taken of the cost of family-planning programs that reduce fertility.[18]

Nevertheless, it is an interesting model, especially as a number of developing countries are aiming at a reduction of fertility by half in fifteen years. This may not be feasible except in favorable circumstances, but they may easily hit this target in twenty-five years.

The final conclusion is especially interesting: total output after

thirty years would be 11 percent higher in the low-fertility case
and would be spread over a population 26 percent smaller.[19]

A continued high rate of population growth means a high number
of dependent children, and other things being equal, not only a
lower per capita income but undoubtedly a lower willingness to
save. It tends therefore to reduce saving and at the same time to
increase capital requirements for food, schooling, and other services. T. K. Burch has shown with reference to mortality and the
burden of family dependence that, other things being equal, parents in low-mortality areas and consequently areas of higher population growth have to spend more to raise their children than do
those in high-mortality areas. For example, this burden increases
by 54 percent as life expectancy increases from thirty to seventy
years. A decline in mortality is sufficient by itself to introduce
substantial changes in the parental role. In this connection Burch
expresses the view that fertility may be causally (not merely in
time) associated with a decline in mortality rates that has already
taken place.[20] This is offset over a period of time by the children
growing up and joining the labor force, provided there are jobs
for them, which, however, is often not the case in the developing
countries.

Reduction of fertility rates would lessen the burden of dependency. There would immediately be fewer children to support. If
the decline in fertility continued, the decrease in the number of dependent children would go on. With a lower dependency burden,
income per head would rise, as we have seen.

The first effect of this would probably be higher consumption,
and there would be a general rise in standards of living. Everyone
would eat better and be better housed; all would have a larger
share in educational and health services. But there would also be

[19] If the figures are not taken too literally, the projections are interesting and illustrative. But those who wish for more technical reservations
should see *Asian Drama*, Appendix 7, Vol. 3, pp. 2068–2075. Myrdal's
conclusion, however, seems broadly similar: "It seems apparent, then,
that the effect of a decline in fertility would be favorable in both economic and broadly human terms and that these effects are very considerable and cumulative, gaining momentum over the years. They would also
be independent of the man/land ratio: the same causal mechanism
would operate in sparsely as well as densely populated countries" (Vol.
2, p. 1467).
[20] Burch, T. K., "Some Social Implications of Varying Mortality,"
World Population Conference, Vol. 2, p. 388.

available more money for savings and investment, and even for
"forced savings" through taxation.

Population growth has an influence on the pattern of investment
as well as the volume. For Latin America, for example, a paper
presented to the World Population Conference found that the population increase requires, among other things, changes in the pattern of investment providing for "increased resource allocation to a
non-active population, greater concern with structural maladjust-
ments, chiefly rural over-population coupled with excess of
organization and with fuller industrialization." The conclusion of
the paper was that "population growth has a direct bearing on
land and educational reform, industrial development, housing programs and methods, etc., and forcibly justifies development planning."

The treatment of Coale and Hoover and of others with regard to
this problem omits, of course, the effect of capital assistance coming from outside sources, and this is crucial. Such capital assistance
is—in the short term, at least—a more powerful instrument for
increasing the supplies of investable resources than are population
controls as an instrument for augmenting domestic savings capacity. On the basis of hypothetical but not altogether improbable volumes of capital assistance flows to the Middle East, and on an assumed capital output ratio as high as four to one, it has been
concluded that "although this factor of capital assistance would almost entirely compensate for population growth, in any event capital assistance would contribute more [to capital formation] than
an unlikely drop in growth rate." [21] Although no one could reasonably argue that population control and capital assistance should be
viewed as alternative and not complementary policies to effect adequate supplies of investable resources, it is useful to have a sense
of proportion as to the relative contribution that may be expected
from measures of capital assistance and measures of population
control.

In other words, capital assistance can give powerful help to a
developing country to supplement its own resources in the difficult
period—probably the next fifteen years—before population measures have any real impact. Even after that, capital assistance

[21] Sayigh, Yusif A., *World Population Conference*, Vol. 1, p. 300. Cf.
Sayigh, "Population Growth, Capital Formation, and Economic Growth
in the Middle East," Vol. 4.

could have a more useful effect from the purely economic point of view and may well be still needed. But, of course, indefinite external assistance should not be envisaged from other points of view. No one would suggest that it was feasible or desirable that foreign assistance should be used so that a developing country could maintain a higher rate of fertility.

Two categories of effects of high population growth on patterns of investment are worthy of attention. In the first place, a more rapid population growth, as we have seen, requires a larger investment in social and economic overheads simply to maintain the same basic services and standards for the increased numbers. Such overhead investments are capital intensive—require a relatively large amount of capital—and therefore are relatively costly in terms of investment resources. Many of the social-overhead investments thought of in this connection have to do with size of population as such, not specifically with the age distribution. The change from that of a stationary or more slowly growing population has distinct consequences for the pattern of investments. A series of expenditure items for the care and maintenance of children, retired people, and other dependents is classified as investments, depending on the extent to which difference in the growth rate of population reflects differences in mortality or in fertility. The patterns of investments in social overheads will also differ. It seems to be a fairly typical characteristic of most of such overhead investments, however, that they need a relatively large amount of capital compared to economic investments. Hence, the demographic development resulting in higher rates of dependency rates requires investment patterns relatively less efficient in terms of economic growth.[22]

With regard to the effect of population increase on technological development, the impact of high rates of population growth is a complex one. The importance of technology (and by technology one does not mean the highly sophisticated technology of an industrialized society but the application of modern invention in a suitable way to the agriculture and industry of developing countries) is of obvious importance for the modernization of the economies of the developing countries. Demographic developments may hinder or hasten the growth of the modern sector of a developing country.

Rapid population growth tends, for instance, to reduce the scope for capital accumulation generally and also tends to favor capital investments of a traditional character rather than more advanced and risky ventures. The traditional sector tends to remain a poor outlet for products of the modern sector and so on. Technological development, in other words, tends to be slow when population growth in developing countries is high, because a poor economy with stagnant or slowly rising per capita income is also a poor environment for the growth of those sectors of the economy that require modern techniques. This statement is nothing more than another formulation of the vicious circle of poverty. Low productivity reflects backward technology and means low incomes; this in turn means that there is little scope for modern technology, which in turn means low productivity, and so on.

There are, of course, some advantages in rapid population growth in relation to technological development and modernization of the economy. Increased population growth, when it reflects increased fertility, implies a younger population and therefore less weight for those groups that represent tradition and conservative attitudes toward social and economic organization. The younger the population, the larger (relatively) is the group with educations of some sort that may make them efficient operators in a more modern production process.

Rapid population growth keeps ratios of labor to land and labor to capital relatively high throughout the economy. In other words, there will be more people for the same amount of land to support and also a greater increase in labor than in the amount of capital. It also means that the modern sector has plentiful supplies of cheap labor from overcrowded urban populations and from the relatively overpopulated subsistence sectors. This mitigates against advanced production methods, in particular those in which modern technology involves a high capital investment. This need not be a disadvantage because there has recently been a reaction against the importing to developing countries of techniques needing large amounts of capital, when labor-intensive methods would seem to be much more suitable. This attitude is behind the whole principle of intermediate technology.

However, there are certain industries in which this does not apply. An example is taken from the brewing of beer. The brewing of beer is a capital-intensive process. There seems to be no efficient labor-intensive substitute process available for adoption in developing countries. On the other hand, activities associated with the brewing process, such as the cleaning of bottles and various transport services, may be done in a very different way and therefore use a lot of labor.

While rapid population growth in developing countries on balance probably tends to weaken the scope and incentive for general introduction of modern technology, it does not make technological advance impossible; while the task of fostering technological development may be made more difficult by the rapid population growth, it is all the more important to strengthen and supplement the forces that nevertheless make advance possible.

INDUSTRIAL- The emphasis to be given to industriali-
IZATION zation in developing countries is subject
to considerable controversy. Because industrialization has proved so successful in promoting economic growth in the developed countries, there is a tendency to think that the same effect will follow from industrialization in the developing countries. As we have seen, this is a fallacy if applied too rapidly at too early a stage of development. The Second Five Year Plan of India, it is commonly agreed now, did rely too much on industrialization and not enough on agricultural production. But provided the principles established in a former chapter on the need for basing economic advance on the agricultural sector are accepted, the need for industrialization must also be accepted, and even stressed from the point of view of economic growth.

The market for primary products, including agricultural products in *developed* countries, only expands slowly as a consequence of the low rate of growth of population, coupled with the advance of technology that is biased against such products. At the same time, exportable surpluses in developing countries may dwindle as a consequence of their own very rapid growth of population. So while the terms-of-trade effect of these forces may or may not turn out to be unfavorable to agricultural products, the potential expansion of trade in primary products does not appear comparable with the needs for imports of developing countries to support the rapid development of their economies they now seek; though there would be better possibilities when regional cooperation and marketing are promoted among the developing countries, such as the Central American "Common Market" and the East African "Common Market" (at present Uganda, Kenya, and Tanzania).

Looking into the future, existing population trends and present land-to-labor ratios strongly suggest that more rather than fewer developing countries will become net importers of food and other primary products and exporters of manufactured goods. This does not mean, of course, that the demographic reasons for industrialization should be considered conclusive in all developing countries, or indeed that agricultural advance is not essential also in those countries that must depend on imports for some of their food needs; but current demographic trends in developed and developing countries certainly seem to suggest that rapid development of the industrial sector is a necessary, though not sufficient, condition of sustained economic growth in most developing countries today.

Having put the conclusions about the relationship between rapid population increase and savings, investment, technology, and industrial growth in a fairly definite way, it must not be thought that all aspects are quite so simple or uncontroversial. At the World Population Conference attention was rightly drawn to the greater pessimism of demographers and sociologists as compared with economists, and to the importance of maintaining a scientific attitude in the study of demographic change in savings and investment.

Nevertheless, there is a wide consensus that high rates of population growth have detrimental effects on rates of saving and investment. It would not be possible to go into all the reservations that one might make or all the dissenting views, but I think it would be true to say that the consensus would apply pretty generally where it came to population growth rates of more than 1.5 percent in a developing country. What these reservations really amount to are a warning against exaggerating the influence of population growth in isolation on savings and other economic variables, not a denial of the fact that it does have a restraining effect.

The decline in the rate of population growth, though important, is not the sole or most important variable in determining economic growth. The demographic phenomenon is one of the many interrelated variables, and while the World Population Conference naturally focused attention on population problems, other variables, which under certain conditions were more critical than that of population change, must always be kept in mind.[23]

It is important to avoid unduly stressing the relationship between demographic growth and savings, investment, industrialization, and technology—the relationship between demographic growth and poverty and underdevelopment. It is still more important to avoid the danger of exaggerating this, often by default in the popular media. Whenever the subject of population comes up, for example, there is generally a full-page advertisement in the *Washington Post* stressing that population increase is the cause of poverty, often signed by a number of very distinguished people. It would be difficult to say that the material in these advertisements is inaccurate, though at times it may seem to be rather overemphasized, but the impression given is surely false, because these advertisements are not followed up by others stressing the need for food production, increased aid, and other positive activities. If such extensive and well-thought-out advertisements appeared in the *Washington Post* with regard to the positive measures of coping with the problems raised by increasing populations and low-income societies, with regard to the vital importance of foreign aid, of technical assistance, of stressing the *needs* of the developing countries, of refuting the "myths" of the anti-aid lobby, it might well be that the attitude in Washington and in the United States generally would be much more positive than it is now, when foreign assistance has been cut radically.

A very useful popular study, *Does Overpopulation Mean Poverty?*, was produced by the Center for International Economic Growth in 1962.[24] This was, on the whole, a very balanced and objective work, and although naturally some of the statistics are very dated, the ideas are still valuable; indeed, they are even more relevant today than they were when first presented, though they would need refinement in view of more recent developments.

The following summary, which may well serve as the summing up of this chapter, is taken from this study, with a few comments added where necessary.

Rapid population growth hinders economic and social develop-

[23] Cf. *World Population Conference*, Vol. 1, pp. 297–316, on which I have relied heavily for the foregoing.
[24] Jones, Joseph Marion, *Does Overpopulation Mean Poverty?*, p. 25. Washington, D.C.: Center for International Economic Growth, 1962.

ment in the developing countries. Underdeveloped countries by
and large have these things in common:

(1) A low per capita income. The average for the 2 billion people
in Asia, Africa, and Latin America is around $100 a year
(as compared to $2,350 in the United States, and about $850
in Western Europe).
(2) A low rate of savings and investment.
(3) Low industrial output in relation to population.
(4) Poor roads, transport, and communications; inadequate supplies of power and light; poor social services.
(5) A very high proportion of the labor force engaged in agriculture.
(6) Widespread hunger and malnutrition.
(7) High illiteracy, low educational level.
(8) High birth rates. In practically all the underdeveloped countries the birth rates range from 40 to 50 per 1,000 population
per year, as compared with 25 in the United States and 16
in some countries of Europe.
(9) High percentage of dependent children.
(10) High incidence of disease; poor health, especially maternal
and child health; inadequate medical services.[25]

There is near unanimity among international economists that the
conditions listed above could be more easily alleviated by reduction in the rates of population growth and that their alleviation
would help to speed economic development and improvement in
average levels of living. A minority view proposed by Professor Albert Hirschman of Columbia University, that "population pressures
are to be considered forces to stimulate development," is admitted
by him to be the least attractive "and least reliable of all induce-
ment mechanisms," that it is "clumsy and cruel," and that "the
spread of birth control is one important form which the reaction to
population pressure can take and one that, if it occurs, brings with
it basic attitude changes that are favorable to development."

An underdeveloped country needs to take certain steps to bring
about economic development and an improvement in living standards. It must bring about enough new investment in agriculture to
increase production and productivity on the farms and enough new

[25] Hirschman, *Strategy of Economic Development.*

investment in industry to increase production and relieve population pressures on the land; but as a concomitant of such new investment there must be greatly increased expenditures for education, health, and a variety of other public services, and more efficient government administration. Increased investment can be made from the voluntary domestic savings of the people, from savings collected by governments by taxation, and from imported foreign capital. Increased development *expenditures* on education and other public services must be financed mostly through local taxation.

The effect of high birth rates (with lower infant mortality) on these factors may be summarized as follows:

(1) High birth rates produce high percentages of dependent children, who are a burden on productivity and increase the burden of near subsistence in relation to income.

(2) High birth rates increase the financial burden of education and other public services in relation to income.

(3) High birth rates increase population pressure on already densely settled land and thus reduce productivity, the capacity to save, and the possibilities of escape from a poverty trap by succeeding generations.

(4) High birth rates create overcrowding, promote disease, and thereby undermine health and reduce productivity; and low productivity means low income and reduced savings.

Although there are exceptions, underdeveloped countries characteristically save and invest less than 10 percent of their national income each year. Obviously then, improvement in living levels is extremely slow and difficult in most less-developed countries with high birth rates, and in some it is impossible. Even a very low-income country, for example, with an annual per capita income of $65, can increase its annual savings rate fairly rapidly if the population growth rate is low, but as the population growth rate increases, savings decline and disappear, as shown in Figure 4-2. Two assumptions are made in this chart: (1) that an investment of $3 is needed to produce an income of $1; (2) that as per capita income increases, one half of annual income is consumed, to provide somewhat better living, and one half is saved for investment.

This is an oversimplified artificial model and the very assumptions tell us not to take it too literally, but it is very useful to illus-

trate the point; a third assumption is, of course, that the country
is not receiving aid from abroad.

With similar reservations, the following model may be used to
illustrate the effect caused by population growth with regard to income and investment.

FIGURE 4-2 [26]

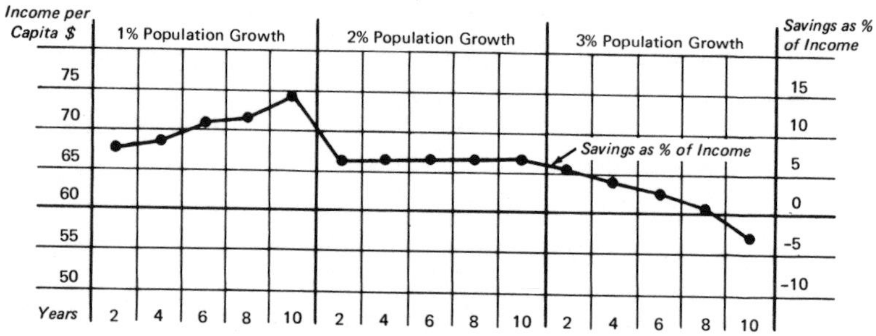

At what rate does an underdeveloped country have to save and
invest in order to make possible improvement in levels of living?

It is widely accepted that, on the average, a fixed capital investment of at least $3 is necessary to increase annual output by $1
annually in the underdeveloped countries, as already assumed in
Figure 4-2. This is a capital-output ratio of three to one. Assuming
this three-to-one ratio, and also assuming that a country is not
receiving any aid or investment from abroad, then:

If the population is growing each year by	A country must save and invest each year at least	In order merely to
1 percent	3 percent of national income	Maintain per capita income unchanged—
2 percent	6 percent of national income	meaning no improve- ment in the average
3 percent	9 percent of national income	living levels

This could be called demographic investment in Sauvy's sense.

Obviously, only savings *in excess of those required to sustain a*

[26] Source: Jones, *Does Overpopulation Mean Poverty?*, p. 29.

growing population at existing levels can be used for investments that will increase per capita income and improve levels of living. Thus, *economic* investment would be:

If the population is growing each year by	*A country must save and invest each year at least*	*In order to achieve an annual increase in per capita income of*
2 percent	9 percent of national income	1 percent
3 percent	15 percent of national income	2 percent

Less-developed countries are, of course, able to supplement their domestic savings with foreign capital imports, most of which reach them in the form of long-term capital investment made by governments, international organizations, and private business. Foreign exchange transfers also occur in the forms of grants, technical assistance, and concessionary food (under the U.S. Public Law 480 Program and the World Food Program). Although developing countries provide 80 percent of their capital investment resources themselves, the 20 percent supplement of foreign resources that is needed is crucial and has often made all the difference in the increase of the annual economic growth rate.[27]

CONCLUSIONS The underdeveloped countries generally confront problems posed by presently rapid rates of population growth, resulting from essentially beneficial, but sudden, declines in death rates. Even in countries that are sparsely populated, rapid increases in population, because of inadequate progress in economic growth, injure both the livelihood of the people and their economic and social advancement. Malnutrition, poor housing, lack of educational opportunities, unemployment and underemployment, and insufficient savings to invest in higher production are consequences.

A rapid rise in population also has consequences for the family and for the quality of life in general. The factors governing the family formation and size are many and subtle, and differ from

[27] *Ibid.*, pp. 29–30.

country to country. They include the prevalent ethos and mores, the level of education, the conditions of health in relation to infant mortality, the status afforded women, and the opportunities available to women for employment outside the home. The development of education for women can make an indispensable contribution to new patterns of family life.

In situations of social change that threaten the family and the truly human development of its members, the first task is to safeguard familial values and the dignity of the human person. A basic contribution to this goal is the promotion of responsible parenthood and family life. Religious institutions can play an important role by emphasizing the duty and right of parents to decide on the number of their children—taking into account, among other things, the claims of the social situation and methods of regulating fertility that are in accord with their conscience and religious convictions. Religious organizations with a deep concern for family life have an obligation to work for the adoption and implementation of programs acceptable to them for responsible parenthood.[28]

As has been emphasized, family planning will not materially reduce the present rate of increase in population in the near future. Even if birth rates are decreased, the falling death rate will keep the rates of population growth at present levels for the time being. The need to limit population now does not imply that in the longer run further expansion in the populations of the sparsely populated regions may not be desirable. Nevertheless, the rapid increase of population in the low-income societies is likely to lead to social, economic, and political problems that may be staggering and perhaps unmanageable. It is therefore a matter of great urgency to curtail the current population explosion, as well as to implement development programs in these societies.

[28] Cf. *Report of the Beirut Conference*, World Council of Churches, pp. 30–31. Geneva, 1968.

Chapter 5

LABOR, EDUCATION, AND HOUSING

THREE VERY IMPORTANT FIELDS ARE often neglected in considering the effect of population growth: labor supply, education, and housing. They have already been touched on, but they are so important that they deserve more extended treatment. Although population growth is not the only factor affecting them, it is useful to consider the effects of rapid population increase on labor supply and education.

LABOR SUPPLY, EMPLOYMENT, UNDEREMPLOYMENT, AND UNEMPLOYMENT

There is a growing tendency to regard the problem of labor and employment as being more important than that of food in a demographic context. The OECD report lays great stress on this factor and gives the impression that there is much more danger of riots and social unrest arising from lack of employment or underemployment, especially in urbanized areas, than from widespread hunger or famines. Perhaps those who hold this opinion have allowed the pendulum to swing a bit too far; perhaps they think that the food situation is in hand and that we need not be too concerned with it. However, warnings such as the following should create great concern: "Unemployment in the large cities of the developing world is staggering. Apart from the waste that this implies that a poor country can ill afford, and from the deep privations entailed, it is a serious threat to the minimum of political stability that development policy requires." [1]

The reason for this widespread unemployment and underemployment is that social and institutional adjustment in a society moving from a traditional economy to urban industrialization is difficult, and present rates of population growth vastly complicate the problem. The most obvious and serious example is failure to absorb the growing labor force. Its absorption in the rural sector is

[1] Ohlin, *Population Control*, p. 58.

held up less by shortage of capital—though this is real—than by the slowness with which methods of cultivation are changed and new lands settled. The resulting exodus to the city aggravates the situation there, which would be critical enough without it, as we have already indicated.

It was reported at the World Population Conference that in Africa, Latin America, and the Far East rates of unemployment varied from 4 percent of the labor force in Thailand to 9 percent in the Philippines and 11 percent in Puerto Rico. In countries such as India even a 5 percent rate involves very large numbers. Despite substantial increases in investment in India during each of its first three development plans, unemployment rose from 5.3 million in 1956 to 8 million in 1961, and was over 12 million by 1966. With a population of 500 million in 1968, a 5 percent rate would equal 25 million.

Because of an inadequate growth of the factors of production in relation to expansion of the labor force, developing economies are also plagued with *under*employment. More than half the inhabitants of Latin America have an income of less than $150 per year, although the per capita average is twice that amount. Percentages of visibly underemployed range from one percent in Israel to 12.5 percent in the Philippines and 22 percent in Pakistan, and higher rates have been found. Increase in population means that there is not enough land to give full occupation to the people on it. In some Latin American countries from 20 percent to more than 50 percent of farms are less than two hectares in size.

In India some 15 to 18 million persons are underemployed (as reported in 1965; the figure was much larger in 1968), and even if the dependence of the labor force on agriculture is to be reduced from 70 percent in 1961 to 60 percent in 1976, a further 23 million workers will still be added to the agricultural force. (The size of the surplus supply of agricultural labor, however, should not be judged completely from the numbers of underemployed in rural areas, since a certain amount of underemployment is caused by the seasonal nature of agriculture.) [2] The rates of population growth of 2.5 to 3 percent in developing countries where there are great unemployment problems, and bad housing and slums in the big cities, obviously compound a difficult situation.

[2] *World Population Conference*, Vol. 1, p. 224.

It is made all the more serious by the fact that total population figures in the decades ahead will not be much affected by declines in fertility. Population increases are going to be large and the labor force will be slower to react for the simple reason that those who will make up the active labor force in 1980 have already been born. But in the years ahead the situation will be aggravated if there is no drop in fertility. The short-run benefits of fertility control are not negligible and may be greater than we at present anticipate if they make themselves felt earlier than, say, the Coale-Hoover model we have considered indicates.

Of course, fertility control alone is no panacea. Positive economic and social measures must be undertaken, with a large amount of capital assistance from abroad. As I have emphasized, the whole problem is linked with general economic development, of which population control is but one factor and not the most important one, nor the one on which immediate impact can be made. But to imagine the labor and urban problems compounded in another twenty years by further high rates of growth, which will happen if fertility control is not immediately adopted, emphasizes the urgency of regulatory population policies *now*.

EDUCATION The cost of education is one of the burdens of dependency that rapid population causes, as we have already seen. But there is another aspect of the relationship. The level of literacy and the proportion of the population of school age being educated are low in the developing countries, and chances of improving the situation are not enhanced by increasing numbers.

The United Nations holds that until at least 50 percent of the population of a developing country is literate, the achievement of self-sustaining economic growth will be extremely difficult.[3] Even if this proportion is regarded as high in view of the possibility of new methods of instructing illiterates, nevertheless there is an urgent need for the expansion of literacy and education in the less-developed regions of the world.

Investment in human resources is as necessary for agricultural and general economic development as investment in the material

[3] *Pre-investment and Productivity*, p. 29. New York: United Nations, Economic and Social Council, 1967.

means to bring these about. No real, truly human progress, no social advance will be possible without raising the standards of overall education in the developing countries. It is one of the most important factors in development. It is, of course, much more than
that. It is a basic human right. As the encyclical *Development of
Peoples* says: "Hunger for education is no less debasing than hunger for food—an illiterate is a person with an undernourished
mind. To be able to read and write, to acquire a professional formation, means to recover confidence in oneself and to discover that
one can progress along with others." [4]

The accumulated knowledge and wisdom of mankind is denied
to the illiterate, even the ability to read simple instructions. The
way to development and progress; the road to a good life, to a reasonable standard of living, to liberation from outmoded social
structures; the ability to escape from the net of fear and superstition, lies through knowledge. Ignorance is the ally and concomitant of poverty and hunger. Knowledge is power. These well-worn
phrases express a truth that is only too well brought home by the
statistics. Education devoted to the full development of the human
personality is an enriching experience. The whole point and purpose of economic development and technological progress is not to
produce things, but to give to human beings a chance of a fuller,
more human life, to promote integral human development. Without
education this is scarcely possible for large numbers in the circumstances of modern life. Basic education is a powerful force making
for national unity and social cohesion. Without it, there can be no
real democracy, no mature participation in the political life of the
nation. The political difficulties of emerging nations—for example,
in Africa—are compounded, even caused, by lack of education. To
give a concrete example, the West Cameroons, where I was a
teacher for ten years, has had no serious political difficulties in
making the transition to independence since the beginning of the
1960's. When independence from colonial rule came in 1961, there
were more than 3,000 highly educated people in the country
(many graduates of the high school of which I was principal, the
first of its kind in the country, which was established only in 1940).
On the other hand, the Congo had but a handful of highly educated people at the time of independence, and its history has been
far different.

[4] No. 35, p. 25.

Improvement in agriculture, improvement of industrialization, improvement in administration—all these things depend on education. At present there is an insufficient supply of trained people of the developing countries for these tasks. That is why technical and capital assistance from developed countries is so important.

An example to illustrate the point may be taken from agriculture and food production. The various measures suggested in Chapters 2 and 3 obviously require people who can carry them out at a high level, but also need people on a lower level, for example, extension officers. But such personnel need basic education plus agricultural knowledge. To get them means competing in the pool of educated people available.

In the advanced countries of the world the literacy rate is between 95 and 99 percent. In the developing countries it is, on the whole, less than 50 percent. In the United States there are 1.7 million teachers at the primary and secondary levels. This is equal to 900 teachers per 100,000 of the population. In Ethiopia the ratio is 22 per 100,000; in Sudan, 91; and in Tanzania, 115.[5]

Nearly half the children of the world do not go to school and have no chance of education. More than half of the world's population over ten has never been to school. Of the inhabitants of Peru, 52 percent are illiterate; of Brazil, 51 percent; of Africa as a whole, 80 percent; of India, 83.4 percent. In Asia illiteracy in the majority of countries is over 80 percent, which explains the scarcity of medium-level and high-level personnel.

The low literacy rate also explains the imbalance, with grave political consequences, already indicated, between a comparatively small educated elite and the mass of the population that is uneducated and illiterate.

In 1963, the director general of UNESCO said that there were 700 million people estimated to be illiterate, namely, two fifths of the population of the world. The great majority are in the less-developed countries.

As regards children (from five to fifteen years) in the underdeveloped regions of Africa, Latin America, and Eastern Asia, 47 percent of the children of school age do not go to school. To take into account the number of those who will relapse into illiteracy—primary school children who will leave before they have reached the decisive age of functional

[5] Cf. Bowe, Gabriel, *The Third Horseman*, p. 154. Dayton, Ohio: Pflaum Press, 1967.

literacy—these regions will have 150 million future adult illiterates. Under present conditions of educational development and population growth in the course of the next six or seven years, 20 to 25 million new illiterates will be added each year to the world's population.[6]

Since then, of course, the population of the world and the proportion of illiterates has grown immensely in spite of all educational efforts.

This brings us to the crucial point to which all these considerations have been leading. Educational efforts are largely nullified by rapid population increase. This is a situation that must be faced by positive means, especially by specific assistance from abroad to the educational plans of the developing countries. But also it indicates the need for fertility control, if the problem is not to become completely unmanageable.

The example of Kenya is a good illustration of my point. According to a report to the Ministry of Economic Planning and Development produced by the Population Council of New York,[7] the rate of population increase in 1965 was 3 percent. It was projected to increase to 3.9 percent by the end of the century, if there is no change in fertility patterns.

The report illustrated the value of a reduction in fertility to the education program by considering the prospects for primary education; a similar argument would also apply with only slight modification to secondary education. Assuming a 4 percent annual increase in school enrollment in accordance with Kenya's current Six Year Development Plan, *the proportion of school-age children in primary schools will increase from an estimated 55 percent in 1965 to merely 62 percent in 1990, if fertility remains unchanged. On the other hand, if fertility were to be reduced by 50 percent in fifteen years, the proportions enrolled would rise at an accelerated pace,* reaching 100 percent shortly after 1985. *However, if fertility were to remain unchanged it is likely that the number of illiterate children* of primary-school age would double in the next twenty-five years, in spite of present plans to improve and expand education.[8-9]

[6] Address to the United Nations Conference on the Application of Science and Technology, p. 12.

[7] August 1965. Compiled by Ansley Coale, director, Population Research, Princeton University; Richmond Sanderson, Population Council; Lyle Saunders, Ford Foundation; and Howard Taylor, Dept. of Obstetrics and Gynecology, Columbia University.

[8-9] *Kenya Population Report*, pp. 28–29.

It seems beyond doubt that a reduction of fertility in developing countries with rapidly expanding populations will give better educational opportunities, even though it will take some time for these advantages to materialize.

Another point with regard to the relationship between education and fertility is that education in the long run also promotes a decline in fertility (though this is not immediately or universally true). An increase in educational facilities will help to strengthen and make successful a program of population regulation. There is a hint of a vicious circle here: population-control measures help to increase education but they themselves are dependent on a certain amount of education. No doubt this is one of the reasons why rapid results cannot be expected, but recent developments seem to suggest that some progress can be made in population-restrictive policies by popular programs without a high degree of education among those who are involved in them.

A certain degree of education makes people more willing to change accepted patterns of social behavior if given sufficient reason to do so. Second, education itself presupposes that a certain change in outlook has already been accepted. The parents are prepared to let their children go to school instead of requiring them to work and become productive either on the farm or in jobs in the city as soon as they are old enough to do so. The fact that education, furthermore, involves expenses for school fees, books, extra clothes, and similar items also means that parents may tend to want fewer children.

The point in the educational process at which it begins to affect fertility varies from the mere attainment of literacy in some areas to a minimum of high school education in others, but it is found that the educational level of women is more significant than that of men. (In towns and cities the effect of education on fertility is more pronounced than in rural areas.) Although higher educational levels generally accompany low fertility, the most highly educated groups in the United States and in some European countries are an exception to this rule. Occasionally, in these countries, particularly low fertility is found among those with a very low standard of education.

Education's effect on fertility is linked with general economic development, conscious motivation to have fewer children, and the means to do so. J. M. Stycos, an expert in Latin American population studies, says on the basis of his studies in Puerto Rico that

most Latin American countries that wait for education to reduce
birth rates may wait for a long time.[10-11]

A family-planning program can only be successful in the midst
of other social and economic changes that cause a veritable intellectual revolution. A family-planning program cannot be pursued
in a vacuum; it must be based on the preexisting desire of the population. Before the population comes to this desire not only have
the advantages of a reduction in fertility to be seen, but even a
completely new idea of existence has to be entertained. A man
must become aware of what he can do with regard to his own fate.
Then there is no longer a fatalistic attitude toward the world,
mixed with superstition, but a reasonable and voluntary one. Man
must see that it is more human to plan his life, even his fertility,
rather than go by instinctual urges or old social patterns, leaving
the result to fate or to "providence" (a falsely conceived Providence).

**HOUSING AND
SLUMS** The disastrous results of overpopulation
are especially visible in the bad housing
and slums in the large cities and towns of
developing countries. Here I can speak from a certain amount of
personal experience, having visited the "barriadas," the "favelas,"
the "barrios," and the "callampas" of Lima, Santiago, Rio, Recife,
Caracas, which surround these South American cities with a belt of
misery; and having seen the slums of East and West Africa, the
Philippines, and Malaysia. Others have examined the slums of
Bombay, Calcutta, and other big cities in India.

Population pressures on the nonmodernized agricultural sector
have heightened the frequency with which families leave the overcrowded, poverty-stricken countryside, hoping to find a livelihood
in the cities. Unskilled labor is abundant and not wanted: hence
the growth of slums like the Ciudad de Dios, about fifteen kilometers outside Lima, to which people from the rural areas flocked,
not only on account of population pressures but because of the social injustice of an outmoded system of land tenure, under which
most rural property is owned by a few absentee landlords. The majority of the squatters in the huge sand dunes, when I was there

[10-11] *World Population Conference,* Vol. 1, p. 209. See also J. M. Stycos,
"Education and Fertility in Puerto Rico," Vol. 4, p. 180.

several years ago, lived in shacks, where public utilities such as water and light were extremely scarce. One young woman with eight children was living in a shelter where one would hardly keep a motorcycle in a more affluent country.

There are other slums, such as the "Poblaciones" of Santiago, which really range from reasonably good working-class dwellings (too small, however, for the number of inhabitants, and where the roads are generally bad) to the "callampas"—mushroom settlements—which are little more than lean-to shelters. In Rio I remember one "barriada" within sight of the luxury hotels of the fabulous Copacabana Beach, where the "main road" was just steps about a yard wide cut out of the hillside, and there were no side roads; one just pushed one's way between shacks, taking care not to lean on them too heavily, for they were so fragile. In these shacks whole families lived with perhaps one source of water supply, a rudimentary tap, for a hundred families. The same holds true of São Paolo.

It gives the lie to those rich people who actually told me that the people of the slums are little better than animals and that they like to live in these conditions. I did not find them so. They were human beings with the same aspirations, the same needs, the same feelings, as their more affluent brethren. That was at once a source of hope and a measure of the tragedy of their surroundings.

I do not wish to strike too gloomy a note. While I was in Rio, I saw a whole hillside that had been cleared and on which good houses were being built as a result of the combination of local effort and the Alliance for Progress. I wished that those isolationists who oppose aid and those intellectuals who despise it because it is "delaying the revolution" could have seen what I saw.

People in the slums often multiply more rapidly than the people in the rest of the cities. In other words, slums are going to double their population in much less than even the short time the average 2.5–3 percent involves. It is this rapid increase that is frightening. Other signs were hopeful, in places like Caracas. The people in the slums seem more self-reliant there, more able to raise themselves than others. Again, the government is doing its best to improve conditions. And I saw a happy example of voluntary service in which thirty Venezuelan university students and thirty American students had formed an enterprise called Acción in Venezuela. They lived for periods in the slums and did not *do* anything for the people but stimulated them to try to improve their own lot, putting them in touch with government and other agencies that could augment their self-help efforts. They had been responsible for a complete water system in one section of these slums, and other sections were being stimulated to do the same.

The slums in Latin America are terrible enough, but some would regard the slums of the East as even worse. I have not seen the slums of Calcutta, but the description of these and the slums in other Indian cities is too well known to need repeating. And it is estimated that if present trends and present birth rates continue there will be 60 million in Calcutta in fifty years' time; the increase will be mainly among the poor and the destitute. Arthur Hopcraft gives a moving description from personal experience of the misery of the slums of Calcutta.[12] He says: "The squatters already nest with the rats on every square foot not built upon. If we imagine their number doubled we are moving towards the unspeakable."

Urbanization has become an acute problem in all the poor countries; it is bad enough in the rich. One sociologist has calculated that in the forty years from 1960 to the end of the century, the populations of Indian cities will increase by something between 100 and 200 million. Bombay has already more than tripled its population since World War II.

Another analyst has predicted that by A.D. 2000, throughout the world, some 4 billion people will be living in urban areas. This will require housing to be built forty times as fast as it is being built today!

So long as opportunities in the city appear to be greater than in the less-developed areas surrounding it, so long will the city attract people to its streets. The overcrowded slums will grow.[13]

These conditions are being aggravated either directly by population increase in the city itself or indirectly by population pressures driving people from the land.

The need for some restriction on fertility and some scheme to better conditions so that this great flow to the cities is stopped appears urgent in the light of such circumstances.

[12] *Born to Hunger*, pp. 105–116. London: Pan Books, 1968.
[13] Llewellyn, Bernard, *The Poor World*, p. 74. London: Zenith Books, Hodder & Stoughton, 1967.

Chapter 6

POPULATION CONTROL

POPULATION REGULATION, RESPONSIBLE PARenthood, restriction of fertility, family planning, birth control, birth regulation, population control are all names for the same thing, but some are more accurate than others, some have less provocative overtones, some have a more positive connotation. They will be used here without any pejorative discrimination to designate programs to reduce fertility and the rate of population growth.

As was pointed out earlier, such programs are no longer seen as a panacea for the problems of developing countries. Indeed, they can only be conceived of as one measure among many, all of which are intended to modify old social and economic structures in view of the changed circumstances of modern life, and to promote needed progress. What can these family planning programs do, what are the prospects of success, what is the cost, and when will they begin to have a significant impact?

I shall try to answer these questions with the most up-to-date information available, but since many of these programs are in their infancy not all the questions can be answered with certainty.

But before trying to do so, it might be useful to prepare the ground by discussing two fundamental points: What is the attitude of the main religions of the world toward family planning? Do parents, especially women in developing countries, want fewer children? There are some preconceptions on both these subjects that closer study may help to dispel.

ATTITUDE OF RELIGIONS TO FAMILY PLANNING Anything as fundamental, mysterious, and awesome as the birth of new life is inescapably related to man's religious instinct. The miracle of birth links the living with the dynamic, the creative element in the universe.[1] All religions, even the most primitive, have in the past

[1] Fagley, Richard, *The Population Explosion and Christian Responsibility*, p. 95. New York University Press, 1960.

linked a concern for fertility with the sacred. This attitude was understandable, since fertility is essential to individual and social
survival. This mysterious and religious aura extended to marriage
and the act of procreation, even in societies where ideas about sexual morality were very different from those of the major religions.

Fertility cults were an expression both of the need for high fertility as a means of survival in the face of high mortality—especially
child mortality—before the era of modern medicine, and also of
the power of the sexual instinct, which, after the instinct for self-
preservation, is the most powerful of human drives.

The major religions tended to absorb fertility cults, to resist the
elements in them that were corrupt and even to react against the
glorification of the "passions of this life." Yet they often retained
the pro-fertility patterns and sanctified them still further.

Children were regarded as a blessing in the natural order, as a
source of labor in subsistence agricultural communities—as they
still are—and as a sort of insurance against old age. At the same
time they were regarded as gifts of God, as the source of filial piety,
as bringing honor to their parents. Often other religious elements
entered in, which also gave value to abstinence and celibacy, and
which attempted, by religious rites and teachings, to modify the
uncontrolled exercise of the sexual instinct.

In the past there was widespread need, on the whole, not for
population restriction, but for increased fertility, and religious
teaching respected and reflected this. Until this century, the idea of
responsible parenthood stressed responsibility for seeing that the
family, the clan, the nation, the human race, should continue. The
opposition, for example, to contraception, of the twenties and early
thirties, was partly because population was declining and birth
control seemed a dangerous means of accelerating and perpetuat-
ing that trend. The encyclical *Casti Connubii* (December 31, 1930),
which registered the Catholic Church's ban on artificial contraception in the strongest terms, was written in that atmosphere.

Religious opposition, therefore, might seem to be an obstacle to
the spread of present population-restrictive policies. In considering
this vital question, two things should be distinguished from each
other: formal doctrine or official teaching as contained in authentic
declarations of the teaching authority, traditions, or documentary
sources; and beliefs, attitudes, and practices of the living religious
community. It is often assumed that differences between the two

mean a lessening of religious faith and a yielding to secular influences. This need not be so. In the application of religious principles to changing social conditions, it is quite normal to find a certain interaction between the community of believers and the religious heritage expounded by the teaching authority. Such a dialogue can be a sign of religious vitality rather than mean a loss of religious interest.[2] These factors must also be related to the availability of cheap and acceptable methods of fertility restriction.

In the past five years changes have taken place more rapidly than might have been thought possible. Even as early as 1963 a study conducted by the University of Kerala in a high-fertility rural area showed signs of changes in attitude beyond, and even contrary to, what the teaching and traditional religious practice of the community would have suggested. This study concerned attitudes to family planning and included members of the major religious groups: Hindu, Moslem, Roman Catholic, and other Christians (mainly Orthodox in background). The result indicated that *one third* of the people studied were not in favor of family planning on religious grounds and *two thirds* were in favor.[3] This finding suggests that changes in religious attitudes in developing countries will take place at a much more rapid rate than has been the case in Western cultures. It is interesting also as showing the importance of empirical data in this field. Such a result could not have been foreseen from the formal religious teaching of the religions represented in these groups.

Hindu teachings on the whole, in spite of their world-renouncing character, lay great stress on the family and caste, and the begetting of sons is regarded as a religious duty. The Hindus had, therefore, a strong pro-natalism and opposed restriction of fertility.

In Buddhist teaching, procreation and family life are matters of secondary importance. There is a strong ascetic element, reflected in the institution of the celibate priesthood. On the other hand, the Buddhist way stresses the middle path, avoiding the extremes of sensuality on the one hand and unprofitable asceticism on the other. But injunctions to marry and generate are lacking in Buddhism and pro-natalist influence in Buddhism stems from extraneous sources.

A strong pro-natalist bias exists in Islam teaching, and this is rein-

[2] Fagley, Richard, "Doctrines and Attitudes of Major Religions in Regard to Fertility," World Population Conference, Vol. 2, p. 78.
[3] Ibid., p. 84.

forced by a strong belief in the active providence of Allah. It is Allah who creates sexuality and determines procreation and barrenness, and the number of souls is predestined. Therefore, the question of deliberately restricting offspring seems to go against the Will of Allah, and to plan the number of children seems an impious distrust of divine providence.

Nevertheless, there is sufficient flexibility in these Eastern faiths for modern reformers within these religions to put forward the case for scientific methods of family planning.[4] Even in Islam, modern religious opinion based on various Islamic principles provides a sanction for contraception, and the statements of heads of governments of Islamic countries give support to family-planning programs. The Shah of Iran, King Hussein of Jordan, Prime Minister Tunku Abdul Rahman of Malaysia, President Bourguiba of Tunisia, and President Nasser all signed the Statement of Population by Heads of State, urging the adoption of family planning on account of rapid population increase.[5]

It appears, therefore, that no general opposition to fertility-restriction policies exists in these religions which would be an obstacle to necessary population-restriction policies. Of course, such a generalization is subject to reservations. More conservative Hindus may well follow the lead of Gandhi, who was completely opposed to any artificial restriction of fertility, and only among more modernized Moslems would the views I have mentioned be general.[6] Nevertheless, if social and cultural factors change in favor of family planning, one would not expect religious opposition to be strong and united.

With regard to the Jewish religion, the Old Testament records strong religious and cultural influences that favored a high level of procreation, and it is probable that family limitation was neither favored nor sought.[7] The new dimension added to marriage by the concept of a loving union of man and woman as a blessing of God meant a curb on unrestricted fertility and concern for the family as a whole, but did not go as far as contemplating the restriction of the numbers in the family.

---

[4]*Ibid.*, p. 82.
[5] Cf. Maudin, W. Parker, *Muslim Attitudes to Family Planning,* New York: Population Council, August 1967, where views of religious and political leaders are collected and various aspects of Islam and family planning are treated.
[6] *Ibid.*
[7] Fagley, *Population Explosion and Christian Responsibility,* p. 118.

In modern Judaism, both doctrine and practice constitute no obstacles to contraceptive birth control. The Rabbinical Assembly of the United States in 1935 stated:

Careful study and observation have convinced us that birth control is a valuable method for overcoming some of the obstacles that prevent the proper functioning of the family under present conditions—proper education in contraception and birth control will not destroy, but rather enhance, the spiritual values inherent in the family and will make for the enhancement of human happiness and welfare. And the practice of birth control seems to have become universal amongst the Jews.[8]

With regard to population restrictions in the developing countries, religious attitudes and their effect on population policies are important. Except for Latin America and countries such as the Philippines (with respective populations of 268 million—slightly more than one tenth of that of the developing world—and 33 million) the influence of non-Christian religions is obviously of greater importance than that of the Christian Churches. Buddhism of one form or another counts between 350 and 400 million Asians. The followers of Mohammed constitute the largest religious group in the less-developed world, with nearly 500 million in Asia and in the Near and Middle East. Hinduism is the major religion of India's 520 million people.

But Christian views, attitudes, and practice are obviously important, not only because of the fact that Latin America is largely Catholic and has some of the highest rates of population increase, but also because of the importance of the attitude of developed countries, especially the United States, and attitudes in international bodies such as the World Health Organization. Christian teaching has a considerable impact, even where practice is lacking, and the United States is a predominantly Christian country with a high level of practice.

The Christian religions, until the last century and the beginning of this century, all held procreation to be the main purpose of marriage. Indeed, in Catholic terminology it was called the primary end of marriage. The Eastern Orthodox Church went further and condemned the nonprocreative use of sex.

The Protestant Churches, although seemingly more pro-natalist

[8] *Ibid.*, p. 122.

than the other Churches, in that they viewed marriage, rather than celibacy, as a religious vocation, nevertheless (some would say because of this), were the first group of Christians to stress responsible parenthood. A cautious and qualified assent to family limitation was given at the Lambeth Conference of leaders of the Anglican Church held in 1930. A much stronger and more positive line was taken in 1958 and 1968 at Lambeth, and the current consensus of Protestant leaders is that companionship and procreation are separable aspects of marriage. Both aspects are important in helping the couple to fulfil "their covenant and serve the one flesh union." The consensus can be summarized as follows:

The nature of this union elevates the question of parenthood above the determinism of lesser species into the realm of freedom and ethical decision. Couples, to whom the power of procreation has been given, have an obligation, in accordance with the concrete circumstances of the marriage, to seek another child or to defer or prevent a further conception. This decision requires that various considerations be weighed: the prospects of health of a future child, the right of children to love and nurture in the full sense, the health of the mother-wife, the claims of the couple's vocation and, some would add, the claims of the social situation of which the family is a part. These are elements in the current Protestant understanding of responsible parenthood.[9]

Some of the higher clergy of Eastern Orthodox Christianity have interpreted patristic tradition to allow only complete abstinence as a means of family limitation. However, in practice the Orthodox tradition is to leave the primary responsibility to husband and wife in this area. The support that Patriarch Athenagoras officially gave to the encyclical *Humanae Vitae* (On the Regulation of Births) of Pope Paul would not alter this position. One bishop, the bishop of Elia, even stated that "the orthodox Confessor is not expected to advise his people to disregard scientific opinion."

In recent years birth control has been the subject of great discussion and controversy in the Catholic Church. The main controversy has centered around *methods* of family limitation but has revealed the development of Catholic attitudes to love, sex, marriage, and the family. Family limitation itself, for personal and population reasons, has come to be officially accepted.

[9] *Ibid.*, p. 80.

The Catholic Church, before the Reformation, was still largely guided by the teachings of the Fathers, especially the rather pessimistic St. Augustine. On the one hand, celibacy and virginity were held in high esteem (religiously speaking, the Middle Ages was the era of the celibate monks); on the other hand procreation was championed as a positive good against the Manichean tendency to regard sex as evil (a tendency revived in the twelfth and thirteenth centuries by the Albigensian heresy). The tendency, however, was to see procreation—the bringing of children into the world—as justifying sex and the marital act.

After the Reformation, the Council of Trent spoke of procreation as the primary end of marriage, but it also assigned importance to the spiritual and moral value of marriage to the couple. Various decisions of the Holy Office, from 1816 onward, condemned artificial means of limiting the number of children. However, the Revised Code of Canon Law of 1917 spoke of the "procreation *and education* of children," a concept that could subsequently be interpreted to justify the separation of procreation from the other purposes of marriage. The famous encyclical *Casti Connubii* (Christian Marriage), issued by Pope Pius XI on December 31, 1930, banned methods of artificial contraception, but added to the concept of procreation in marriage the cultivating of mutual love. Though it kept the terms primary (namely procreation) and secondary ends of marriage, in one passage it seemed to exalt this mutual love in a certain way above procreation.

Pope Pius XII went further and in 1951 recognized that there were medical, social, economic, and eugenic circumstances that might justify the separation of the procreative from the other ends of marriage. Nevertheless, he did not sanction the use of artificial contraception. The only way for Catholics to achieve this separation and yet retain the physical relationship in marriage was by the method of periodic continence.

The method of periodic continence, also called the rhythm method, or the method of the "safe period," is based on the physiological fact that only for a short time each month, probably about forty-eight hours, is it possible for a woman to conceive. This fertile time is calculated either by the calendar method, based on the monthly cycle, or by the temperature method, which fixes the time of ovulation through a slight rise in temperature. It is then possible to avoid conception by restricting love-making to the infertile periods of the cycle. According to an article in the British medical periodical *The Lancet,* the rhythm method practiced by well-instructed and highly motivated couples is as successful as most contraceptive methods and more successful than some in use.[10]

The statement of Pius XII firmly established the idea of responsibility in parenthood and made it clear that the Church did not stand for "an ungoverned spate of unwanted births." Nevertheless, even until the beginning of the Vatican Council in 1962, among many Catholics the ideal of the good Catholic family was the large family. On the other hand, numbers of Catholics had left the active practice of their religion either because they could not, or did not want to, practice the rhythm method, but still did not want a large family.

During the early sixties, and especially during the Vatican Council,[11] an important minority of bishops, theologians, and lay people came to the view that responsible parenthood, being a positive and approved value, could be practiced by any effective artificial means, short of surgical sterilization or abortion, as well as by the use of the rhythm method. This view has spread so much since the Council that it could hardly be called a minority point of view, at least in the developed countries; and many married couples have been following it without condemnation from their priests and even with their active encouragement. The Council produced a very fine treatise in miniature on marriage in Chapter 1, Part II, of the Pastoral Constitution, *The Church in the Modern World,*[11a] in which the couple's personal relationship and the family are seen as two equal aspects of marriage and the old division into primary and secondary ends is deliberately avoided.

However, the vexed question of artificial methods—methods "against nature," as *Casti Connubii* described them—remained and was not then discussed, still less decided, at the Council. Pope Paul had reserved the ultimate decision to himself when on June

[10] Marshall, Dr. John, in *The Lancet,* July 6, 1968. Dr. Marshall gives an interesting comparison of the effectiveness of the different contraceptive methods: Pregnancies per 100 women years: Temperature method using first and second phases, 19; calendar method, 14; condom, 11; diaphragm or cap and cream, 8; temperature method using second phase only, 6; intrauterine device, 3; oral contraceptive, 0.1.

[11] October 11, 1962–December 8, 1965.

[11a] Published in *Documents of Vatican Council II,* ed. Walter Abbot, S. J. New York: America Press, 1966.

23, 1964 (between the second and third sessions of the Council), he appointed a special commission to study the subject of population and family planning (this commission extended the work of the one that had been set up in 1963 by Pope John).

The papal commission reported at the end of June 1966. Its report was leaked to the press and showed that a large majority of the commission, in origin a conservative body, was in favor of change and no longer accepted the ban on contraception for the two main reasons hitherto advanced, namely, that contraception was against the natural law and against tradition. The argument from authority, i.e., from the solemn statement of the Pope in *Casti Connubii*, believed by some to be an infallible pronouncement, remained as the basis for a continued ban. In October 1966, the Pope declared that he needed more time for study, but in the meantime, the traditional teaching had to be followed.

The papal encyclical *Humanae Vitae* (On the Regulation of Births), published on July 25, 1968, caused controversy unprecedented in the modern Catholic Church. Instead of the easing of the Church's position as had been expected, Pope Paul reiterated the ban on artificial contraception. He did, however, assert the need for responsible parenthood both for the good of the individual and of society. With regard to population, what he said must be understood in the light of his previous encyclical, published in 1967, *Populorum Progressio* (On the Development of Peoples).[12] Although that encyclical seems very concerned, and rightly so, with possible abuses in population policies, at the same time, problems of increasing population are frankly stated in the first sentences of paragraph 37.

It would obviously be out of place in a factual book such as this to go into the controversy that the encyclical *Humane Vitae* has raised: one can simply note the fact of the controversy without speculation at this stage as to what the longer-term effects of it may be. What follows in this chapter is, then, purely a record of facts. The author does not intend to state any position in this controversy, and such recording of facts with regard to this and to population programs is without value judgments or advocacy of particular programs or methods. But a few general remarks with

---

[12] Both encyclicals are available from the United States Catholic Conference, 1312 Massachusetts Avenue, Washington, D.C.

regard to the Catholic position on development and population may be in order.

Very many—perhaps most—population experts were disappointed by the encyclical, for they viewed its ban on artificial contraception as an obstacle to much-needed population restriction policies, especially in Catholic countries such as Latin America and the Philippines. Indeed, the population problem in these countries must have been one of the principal causes of the anguish that Pope Paul tells us he experienced in doing what he felt he had to do, for moral reasons.

Most moderate demographers and those organizations concerned with coping with population problems and aware of their complexity, while strongly regretting the official stand of the Church, reiterated by Pope Paul, have been anxious to understand the problems for Catholic demographers that the encyclical has raised and to help the Church constructively to play its part.[13]

The constructive and realistic thing to do is surely to intensify efforts to make the means of population control recognized by the Catholic Church as effective and easy to use as possible. A breakthrough on the rhythm method would be a boon, not only to Catholics, but to all who have misgivings about present contraceptive methods. On the other hand, it is completely in keeping with the teaching of Vatican Council II that those outside the Catholic Church who honestly believe contraceptive practices for population control to be legitimate should not be hindered by the Church, even in Catholic countries. Moreover, a close study of the encyclical shows understanding and compassion even for those Catholics who find the high principles of the encyclical difficult or impossible to put into practice. This must be true of many millions of poor people in the developing countries who are not able to be instructed in the rhythm method, feel unable to practice complete abstinence in marriage, and yet abhor abortion, which is often the scourge of those countries where adequate family-planning facilities are not available. That many devoted Catholics in developing

[13] A group of German scientists were much more balanced than the American scientists in their views. Cf. Federation of German Scientists, *Welternährungskrise* (provisional translation: World Food Crisis, or Is Famine Inevitable?), pp. 92–97. Hamburg: Taschenbuch Verlag (Rowohlt paperback), 1968.

countries feel themselves to be in this position is clear from statistics of practicing Catholics who do use contraceptives.

The pessimistic reactions to the impact of the encyclical on population policies were, perhaps, premature. Possibly, the clarifications that have come out since the encyclical may allow Catholics to cooperate in population programs that use unapproved methods and may even allow governments in Catholic countries to have population programs.

Even high ecclesiastical circles and theologians known to be uncompromisingly in favor of the encyclical seem to be favoring an easing of the position in practice. To many outside the Church and to some inside, these positions may seem to be theological subtleties, but our concern here is only with the practical consequences.

It is reported that even some of those in high positions in the Catholic Church who have shown the utmost loyalty to the teaching of *Humanae Vitae* in the controversy, have given their approval to the following view of the encyclical:

According to the teaching of the Church the encyclical represents the "ideal" of Christian marriage, but couples who have genuine problems about birth regulation could use "artificial" methods for this purpose without sin or scruple of conscience on the ground that their objective situation prevents them from attaining the practice of the ideal or noncontraceptive marriage.[14]

Whatever may be the truth of this report, a leading theologian who is widely credited with a major part in the compiling of the encyclical, the French Jesuit G. Martelet, has written two lengthy articles in a Louvain periodical.[15] He makes a distinction that could be of great importance for the participation of the Catholic Church in population programs. He asks the question: Does the encyclical in condemning contraception as an objective disorder also condemn by this very fact someone whose conscience causes him to have recourse to such a deviation as being in his view the lesser evil? Father Martelet says we must frankly answer this question in the negative.[16]

[14] *Herder Correspondence*, "Roman Reactions to the Reactions," London, Vol. 16, No. 1, Jan. 1969, p. 28.
[15] Martelet, G., S.J., "Pour mieux comprendre L'encyclique *Humanae Vitae*," *Revue Nouvelle Théologique*, No. 9, Nov. 1968, pp. 897–917, and No. 10, Dec. 1968, pp. 1,009–1,066.
[16] *Ibid.*, p. 1053.

Surely this statement suggests the legitimacy of individual Catholic support and even Catholic government sponsorship of family-planning programs. The "lesser evil" in Latin America is surely contraception rather than abortion. Using contraceptives to remedy the plight of those poor millions who do not have access to the rhythm method and cannot (and should not) practice complete abstinence is surely a lesser evil than leaving them to procreate irresponsibly and without any means to regulate their fertility.

Adopting the principle of the "lesser evil" would also have the very desirable effect of making Catholic teaching concur with Catholic practice. A recent study has shown that although the Church's teaching has some effect on the fertility of Catholic couples, the sociological factor, especially the level of development, has a much greater effect.[17] In developed countries, for example, Catholics do have a fairly low fertility rate comparable to that of non-Catholics, and surveys have shown that a high proportion have used contraception and a comparatively high number think it should be allowed. The compromise suggested above could be a practical way of easing the tension of good Catholics who practice contraception, but who suffer from going against the official position of their Church, and of those who leave it simply because they are unwilling or unable to accept this tension.

This sketch of the position of the Christian Churches shows that they are firmly committed to the principle of responsible parenthood. They therefore favor policies regulating fertility where these are necessary. A considerable number of Catholics would be in favor of using artificial means as well as the rhythm method to implement population policies. This has meant in practice that Catholic opposition in recent years to official family-planning programs of governments and of the United Nations has often not been as strong as in the past. In some countries, e.g., in the United States, Catholics have acknowledged the right of governments to promote birth control even with techniques not officially allowed by the Catholic Church, though such tolerance has been more widespread in developed than in developing countries.

---

[17] *Studies in Family Planning*, "Roman Catholic Fertility and Family Planning," No. 24, Oct. 1968. This is a very interesting and fair review of the events leading up to *Humanae Vitae* and a review of research literature on Catholic practice in regard to contraception. It does not consider the suggestion I have made but would obviously fit in with this.

On the whole, as already indicated, the rhythm method of family planning is not used very much even in the Catholic countries, although it is the only method endorsed by the Church. This is often because the method has not been given a fair trial. Taking into account the difficulties and problems of methods so far available, this method has a part to play in population policies, especially if its effectiveness is improved. If as much money had been spent on research into it as was spent on the "pill" or in trying to get I.U.D. accepted, perhaps the rhythm method might have had a much more important role in family planning than it has at present. One would hope that those Catholics, and especially governments of Catholic countries who loyally accept the encyclical *Humanae Vitae* and regard the method of periodic abstinence as the only legitimate one for population control, would launch research projects to improve the rhythm method; this would be a real test of their sincere concern. However, with one or two exceptions,[18] little research has been carried on into feasible improvements of the rhythm method. There are about eight possible lines of research and if enough money, equipment, and personnel were available a scientific breakthrough valuable in itself and of great use to population-control programs might well occur. If the rhythm method were to be made effective and easy to apply it would have many advantages over the present methods, all of which have some disadvantages in use.

THE DESIRE FOR FEWER CHILDREN It used to be thought by many, and it was used as an argument by some, that people in the developing countries, especially in rural communities, always wanted large families and would not take kindly to the idea of a reduction in fertility.

There were a number of valid reasons why parents wanted many children, some of which still hold true in certain circumstances. Roger Revelle has suggested that the main reason for such an attitude is the high infant mortality rate that until recent decades has obtained in the less-developed countries. Lower mortality, while

[18] For example, Professor J. Ferin of Louvain has been researching ways of identifying the time of ovulation or even anticipating it, since 1964, with a Ford Foundation grant. In 1969 Cardinal O'Boyle of Washington set up a $1,000,000 fund for this purpose.

birth rates remain high, is the main reason for the population expansion, but Revelle defends the paradox that it is this very factor of lower mortality that makes people more willing to limit their families.

The desire for a large family lessens as social change and modern ideas filter into the urban areas of developing countries, and into the rural areas as well, although more slowly. Lower mortality rates have already begun to cause a change in attitudes. For example, in the fifties Ceylon's death rate was halved. This is one reason why there appears to be a more ready welcome for family planning there than was expected. At all events, surveys conducted in developing countries about the number of children desired, as well as the actual successes of family-planning programs, show an openness to the idea of lower fertility. These surveys are not complete, but they do enable us to give partial answers to the question we set out to answer.

First of all, it is clear that even in most pre-modern societies fertility was and is below the physiological maximum.[19] In other words, it is less than is physically possible, and so some restrictions of fertility, even if minimal, actually took place and are taking place. Human fertility in these countries has been kept down by social and religious factors: the postponement of marriage, permanent celibacy, taboos on sexual intercourse at certain times, and other institutions surrounding sex and childbirth. Induced abortion, infanticide, some form of contraception, and especially *coitus interruptus* have a long history in most societies.

However, it seems clear from the surveys that have been carried out that people in pre-modern societies are now far readier than was imagined to have fewer children, even though they may not have taken steps to do so. In the past the mere survival of a society required the full utilization of its reproductive powers. If this was true of society, it was even more true of individual families, clans, tribes, and smaller kinship groups, which ran high risks of being wiped out by the waves of epidemic mortality that characterize a high-mortality situation. It is therefore not surprising that traditional values and institutions in pre-modern societies favor early marriages and large families. A large number of other reasons are also often cited: children may, for instance, be regarded as eco-

---

[19] Ohlin, *Population Control*, p. 65.

nomic assets both in their adolescence, when they contribute their labor to the family's upkeep, and in adulthood, when they support their aged parents.

Surveys taken in developing countries in recent years to learn by more direct means what the prevailing attitudes to fertility actually are, have radically changed the picture. Instead of confirming the notion of vast continents committed by ingrained values to the maintenance of maximum fertility, these surveys have revealed that in almost all parts of the world parents of many children would prefer to have no more and that those who have heard of birth control are anxious to know more about it.

Fertility studies are carried out on a sample basis, usually containing up to 2,000–3,000 individuals. Many have been undertaken on a limited basis, covering only a town or a region, but there are already more than twenty studies covering national populations in underdeveloped countries. Sometimes referred to as KAP surveys, because they typically aim at investigating knowledge, attitude, and practice in regard to family planning, the intimate character of their subject obviously requires highly competent interviewers. The results already amount to an impressive body of comparative sociological statistics, and they are extraordinary in their uniformity. Regardless of nationality, religion, or race, the large majority of men and women in the underdeveloped countries do not seem to want more than four children, do not know about family planning, and say that they wish to learn.[20] Those who already have four children do not, as a rule, wish to have more. Among those with five children or more, increases in the family are even less welcome.

Table 6-1, on page 170, gives a summary of the findings of such surveys.

According to this table, attitudes to family size in developing countries are not very different from those in the United States. It is true, however, that questions about the "desired" number of children seem to show that the ideal family size in most developing countries, though moderate, is larger than in industrialized countries.

Of course, the concept of "desired" family size is not straightforward, and attitudes to family size are often ambivalent. Survey

[20] *Ibid.*, p. 71.

questions have been differently worded and have usually evaded
the crucial problem of infant and child mortality. Nevertheless, it
is clear that in general inhabitants of developing countries do not
believe that the ideal family is the largest possible one.[21]

In spite of the difficulty of getting accurate replies in surveys on
this subject, for example, on the use of contraceptives, it is extremely important that these studies have shown both among men
and women in developing countries attitudes toward family limitation that are more positive than could have been expected only a
decade ago.

TABLE 6-1: Percentage
Not Wanting More Children [22]

Country	Number of children		
	3	4	5 or more
Ceylon	57	69	88
India	43	74	88
Pakistan	42	67	74
Taiwan	54	76	88
Thailand	71	85	96
Turkey	68	67	76
Philippines	56	68	85
Korea	65	81	94
Tunisia	44	68	87
Brazil	95	93	93
Colombia	67	79	93
Costa Rica	67	78	86
Mexico	64	76	86
Panama	70	86	94
United States	62	81	74

The World Population Conference in 1965 made much of the
conditions necessary for a decline in fertility; developments since
then have allowed a more optimistic assessment of the time it takes
for a change in attitude with regard to family size, without such a

[21] Ohlin, *Population Control*, p. 71.
[22] Source: Berelson, Bernard, "KAP studies on fertility" in *Family Planning
and Population Programs*. Chicago: University of Chicago Press, 1966.

degree of economic development as was postulated in some of the discussions. But for the millions and tens of millions who will have to adopt family limitation if a really significant impact is to be made on rates of population growth in the developing countries, several factors do need to be in operation and recognized to be in operation before such an impact will occur.

First, mortality must be relatively low for some time before parents become aware of the problem of excessively large families and before they realize that they do not need to have many babies in order for a minimum to survive.

Second, some kind of social and economic development, some kind of modernization or contact with modern ways that lessens the ties of tight-knit extended families of subsistence economies, seems to have a big influence.

A large family is burdensome only when it makes a difference to the realization of ambitions to improve or defend some social or economic position. Nothing is known about the precise importance of such factors, although it is universally recognized that fertility change occurs first in the urban, educated, and generally modernized sectors of a population. This may, to a large extent, be due to superior knowledge and communication. As indicated by the fertility studies already cited, traditional ideas of desired family size are upset by declining mortality in rural areas as well, and there is no reason to assume that traditional values attach merely to fertility and not to norms of family size.[23]

Elsewhere in this book the importance of general economic development has been noted, and it still seems to me that such development is a condition of a general reduction in fertility, i.e., not one where special efforts have been made at a cost in personnel and materials impossible to extend to a general family-planning campaign. But some demographers feel, on the basis of surveys and successful campaigns already undertaken, that it may be possible to hasten a fertility decline "by an organized, large-scale effort, which is focused on information" and that "this may find a readier response in rural and under-developed areas than their degree of economic development would have led one to expect." [24]

However, the optimism of some demographers who predict rapid

[23] Ibid., p. 73, summary of views of World Population Conference discussions.
[24] Ibid.

fertility declines in five or ten years must be tempered by the consideration that large-scale *implementation* of family-planning programs is important and that this involves far more than attitudes. It involves all the supporting services for such programs, including the medical or paramedical personnel, which in some Eastern countries is in short supply. And while it is true that fertility declines have begun in some Eastern countries, there is no sign of this yet in Latin America. There is no doubt that official religious and political opposition to contraception are partly responsible. Even though practicing Catholics are in the minority, these countries are regarded as Catholic countries, and there is no doubt that the official attitude with regard to contraception in the Church has had a considerable effect at government level. But apparently, not at the level of ordinary parents, as Table 6-2 shows.

TABLE 6-2: Use of Contraceptives by Married Women in Relation to the Frequency of Their Attendance at Church [25]

Frequency of Church Attendance	Percentage of Women Using Contraceptives		
	Panama	Rio de Janeiro	San José
Once a week or more	59.3	57.9	65.2
Once a month or more	64.4	47.1	54.2
Sometimes in a year	. . .	51.1	53.2
Once in a year	58.2	59.7	62.4
Once in years	. . .	64.0	78.0
Never	50.0	58.0	71.9

These figures show clearly how far married women who call themselves Catholics are deviating from the known laws of the Catholic Church. What is statistically most significant is that most of those who go to Church use contraceptives. It does look as if the Church's ban has been superseded by the judgment of conscience, especially after the birth of the third child.

A survey done in 1967 in five countries of Latin America (Brazil, Chile, Colombia, Mexico, Venezuela) in view of the expected papal pronouncement on the regulation of births produced the fol-

[25] Source: CELADE (The Latin American Demographic Center of Santiago de Chile), 1964, reproduced in Ohlin, *Population Control*, p. 75.

lowing results: 80.5 percent of Catholic lay people hoped that the Pope would leave freedom of choice regarding the means of birth control to the marriage partners. If the traditional doctrine of a ban on artificial contraception were reaffirmed, 62 percent of lay people and 68 percent of Catholic action leaders would be disappointed (87 percent in Chile, 52 percent in Brazil). If the ban were lifted, 45.3 percent of the clergy and 35.4 percent of the laity considered that such a change would bring the people nearer to the Church. No lay person and only four priests felt that such a change would drive the faithful away.

Only 16.2 percent of the laity and 12.5 percent of the priests thought that the faithful would obey a papal directive reaffirming the traditional teaching.[26]

In the more progressive circles in Latin America, reconsideration of the Church's teaching on this subject is intense. For example, the bishop of Cuernavaca, Mexico, has openly declared that the methods of contraception are a matter for each person's conscience, and his view has been quoted with approval, not only in Latin America, but also in progressive circles in Europe. Ohlin sums up the situation in Latin America by saying that "opposition may have been founded on erroneous notions of popular attitudes and will switch to overt advocacy when a vocal demand for government action is heard." [27]

REGULATORY POPULATION POLICIES AND PROGRAMS With regard to government policies on fertility restriction there have been developments in recent years shown by changed attitudes in the United Nations and by the fact that well over half the governments of developing countries now have policies and programs of varied effectiveness and at various stages.

A study of these programs will help us to assess the possibilities of a decline in fertility in the near future.

Family-planning programs in more than half the developing

[26] Cf. Ramirez, G. Perez, "Les Attentes vis à vis la déclaration pontificale sur la régulation des naissances en Amérique latine en 1967," *Social Compass,* Vol. 15, No. 6, 1968.

[27] Quoted in Ramirez, G. Perez, "Family Planning and Latin American Problems, Perspectives in 1965," *Concilium,* Vol. 10, No. 1, Dec. 1965, p. 79. Reprint of an address given to the first Pan American Conference on Population, August 1965.

countries testify to a growing awareness in these countries of the need for population-restriction policies.[28] It is too early to assess them, with regard to their potential for a serious impact on rates of population growth in the developing world. As I have indicated, ten to fifteen or even twenty years will probably be necessary for this, even taking the most optimistic view of their successes.

The best short informative summary of these programs throughout the world is contained in *Population Program Assistance*,[29] which describes the situation in twenty-one countries in Latin America, ten countries in the Near East and Southeast Asia, twenty-four countries in Africa, and nine countries in East Asia, with a special section on Vietnam. This is done with special reference to United States AID participation, but there is a mine of condensed general information.

There is a good deal of financial and technical assistance supplied by the United States to these programs,[30] but other countries are increasing these partnership efforts and the United Nations is a channel for increasing multilateral assistance. It has recently set up a fund for this purpose.

The programs use a wide selection of methods, with emphasis on particular methods according to circumstances: various forms of the contraceptive pill [31] and I.U.D. [32]—the new methods of the 1960's—conventional contraceptives, the rhythm method where instruction is available, and sterilization. Most programs do not include abortion. Indeed, one of the strongest reasons for these programs is to prevent recourse to abortions. This is especially true in

[28] "A decade and a half ago, few of the less-developed countries were aware of the rapidly mounting rates of increase. Now more than 70 percent of the population of the newly developing world lives in countries that have adopted policies designed to reduce birth rates; many more are moving in that direction." *Population Council Report*, Washington, D.C., p. 11.

[29] Agency for International Development, Office of the War on Hunger, Population Service, Washington, D.C., September 1968.

[30] Cf. *Population Program Assistance*, pp. 48–53 and *passim*, and publications of the International Planned Parenthood Federation and Population Council.

[31] Cf. Jones, Gavin, and Maudin, W. Parker, "Use of the Oral Contraceptive," *Studies in Family Planning*, No. 24. New York: Population Council, Dec. 1967.

[32] Cf. "Retention of I.U.D.'s: An International Comparison," by W. Parker Maudin *et al.*, with supplement by Dr. Christopher Tietze, "Intra-Uterine Contraception—Recommended Procedures for Data Analysis," *Studies in Family Planning*, April 1967.

South America. In Uruguay a Christian Family Movement survey done several years ago reckoned that 75 percent of conceptions were terminated by illegal abortions. In 1964, when I was in Santiago, Chile, I was told by one of the leading doctors of the University Medical Faculty that women lay on the steps of the University College Hospital waiting for a place in the overcrowded wards (sometimes more than one to a bed) to be treated for crude abortions that had caused serious illness.

Some countries have official government programs. This is especially true in the East. In other countries voluntary organizations, such as Family Planning Associations, with the help of the International Planned Parenthood Federation, have sponsored programs. Almost all programs have started as volunteer efforts, and the contribution to population-regulatory policies of the Federation and its affiliates, which have started such programs and prepared the way for official involvement, has been very great indeed.[33] The Population Council of New York has for many years fostered high-level research that has been of use in these programs and has aroused awareness of the situation, especially in the United States. The Ford and Rockefeller foundations have taken a special interest, financial and technical, in such programs.

What follows is a brief account, with some attempt at evaluation, of selected programs in certain developing countries.

INDIA India is the country with the largest population problem. Her population is over 520 million, one seventh of the world's inhabitants. (If Pakistan is included, the Indian subcontinent has nearly 700 million out of a world population of 3.5 billion—one fifth of the world total.) This population is increasing by a yearly rate of at least 2.7 percent, which means a doubling of the total Indian population in twenty-six years.

For a family-planning program to be successful at least half of nearly 140 million couples would have to be reached, 80 percent of them in the 567,000 villages of India.

The government became interested in family limitation earlier than in any other developing country. Already, in the First Five

[33] Cf. *Population Program Assistance*, pp. 48–53 and *passim*, and publications of the International Planned Parenthood Federation and Population Council.

Year Plan, which began in 1951, provision was made for family planning when the population was less than 400 million and the rate of increase was 1.3 percent. In all, $64 million was allotted in the three Five Year Plans, which ended in 1966. By the time these plans ended population had increased to 500 million (August 1966) and the rate of increase was double what it had been at the start. The reasons for this were, first, the basically conservative attitude with regard to this very personal matter; second, the lack of a safe, cheap, reliable, simple, and acceptable contraceptive; and, last, and perhaps most important, the lack of trained personnel to administer the program. Since then, more intense efforts have been made using the new methods put into use at the beginning of this decade: the intrauterine contraceptive device (I.U.D.) and the anovulant contraceptive pills.

An evaluation of the Indian family-planning program was undertaken in 1965 by a United Nations team at the request of the Indian government. That evaluation and that year gave new impetus to the program.[34]

The Fourth Five Year Plan extended for 1966–71 allotted $306 million to the new Department for Family Planning created in 1966. Family planning was given very high priority, second only to agricultural production (a big change with regard to both from the Second Five Year Plan). The amount allotted to it in the budget was a sensational stepping-up by eightfold of the amount in the Third Five Year Plan, the equivalent of $3.50 for every couple in the reproductive age. At the beginning of February 1968, the United States Agency for International Development gave a further $26 million grant to help this crash program, on top of the $1.3 million given in 1967.

This program stands a better chance of success than many because of the commitment of the central government and the top leadership of the country. The program is very highly organized and the training of personnel, the use of qualified people, and programs of education are good.[35] Some less desirable features seem to be suggestions of compulsory sterilization in some states and undue pressure especially on the very poor, the former Untouchables.

[34] Cf. *Studies in Family Planning*, No. 12, June 1966.
[35] Cf. "India, The Family Planning Program Since 1965," *Studies in Family Planning*, No. 35, Nov. 1968.

Otherwise the choice of contraceptive is left to the individual. Condoms seem to be the most popular in spite of a big campaign based on the Lippes loop—a special type of intrauterine contraceptive device. This got off to a good start in 1965 and much—perhaps too much—was expected of it. It is simple and cheap, but it had some disadvantages. The target of 1966–67 of 4 million was not reached; indeed, less than one million insertions took place. The loop has been improved, and it was hoped to have 2 million insertions in 1967–68. Nine hundred thousand sterilizations were performed in 1966 (nine males to one female), and one million in 1967.

The use of contraceptive pills is also being considered. They are somewhat costly, about 11 cents per woman per month, and need to be taken under supervision; they are therefore hardly suitable for the more than half a million villages and they are not yet used in the official campaign. But the 20–30 percent who cannot tolerate the I.U.D. could find them useful provided adequate medical supervision were available.

The immediate object is to reduce the birth rate from 41 to 25 per 1,000. Three million sterilizations a year would prevent 4.5 million births. The use of contraceptive methods by 15 million families would eventually prevent 4 million births.

That would cut the birth rate in half in ten years, and pursuing the same plan through 1985 would stabilize India's population at 680 million in 1985 (unchecked it would be one billion).

The reasons for the urgency of the campaign is, in a nutshell, that the expanding population demands 1.5 million tons of additional food grains per year, 2.5 million houses, and 4 million jobs.

The optimism of the early stages of those who believed a crash program combined with newer methods would have sensational results has not been justified.

It is true that such a huge program in such a difficult field, affecting 140 million people in the most personal aspect of their lives, could not be expected to run smoothly, especially in the early stages. What is most significant is the widespread realization of the urgency of the problem and the commitment of the political leadership of the country to do all that is possible to achieve the target. It is widely admitted in India that there have been and will be snags, disappointments, difficulties, and setbacks. At the beginning of 1968 Kasturi Rangan, writing in *The New York Times* under the headline "Population Problems Defy Indian Drive," stated that in spite of the massive birth-control campaign India was still baffled. The reason for this was the growing unpopularity, due to bleeding and pain, of the cheap I.U.D. loop, which had been expected to cause a breakthrough. However, more intensive efforts are being made to use condoms and other methods, and in spite of this initial failure, the energetic and widespread propaganda may well overcome the formidable obstacles.

It is, then, too early to say if the above objectives will be reached. The problem is made difficult by the lack of trained doctors and nurses. More than 13,000 nurses and 1,700 health visitors are at work, but tens of thousands more will be needed. The ordinary medical needs of the country have also to be considered.

However, it is possible that a significant impact will be made on population growth rates within the next ten or fifteen years—something that would hardly have been envisaged even three or four years ago.

KOREA Korea, with a population of 42,484,000,[36] has had an intensive and very well organized birth-control campaign since late 1964.[37] The years 1966 and 1967 were very successful from the point of view of I.U.D. insertions: 400,000 for 1966, just over 320,000 for 1967, and nearly 20,000 male sterilizations (vasectomies) for 1967. By the end of 1967, 27 percent of the estimated married women had tried the loop and 3 percent of the married men had undergone vasectomies. The cost of each birth prevented has been estimated at $7.66. The government allotted $1.75 million in 1967 to the program. Training was stepped up in 1967—a necessary procedure, since demographers and medical people were worried about unqualified people being responsible for insertions.[38]

The program has been pursued with great enthusiasm and zeal

---

[36] *United Nations Demographic Yearbook, 1967*—adjusted midyear estimate 1967.

[37] For further information cf. Victor-Bostrom Fund, *How Family Planning Programs Work, Will They Succeed?*, pp. 8–10. New York: International Planned Parenthood Federation, Report 10, Fall 1968.

For a more sophisticated evaluation cf. *Studies in Family Planning*, No. 29, "Korea and Taiwan: The Record for 1967," April 1968.

[38] These misgivings were expressed privately to me by some members of the UN Population Commission meeting in Geneva, Nov. 1967.

on the part of the promoters and the government, with the collaboration of Seoul University and especially of maternity and child welfare agencies.

Accumulated loop dropouts, however, constitute such a large group that it seems unlikely that the target of one million women using the loop will be met by 1971. What is needed is an effective followup method. The conclusions seem to be that because the loop gives only temporary protection (about thirty months at the maximum), it will probably have to be followed up by the pill, which even at 11–13 cents per cycle, is relatively expensive.

In spite of the enthusiasm, it seems that family planning does not have a one-step, reversible, cheap, attractive method to offer to large populations.

Nevertheless, it is obvious that the campaign has had significant results. There is evidence from a number of surveys that fertility is falling; there is a rise among couples who are using contraceptive measures; and there is an improvement in the KAP [39] indicators.

How much fertility decline is specifically due to the *campaign* for use of the loop is difficult to say. The following analysis is quoted from Population Council data.

BIRTHS PREVENTED

In both Korea and Taiwan the fertility of loop acceptors fell heavily, perhaps as much as 70 percent, in the year or two after insertion. This was due both to the protection afforded by the loop itself and by independent action, partly induced abortion, taken by women who lost their loops. It is highly unlikely that these women, most of them rural and uneducated, would have experienced such sharply reduced fertility without the loop program. Further, the impact on the total population must be substantial, considering that roughly a fourth of all married women of childbearing age in Korea and Taiwan have had loops inserted and that they seem to be the most fecund members of their age groups.

To estimate how much decline above what would otherwise have occurred could be credited to adding the loop to the campaign, Professor Robert Potter [40] used Taiwan data to compare fertility after insertion to three standards: the fertility level experi-

---

[39] Knowledge, Attitude, and Practice of Contraception.
[40] Potter, Robert G., "Estimating Births Averted in a Family Planning Program." University of Michigan Sesquicentennial Celebration, Nov. 1967.

enced before insertion by acceptors who had never used family planning, the level experienced by all acceptors combined, and the level experienced by those who had definitely used family planning before the loop. The comparison of fertility levels before and after insertion showed the average loop preventing .94, .64, and .43 births per woman in the three groups respectively. Taking the medium figure as a rough standard for Korea's one million acceptors, there would be approximately 640,000 births prevented (over the period of years during which the loops had been and would be worn, starting from late 1964) compared to a base of about 1.1 million births annually. A similar calculation shows about 238,000 births prevented in Taiwan, over a corresponding period of years; the annual birth rate is about 420,000.

Putting the calculation on an annual basis, W. Parker Maudin estimated that the number of I.U.D. wearers was sufficient at the start of 1967 to reduce the birth rate by 3.7–5.3 births per 1,000 population per year in Korea and by 3.0–5.0 per year in Taiwan, with certain qualifying assumptions.[41] These figures will rise as long as the number of wearers continues to rise, as they will for a few more years before annual loop dropouts begin to outnumber annual new insertions.

The experience of Korea shows that there is certain justification for increased optimism among those concerned with family-planning programs. However, it is too early to come to hard conclusions with regard to the possibility of early success in significantly reducing rates of population increase in the developing world as a whole.

PAKISTAN In Pakistan there has been a vigorous program of family planning, especially since 1960 when President Ayub Khan warned of the "frightening prospects" of rapid population increase. His concern stemmed from the demographic figures in this century for the area now known as Pakistan. The population was 46 million in 1901, 76 million in 1951, and 113 million in 1965. At that time the rate of natural increase was 3 percent; i.e., without a change in the rate of population growth there would be 226 million by 1988, nearly a fivefold

[41] Maudin, W. P., *et al.*, "Retention of I.U.D.'s: An International Comparison," *Studies in Family Planning*, No. 18 (and supplement), April 1967.

increase since the beginning of the century, with more than 100 million more people to be added by the end of the century.

Family planning since 1960 has been given top priority in the plans for socioeconomic development. Already $10 million had been allocated for this purpose in the First Five Year Plan (1955–1960), and the same amount was allocated in the Second Five Year Plan. The work during the Second Five Year Plan was still in the stage of pilot projects but it did establish a number of family-planning clinics and a cadre of trained workers. The Third Five Year Plan (1965–1970) allotted $60 million to family planning. By mid-1968 over 100,000 personnel were involved in family-planning programs and all districts of the nation were covered.

The population-restriction policy of Pakistan is based on public relations and public understanding; the approach is not merely clinical. The main methods of the program have been I.U.D. and male sterilization, but recently the pill has gained in popularity. Between July 1965 and June 1968 there were 1.6 million I.U.D.'s inserted and nearly 300,000 male sterilizations. The monthly sale of conventional contraceptives averages 14 million; the total between 1965 and 1968 was 350 million in the three-year period.[42]

Due to the extensive educational campaign in Pakistan, a change of attitude has taken place. Family planning has become respectable. The ideal of a very large family is being replaced, and the value of low fertility in the population situation of Pakistan is being accepted. It is estimated that about 3 million couples are practicing family planning effectively. The aim of reducing the birth rate by 20 percent by 1970 may not be achieved but will be approached. In order to achieve this aim about 5 million of the nearly 20 million fertile couples would need to be practicing birth control.

TAIWAN Taiwan is an example of a very successful program [43] and it is also is a good illustration of the fact that economic development (partly the result of

---

[42] Victor-Bostrom Fund, *How Family Planning Programs Work*, p. 12.

[43] Cf. Bostrom, *How Family Planning Programs Work*, p. 11; *Studies in Family Planning*, No. 29, April 1968; Robert G. Potter, Ronald Freedman, Lung Ping Chow, "Taiwan's Family Planning Program," *Science*, Vol. 160, May 24, 1968; Albert I. Hermalin, "Taiwan: An Area Analysis of the Effect of Acceptances on Fertility," *Studies in Family Planning*, No. 33, August 1968.

massive American aid) makes the acceptance of family planning much easier.

At the end of World War II, the population was just over 6 million. This doubled in a little more than twenty years. Of course, a large part of the increase in the early years was due to the influx of Nationalists to the island from the mainland after the victory of Mao Tse-tung. The average rate of population increase was 3.6 percent between 1953 and 1960.

In 1963 the Taiwan Health Department began family planning based on the use of the loop. By July 1967 one out of five fertile mothers between the ages of twenty and forty-four used the loop. The estimated birth rate was down to 28.5 per 1,000, and with the death rate down to a little more than 5 per 1,000 the rate of population increase had declined to 2.3 percent by the end of 1967.

A feature of Taiwan's program is that all aspects are completely voluntary, with public and private agencies cooperating. Also it is integrated into a development plan based on remarkable agricultural progress, which has enabled Taiwan to win the race between food and population increase.

PUERTO RICO Family-planning programs in Puerto Rico have caused a significant drop in the birth rate since 1956.[44] In the previous twenty years such programs had not been very successful.

In the ten years between 1956 and 1966 the birth rate fell from 34.8 per 1,000 to 28.3—a drop of nearly 20 percent. In 1966 the Antipoverty Program included family planning, and in 1967 the birth rate fell an additional 9 percent. But the natural rate of increase in Puerto Rico is still fairly high at 2 percent per year.

A feature of the family-planning program of the Federal Office of Economic Opportunity of Puerto Rico are the two principles that are a model for any such program: (1) No individual will be provided with any information, medical supervision, or supplies which such individual states to be inconsistent with his or her moral, philosophical, or religious beliefs. (2) No individual will be provided with any medical supervision or supplies unless such individual has voluntarily requested such medical supervision or sup-

[44] Bostrom, *How Family Planning Programs Work*, pp. 21–26; J. Mayone Stycos, *Human Fertility in Latin America*, pp. 57–114. Ithaca: Cornell University Press, 1968. This is especially valuable for study of attitudes.

plies. (Incidentally, the Antipoverty Program does not permit sterilization.)

The dramatic fall in rates of population increase in Puerto Rico shows how successful a well-organized family-planning program can be. However, Puerto Rico has many advantages denied to other developing countries. Its proximity to the United States and its special relationship to that country, which has been a pioneer in family planning, and the fact that it is a compact island and that no woman is more than walking distance from very well-equipped clinics have been crucial factors in the success. The contraceptive pill, for example, was given extensive trials there by Dr. Gregory Pincus in 1955–58 and there has been intense interest and pressure for family planning from the Family Planning Association of Puerto Rico, strongly supported by the International Planned Parenthood Association.

SINGAPORE Singapore is in the category of special cases, being an extremely small state with most of its population concentrated in the busy and prosperous port of Singapore. Situated at the tip of the Malay Peninsula, with an area of 224 square miles, it has an overall population of just under 2 million and a population density of 3,367 per square mile.[45] The population density of Singapore city is about 8,000 per square mile. Now that it is separated from Malaysia, it can hardly be ranked as a developing country, though its inhabitants are drawn from the same races as those of neighboring developing countries.

Its family-planning program, sponsored by the government since 1965, has had the special problem of being confronted with an extremely high population density and rate of population increase (about 2.7 percent in 1964).[46] It is not typical of most developing countries in that its medical services and family-planning services are highly efficient and highly effective. It will suffice, therefore, merely to note results and one very interesting feature with regard to use of method. The initial emphasis was on I.U.D. as the

[45] *Demographic Yearbook, 1967.*
[46] Bostrom, pp. 18–20; Dr. K. Kanagaratnam, Deputy Director of Medical Sciences (Health), and Chairman, Family Planning and Population Board, Singapore, "Singapore: The National Family Planning Program," *Studies in Family Planning*, No. 28.

method of choice for 80 percent of those participating in the national program. However, there was a sudden change quite early in this program: within a year I.U.D lost its popularity because of side-effects. These side-effects were exaggerated, it is true, but in a family-planning program it is generally not the facts with regard to acceptance of methods but popular beliefs that affect decisions. The bleeding, cramps, perforation, and failures of I.U.D., admittedly overemphasized by popular rumors, caused a switch to the contraceptive pill and conventional contraceptives, as shown in Figure 6-3.

FIGURE 6-3: Methods of Family Planning Adopted
by New Acceptors, 1967 [47]

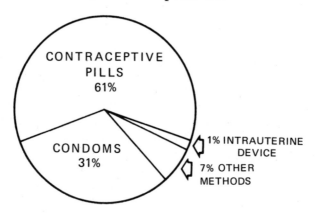

The success of Singapore's program can be gauged from Table 6-4. Its aim was to reduce its birth rate increase from 30 per 1,000 in 1966 to 20 per 1,000 by 1970. After two years of its Five Year Plan (1966–1970) it had succeeded in half its objectives.

It looks as if Singapore will reach its target, and without recourse to abortion (which helped produce Japan's sensational decline in birth rate in the fifties) will achieve the relatively extremely high decrease of one percent in population growth rate. But as I have indicated, Singapore can hardly be regarded as a model.

[47] Source: Singapore Medical Services, in Bostrom, p. 19.

TABLE 6-4: Singapore's Five-Year Family Planning Plan,
1966–1970 [48]

Year	No. of Acceptors Under the Plan	Actual No. of Acceptors	Total No. of Births	Birth Rate
1965			55,725	29.9
1966	25,000	30,410	54,680	28.6
1967	30,000	30,935	50,560	25.9
1968	35,000	16,896	23,095	23.1[a]
			(6 months)	
1969	45,000	—	—	—
1970	45,000	—	—	—

[a] Note: (1) Birth rate for 1968 based on data for the first six months projected for the year. (2) It is estimated that since the plan commenced in Jan. 1966 until the end of July 1968 nearly 80,000 women have accepted family planning from the Board.

SUCCESS OF FAMILY PLANNING PROGRAMS It is too early to evaluate completely the success of the programs that have been sketched here—among the most promising, except for India—or to forecast ongoing effects.[49] Still, the intense efforts and partial successes of these programs do justify to a considerable extent the conclusion of Frank Notestein, former professor of population studies at Princeton and president of the Population Council:

No one, ten years ago . . . would have forecast the rapid changes of the past decade in policies, in contraceptive technology, in public interest and in programmatic successes. We must assume that the future will bring an accelerated pace of change. We have already moved from a position of public apathy to one of deep concern by many people. Today, governments, international agencies and private organizations are talking a great deal about major efforts and new groups are entering the discourse every day. Everything on the horizon suggests a further deepening of interest, both public and private. Our estimate of the future

[48] Source: Singapore Medical Services.
[49] Cf. Maudin, W. Parker, "Births Averted by Family Planning Programs," *Studies in Family Planning*, No. 33, Aug. 1968. This gives approaches to methods of evaluation, with special reference to Taiwan.

possibilities should be based on the premises that we are at the beginning of an accelerating trend. Almost all of the actual work, national and international, remains to be done. If our efforts are commensurate with our opportunities, however, we have reason to believe that by the end of the century the specter of poverty perpetuated by population growth can be lifted from the earth.[50]

THE SPECIAL CASE OF INDIA Results, in India, do not yet seem to be in proportion to the size of the more optimistic forecasts of administrators of the program. The comparative failure of acceptance of I.U.D. has been for roughly the same reasons as those in Singapore but with the added problems of India (such as huge, scattered population, difficulties of communication, more firmly established religions and social taboos, and a greater illiteracy rate). Dr. Sripati Chandrasekar, the minister in charge of the Indian program, has openly acknowledged the failures of the family-planning program, especially those connected with I.U.D. Indeed, in December 1968, he appealed to Indian couples to observe 1969 (Gandhi Year, during which this legendary figure is being honored throughout India) by abstaining from making love, a more stringent demand than that made even by the rhythm method.

KENYA African countries as a whole, at least tropical African countries, have not made much advance with regard to family-planning programs. This is partly because many tropical African countries are underpopulated rather than overpopulated, with some of the lowest population densities in the world. Until recently, also, infant and child mortality rates have been high, with the result that population growth rates were not excessive. Even now there are only one or two countries, e.g., Zambia and Kenya, with rates of over 3 percent, and fourteen countries are below 2 percent. Also, absolute numbers of population are small, only five countries having more than 10 million inhabitants in Central, East, and West Africa. So far, the full force of the population explosion has not hit Africa. But population rates of increase are rising, and even countries with relatively sparse populations can hardly bear a very rapid increase such as 2.5 or 3 percent.

[50] *Foreign Affairs*, Oct. 1967.

An example of the problems African countries are now facing is in Kenya. The Population Report, in 1965, already mentioned, showed that a regulatory fertility program was necessary for Kenya.

The population of Kenya was about 10.2 million in mid-1967; [51] its rate of population increase was given then as 2.9 percent; it is probably more than that now.

The population density is less than 10 per square mile, but a large part of the country is desert, mountains, or marginal land. The Population Report estimated that the density on good cultivable land would be about 300 per square mile.

Kenya is a poor country (euphemisms such as "less developed," "developing," and "peripheral" cannot disguise this fact). It has a gross national product of $113 per head. The strain of a high rate of population increase on the development of the country is great.

In 1965 the government published a report on economic problems facing the ambitious 1966–1971 Development Plan and approved of family planning, provided it was voluntary and respected the religious, cultural, and social convictions of the recipients.

The government officially inaugurated a policy of family planning in 1967. It is too early to make any judgment about the success of the program, but it will be watched with interest not only by those who are concerned with Kenya's development but by other African governments.[52]

Although no doubt the main drive of recent policies directed against Asians and causing widespread emigration was largely political—and even racial, aiming at more Africanization—population pressures undoubtedly played a role, especially due to the large number of young Africans being thrown each year on a labor market unable to absorb them.

LATIN AMERICA Latin America has the smallest population of the three main areas of the developing world: Asia, Africa, and Latin America. Nevertheless its present population is about 273 million. At present high rates of increase

---

[51] *Demographic Yearbook.*

[52] Ghana (with a population of over 8 million and a rate of national increase of 2.7 percent) is another African country taking its population problems seriously. Cf. *Studies in Family Planning*, No. 25, Dec. 1967, p. 10.

—the highest of any region of the world, at an average of 3 percent—the population, which is increasing by 8 to 10 million per year, will be 690 million by the end of the century. Food production is increasing at a much lower rate.

A glance at a table of population densities shows Latin America, especially South America, to be an empty continent. A glance at the population of its main towns and cities shows urban overcrowding in the midst of this emptiness. There are vast resources waiting to be exploited and vast social injustices waiting to be redressed.

Too much emphasis on population policies could mask these facts. On the other hand, the facts do not provide a valid excuse for neglecting much-needed population programs to slow down the rate of increase, which is excessive for the countries of Latin America to absorb, especially since it is happening mainly among the poverty-stricken masses.

Family planning in Latin America, except in special cases such as Puerto Rico and Mexico, has met many obstacles—political, social, and religious.[53] There are no official government family-planning programs [54] and the publication of *Humanae Vitae* had a negative effect on some that were proposed. A plan for a government-sponsored program had to be dropped, for example, in Colombia.

However, considerable progress has been made by public and private organizations with regard to population study and family-planning facilities. Some form of organized family-planning activities and related population studies is underway in all Latin American countries. The Population Council estimates that nearly 2 million women in Latin America were using oral contraceptives in 1967, compared with 500,000 at the beginning of 1965. This would amount to about 6 percent of women in the reproductive years, compared to 40 percent in Australia, 25 percent in the United States, and 10 percent in England.

In these circumstances, I have not included specific Latin American countries (except for Puerto Rico) in a description of the selected family-planning programs of different countries.

However, it seems only a question of time, in spite of the papal

---

[53] Cf. Stycos, *Human Fertility in Latin America.*
[54] Only five governments encourage or condone family-planning programs.

encyclical, before full-scale family-planning programs are accepted at least in some Latin American countries. The meeting on Population Policies in Relation to Development in Latin America, held in Caracas, September 11–16, 1967, is regarded by many as a break-through.[55]

This meeting was sponsored by the Organization of American States (OAS) and other bodies. It was attended by ministers and other high officials from family-planning, health, education, labor, and urban and rural development agencies in the member states of the OAS—altogether nearly 200 people from eighteen member states and a wide variety of institutions and organizations.

The theme of the conference was expressed by Dr. Walter Sedwitz: [56] "There is no population policy without a strategy of development, neither is there development without a population policy."

The human background to the conference was sketched by Dr. Jorge Eliézer Ruiz.[57]

No sociologist would dare to ignore the reality of a population which increases by tremendous marginal accumulations in all large Latin American cities, and which brings with it such overwhelming indices of promiscuity, juvenile prostitution, crime, and underemployment. No proponent of public health can deny that, although there has been a vertical drop in mortality, at the same time the infant mortality rate has remained constant, abortion is still the most frequent cause of maternal death, and the general condition of the population is little more than subhuman. No economist, finally, would seriously attempt to ignore the fact that it is impossible to achieve the economic surplus necessary for the take-off towards development in societies where the new beings which enter life continually use up this surplus, so painfully obtained, for their own physical survival.

The recommendations of this meeting emphasized the importance of demographic and social factors with a view to immediate action. The forty-seven recommendations put these factors in the

[55] Cf. *Studies in Family Planning*, No. 25, Dec. 1967.

[56] Assistant Secretary for Economic and Social Affairs of the OAS and Executive Secretary of the Inter-American Committee on the Alliance for Progress, quoted in *Population Bulletin*, Washington, Vol. 24, No. 1, Feb. 1968.

[57] Director of the Latin American Office of the Population Reference Bureau, Bogotà, *Ibid*.

context of overall development and made it clear that the approach to demographic and family-planning programs should be multidisciplinary and interdisciplinary, thus avoiding the pitfall of regarding population expansion as the main or only obstacle to development.

I quote the first two recommendations to underline this point:

(1) That the Latin American governments, the private sector, university institutions, public information media, and public and private international organizations promote the broadest possible review and study of population problems within the context of economic and social development trends and policies, taking into account the complex interrelationship between population growth and other aspects of social evolution and change in Latin America.

(2) That the action programs already under way in any field affecting the demographic variables—whether in health and family planning, education, the labor force, agricultural development, regional or urban development, or any other—be evaluated periodically in terms of the general criteria and propositions adopted at the present meeting, in order that they may be adjusted to the objectives of the population policies within the framework of the plans, programs, and activities designed to accelerate economic and social development and to take full advantage of material and human resources to the benefit of the Latin American peoples.[58]

The balanced view of the conference is reflected in a passage in the final report:

Though it cannot be said that the lack of success of many of the plans and programs for economic and social development is due to the magnitude and characteristics of the demographic trends, there is no doubt that much of each country's effort to raise its levels of productivity and employment and improve social conditions is eaten up by being extended to a growing population that demands the services it has a right to, without the existing population's receiving enough of the benefits of public and private action. Whatever the rate of population growth, of course, the Latin American countries have an obligation to increase their investments in education, health, and welfare, and to improve their efficiency and also to develop their over-all productive capacity. It will constantly be necessary to contrast the present situation and trends with the

[58] *Studies in Family Planning*, No. 25, Dec. 1967.

long-range objectives and determine the effects of the population phenomenon on the achievement of these objectives.[59]

JAPAN Japan is often cited as a country that has
successfully coped with its population
problem, and it is sometimes put forward as an example for developing countries to copy. It is, of course, a developed country and
has not been included in our selected cases.

There is no doubt that after nearly twenty years of intensive
family-planning efforts Japan has a lot of experience to offer. But
some of it is of a negative character, and considerable reservations
must be made not only with regard to moral aspects but with regard to economic and social factors. These must be borne in mind
when one tries to apply Japan's experience to other developing
countries.

Between 1948—when the Eugenics Law was passed, which legalized abortion in some cases—and 1958 the rate of population
increase in Japan was reduced from 1.7 to .9 percent as the result
of a very intensive campaign in this highly industrialized country.

These years were the basis of the population control that Japan
has achieved. But it was a success for abortion, not contraceptives,
in spite of the fact that in 1952 the government provided birth-control education for couples on a nationwide basis and made contraceptives available free of charge. The abortions themselves were
made possible by a comparative surplus of doctors and medical facilities, which is the opposite of conditions in most developing countries.

In the nine months following the passing of the Eugenics Law in
1948, the number of legal abortions recorded was 246,000. By 1954
the number was over one million. In 1958, in a total population of
nearly 100 million, there were 1.1 million legal abortions, according to a Japanese White Paper, and an estimated number of illegal
abortions exceeding one million, compared with 1.2 million live
births—roughly two abortions for every live birth. Health authorities were alarmed, and the campaign for more effective use of contraceptives was intensified. Sterilizations increased, and the number of legal abortions declined to well below the million mark in

[59] Quoted in *Population Bulletin*, Vol. 24, No. 1, Feb. 1968, p. 11.

the early sixties. Japan's current rate of population growth is 1.1
percent; merely from the point of view of the numerical success of
the population policy, without making any value judgment, this
seems satisfactory. However, apart from moral and health considerations of the tremendously high abortion figures, which most people
would regard as a scourge, the situation is, to say the least, ambivalent.

Japan's economic growth is very great, but it is by no means certain that this has been due to drastic population decrease (even
though this is much more considerable than it seems, because if
population had grown unchecked, it would obviously have been
higher than the 1.7 percent increase of 1948 and the current figures
indicate).

Now Japan is faced with a labor shortage. There is at present a
movement to persuade parents to have more than the two children
they have been trained to desire. Furthermore, Japan, within thirty
years, will have a greater number of aged people than any country
in the world.[60] This will impose a great burden on the economy.[61]

Among the advantages of the Japanese people in reducing their
numbers was the high rate of literacy, which is often a crucial factor in the success of family-planning campaigns. In Japan the illiteracy rate is 0.2 percent; in most developing countries of the East,
as we have seen, it is well over 50 percent. (It is even 40–50 percent in Singapore, while in Malaysia it is 70–80 percent.)

An interesting feature of the Japanese program was the high
percentage of users of the rhythm method (over 30 percent). This
was no doubt due to the fact that Dr. Kyusaku Ogino, the co-dis-
coverer with Dr. Hermann Knaus of the safe period and the calendar method of computing it, was a high official of the Japanese
Health Ministry. Also the high rate of literacy and standard of education made this method more feasible.

MAURITIUS Mauritius, a medium-sized island in the Indian Ocean, between the southeast coast of
Africa and the west coast of India, illustrates the population explo-

---

[60] Confirming a forecast made nearly ten years ago in my book *People,
Space, Food.*

[61] Cf. Hon. Nobusake Kishi, Chairman of Japanese Foundation for International Cooperation in Family Planning, in "The Road to Hope from Distress,"
Victor-Bostrom Fund, *How Family Planning Programs Work,* p. 7.

sion in microcosm. Its population of 800,000, with a density of 407 per square kilometer (or over 1,000 per square mile) has been increasing rapidly for a number of years. It received independence March 12, 1968. There are hardly possibilities for emigration. The economic situation makes the situation more difficult, since Mauritius is a classic example of monoculture, or dependence on one single agricultural product, namely sugar, the cultivation of which occupies 45 percent of the total land area of 85,000 hectares (about 210,000 acres), which is 90 percent of the cultivable land available. This crop constitutes at least 93 percent of total exports and gives work to 34 percent of the employable population.

Rapid population increase in these circumstances tends to aggravate the unemployment problem. In 1966 there were about 14,000 unemployed, plus 1,900 relief workers.

Looking into the future, it is reckoned that 60,000 new jobs need to be created by 1972. The Development Plan envisaged 3,000 new jobs for 1966. This target, small enough compared to the size of the problem, was not realized, and there will be more unemployment each year as more young people, the fruits of the population explosion, enter the labor market.

For these and other reasons family planning has won wide acceptance from the government and religious bodies. The Catholic Church is strong in Mauritius, but the ecclesiastical authorities have made very serious efforts to cooperate in reducing the rate of population increase. Indeed, the rhythm method has been spread by the Family Action Movement as part of a very thorough, integrated movement of education in sex, parental responsibility, and respect for the values of marriage and family life. As an educative force, the implementation of this family-planning program is really a model of a truly human treatment of the problem. It is a rather lengthy and slow process to fully educate the people to responsible parenthood as the group is doing, but it is perhaps as valuable as more hasty solutions. We are fortunate to have a description of the work of this movement, sponsored by the Church, by two French doctors, François and Michèle Guy, a married couple who spent two years in Mauritius to give their professional help to the program, especially in the teaching of the temperature method of periodic abstinence.[62] They had already had ten years of successful ex-

[62] Guy, Drs. François and Michèle, *Île Maurice*. Lyon, France: Éditions Xavier Mappus, 1968.

perience in this work at Grenoble. A very good idea of the
philosophy of the movement and its widespread organization
throughout the island emerges, but not so clear an idea of its effectiveness in actual impact on the birth rate. However, thanks to the
government programs and those of private bodies, the following reductions in the birth rate and the rate of population increase have
been achieved.

TABLE 6-5 [63]

Year	Number of births	Birth rate (per 1,000)	Death rate (per 1,000)	Rate of population increase (per 1,000 and percent)
1963	27,978	39.9	9.6	30.3 or 3.03%
1964	27,528	38.1	8.6	29.5 or 2.95%
1965	26,279	35.5	8.6	26.9 or 2.69%
1966	26,817	35.3	8.8	26.5 or 2.65%
1967	23,499	30.4	8.5	21.9 or 2.19%

A reduction of the rate of increase by .8 percent in five years is
certainly very satisfactory.

As I have indicated, it is not possible to calculate the exact contribution of the rhythm method to these results, but from questionnaires and charts of couples actually using the method some idea
can be obtained, especially by checking the failure rate. We must
bear in mind also, as we have already said, that the ongoing educative process will take time to have its full effect.

Table 6-6, on page 195, gives figures of the number of couples
reached by the Family Action Movement.

There is obvious overlapping in one or two of the items, e.g.,
1 and 3. Allowing for this, there were 5,695 enrolled couples at the
end of 1967. To these must be added 1,020 couples who had not
completed three months of the course (these are not yet regarded
as being on the register) and 259 independent couples, i.e., who
followed the method on their own. It is interesting to note that
nearly 40 percent were non-Catholic.

On the basis of answers to questionnaires and the charts used by
couples themselves, a failure rate was worked out, calculated on

[63] Central Statistical Office, Mauritius, 1968. Quoted in *Île Maurice*, p. 261.

100 women years, i.e., 100 women using the method for twelve months.

The result was quite good. The method followed with absolute precision is regarded as 100 percent effective; the result takes into account the failures for practical reasons, i.e., those couples who, in practice, did not use the method correctly.

TABLE 6-6 [64]

1. Couples under instruction 1967	1,727
2. Couples already instructed 1965–66	1,621
3. Number of *foyers éducateurs*[a]	250
4. Couples who finished their course in 1967	937
5. New couples enrolled during 1967	2,045
Total	6,580
6. Number of dropouts in 1967	885

[a] Couples who have already been trained and who themselves give instruction.

Perhaps one of the best assessments of what the Family Action Movement is trying to do was given by *L'Express* of Mauritius in February 1966.

Family Action has certainly not chosen the easy solution to the problem of overpopulation in Mauritius. No one can ever accuse them of that. It is good to remember this as the report for 1965 bears witness to intense activity but does not contain any sensational results. Family Action has chosen the way of the tortoise, but it is well known that the tortoise sometimes beats the hare.

The Family Action Movement, although geared to the rhythm method, could well be a model for all family-planning programs in developing countries because of its integrated human approach and because of its respect for the dignity of even simple people and for the values of love and knowledge in marriage and the family.

[64] Guy, *Île Maurice*, p. 259.

EVALUATION OF THE PROGRAMS DESCRIBED AND PROSPECTS FOR THE FUTURE From the above descriptions of projects in various countries, mainly ones where the most progress has been made in family planning, it will be seen that the outlook is still far from clear. There is very much more educational work to be done and there is a great need for more effective, cheap, and morally acceptable methods of family planning. There is also a great need for more scientific evaluation of programs of an ongoing basis; this need is recognized by most of those concerned with family-planning projects, and a certain amount of progress has been made. However, it must be recognized that reports about the success of family-planning projects in certain areas are very often given by those who have a vested interest in the success of such programs, and these reports are inclined to take a more optimistic view of the situation than an objective outsider would. This is stressed in Parker Maudin's excellent article on this subject, already referred to.

But, of course, an even more serious question arises. In this chapter so far, except for brief references to Mauritius, we have described the success or failure of methods and of population policies from a purely demographic or methodological point of view. No value judgments have been passed on the means by which the family-planning programs are being operated. However, to avoid judgment on the moral or medical desirability of the ways a program is carried out would be undesirable, as relegating a very human problem to the realm of the purely scientific. It cannot be a matter of indifference, even to a population expert, whether numerous abortions are encouraged or are provoked. Many religions apart from the Christian ones are reluctant to agree to the morality of abortion. Those who support contraception often do so because they hope that it will help to avoid the terrible moral and medical scourge of abortion. Japan carried on its program for the first twelve or fourteen years largely by legal abortions, which only sank below the one-million mark in 1962.

Western observers who are keen on reduction of population increase at any price are inclined to say that people belonging to Eastern religions have not such a great horror of abortion, nor do they regard it as very morally wrong. But this is not true in many, possibly in most, cases. A survey made in 1964 by gynecologists in Nagoya among 153 married women who applied for abortion indicated that only 8 percent did not think this morally evil; 17 percent thought it was evil rather than good; 16 percent thought it was quite evil; and 59 percent thought it was very evil. They went through the abortion because they thought there was nothing else to do considering the present state of public opinion, housing problems, and so on. A survey during the previous year, in the same city, showed that only 20 percent had confidence in contraceptives, and 50 percent had no confidence (30 percent failed to reply).[65]

The difficulty and time needed for contraceptive programs to be accepted in developing countries is the reason why there is great pressure on the part of the more extreme adherents of family planning to have abortion legalized and to use this method of restricting the number of births.

Apart from the morality of this, the medical consequences in developing countries, where health services are not nearly as good as they are in Japan, should certainly give cause for concern. First of all, in developing countries there is a very great shortage of doctors and hospital facilities. These countries would not be able to support abortion campaigns at all, or only at grave cost to other branches of the health services. Second—again, apart from the medical and moral consequences—undoubtedly some of the propaganda for family planning has in the past been far too optimistic and has made promises that could not be fulfilled in regard to contraception. It has also been contradictory, because some advocates have stressed the need for contraception in order to avoid the great scourge of abortion, and yet others have presented abortion as a logical consequence of the failure of contraception. For example, Professor William McElroy [66] has said that he is in favor of altering abortion laws to liberalize and promote free abortions: "It is perfectly true that even in families which practice family planning through the use of current contraceptive technology, mistakes are made and the wife becomes pregnant even though she had no desire to be so. The logical extension of the concept of a baby 'only when you want it and if you want it' would allow the person to

[65] Cf. Zimmerman, A., S.V.D. *Report*, p. 58. Teckny, Ill.: Divine Word Publications, 1966.

[66] Chairman, Department of Biology, Johns Hopkins University; president, American Institute of Biological Sciences; chairman, Committee on Population of the National Academy of Sciences, in an article in *Science*, Feb. 23, 1968.

make the decision to have an abortion." It is precisely this attitude which stimulates much of the opposition to contraceptive birth-control programs not only in the Catholic Church but among other Christian bodies, not all of whom favor contraception, and even among those who have no particular religious opposition to contraception. While not suggesting a solution to this impasse except the better implementing of family-planning programs by perfection of methods and by thorough education, I do feel that if it is made clear that people will have to accept frustrations and difficulties that come from the imperfections of present family-planning techniques, they will not be so inclined to have recourse to abortion, which certainly in the opinion of many should not be promoted by the state. From a population point of view the failure rate of contraception of any kind is not so great as to jeopardize the policy if earnest efforts are made to implement it. The reason why, in Japan, there were mistakes and there may be the prejudice about contraception is possibly because until 1962 there was much more emphasis on abortion than on other methods of regulating the number of births. We must keep our perspective with regard to the population explosion and not regard it as something that must be coped with by whatever means and at whatever cost in health, either physical or moral.

WILL FAMILY PLANNING SOLVE THE POPULATION PROBLEM? Some scientists believe that family planning will fail to solve the population problem.[67] Among them is Dr. Kingsley Davis, who advocates stronger measures, such as a target of zero increase, which certainly would hardly be accepted by most people in developed and developing countries. Therefore the very suggestion is counterproductive. Moreover, the necessity he alleges for these stronger measures seems to me to stem partially from a very pessimistic attitude toward the population explosion and toward the possibility of population programs succeeding in the rapidly changing social conditions of the developing countries. We really are only at the beginning of these programs, and to prejudge their failure at this stage is to my mind not completely in keeping with the scientific attitude. The target to be aimed for should be a considerable re-

---

[67] For a brief account, cf. Bostrom Report, p. 17.

duction in the number of children in the average family in developing countries. It seems much more reasonable to aim at the reduction of really large families of say ten, eight, or six children, to a size of three or four children, and then to assess the economic and social consequences.

Precisely because really intensive family-planning programs are still in an embryonic stage, it is not possible to be more definite and clear than we have been with regard to their effectiveness and prospects for the future. As we have seen, even quite successful projects have their setbacks. But it seems to me that research and effort to make them more successful, and in keeping with the moral, religious, and social convictions, of those who have to practice them, is a necessity.

For social and political reasons, also, family-planning programs should not be seen to be coming from bodies outside the country or from bodies inside the country inspired from abroad without regard to the culture of the receiving country. Still less should they be imposed as a condition of aid either by governmental or private organizations. It is here that the true spirit of partnership between developed and developing countries should be sincerely cultivated, and brash and extremist propaganda avoided. The opposition to some family-planning programs in Latin America, for example, is much more due to social and political factors than to religion.

There is a danger otherwise that political or even racial aspects will be introduced into a problem that is a concern of the whole human race. To oppose family-planning programs as a form of anti-Americanism or from an ideological affinity for Communism, or to regard family-planning advice coming from developed countries as a means of keeping the numbers of the poor or the colored down, would be very regrettable. This is far too serious a problem, and too well established by experts from both developing and developed countries, to be subject to such unworthy hindrances. Those who try to defend the papal encyclical, by giving the impression that developing countries do not want contraceptive birth control because they regard it as a plot by developed countries to keep their numbers down for political or racial reasons, do no service to the truth, or the cause of international cooperation.

The most important point to stress with regard to population policies is the attitude toward them. The focus of such policies must be the quality of human life, of family life, and of the human dignity of the individual, which excessive population growth places in jeopardy.

The population problem is part of a much wider problem of dignified human development and stable family life; neither studies nor policies in relation to it can be separated from the broader context. Some groups do precisely this, stressing family planning with messianic fervor and with little attention to wider human needs and responsibilities. This imbalance leads to a concentration on quantitative policies aimed at restricting population and a neglect of positive and qualitative policies for housing, schools, jobs, and family welfare.

It is essential to view the population issue in its integrated context. It is part and parcel of the development problem. It has relevance for nations, but above all for families. It is somewhat disturbing to encounter those specialists on development who can only discuss and recommend in terms of optimal economic growth rates. They tend to forget that nations consist of families and individuals. It is equally unrealistic to define the population problem as one solely concerning the marketing of birth-control devices.

THE U.S.S.R. AND POPULATION CONTROL The Soviet view of family planning is interesting, not only with regard to what has happened in Russia but also on account of Soviet influence in some developing countries.[68] The official line is that family-planning programs are unnecessary. For a Communist, absolute overpopulation is a bourgeois phenomenon caused by the means of production lagging behind the growth of population. But in reality there is only relative overpopulation, due to the fact that capitalistic production is subjected to the interests of capitalistic ideology and to meeting the demands of population. In socialist countries, where, for the purpose of meeting the steadily growing material and cultural demands of the entire society, production is incessantly developing and expanding, employment of the entire productive population is ensured and consequently the problem of relative

[68] Podyashchikh, P., Soviet Representative on the UN Population Commission, "Impact of Demographic Policy on Population Growth." Cf. Bostrom Report, p. 27.

overpopulation is eliminated. This represents the main difference between the demographic law of socialism and that of capitalism.[69]

This is a rather doctrinaire and oversimplified attitude to the population situation, which, despite their great competence, Soviet demographers have difficulty in proving; it obviously affects the objectivity of their thinking. Whatever the merits of it, it does not seem to be for export; Cuba, for example, since Castro came to power, has hardly shown the economic advance that would correspond to the idyllic picture presented above.[70]

TABLE 6-7: United States and Soviet Rates Compared [71]

	U.S.	U.S.S.R.
Population mid-1967	199,118,000	235,543,000
Birth rate (per 1,000)	17.9	17.4
Death rate (per 1,000)	9.4	7.6
Natural rate of increase (per 1,000)	8.5	9.8
Annual rate of growth, %		
1966–1967, including migration	1.1%	1.0%

Actually, reduction of birth rate and population rate of increase have been pretty much the same in the Soviet Union as in capitalistic countries, although, according to Mr. Podyashchikh, the Soviet delegate to the UN Population Commission, no measures have been taken to propagate artificial restriction of births; on the contrary, people have been urged to increase their number.

The comparatively small birth rate and rate of population increase have been achieved in the Soviet Union since about 1930,

[69] In considering the terms "capitalist" and "socialist" in this context, it is well to remember that pure capitalism and pure socialism do not exist. In capitalist societies like America there is much planning and concern for equitable sharing; in the U.S.S.R. the emergence of the profit motive and other differentials in society make so-called socialist societies much nearer to capitalist ones than the theory would lead one to suppose.

[70] The Population Council, reviewing developments over the past fifteen years, says: "Then, the ideological clash between the Communist and non-Communist worlds on demographic matters was sharp. Today, both sides have essentially similar interpretations of the demographic situation and differ mainly about the emphasis to be given to spread family planning as one of the means of dealing with it." (*Annual Report, 1967,* p. 11. New York: 1968.)

[71] Source: *Demographic Yearbook, 1967.*

for in prerevolutionary Russia and in the first years of the Soviet Union the birth rate was even higher (4.4 percent in 1926, for example) than it is today in many developing countries. The methods by which the parity with the United States in population increase was achieved are not so clear, and the means by which the Soviet economy grew, including industrialization and forced collectivization of farms, have negative aspects, which Mr. Podyashchikh does not mention. But there is no place here for a detailed discussion.

An article in *Population Bureau* [72] makes it clear that Soviet thinkers have changed, at least since 1966, and in international bodies are adopting a neutral policy, while more and more demographers are taking the view that some restriction of population on a national and world level is necessary.

But the stress on positive economic progress and (at least theoretically) more equitable distribution of wealth are valuable elements in a demographic policy from which the more extreme Western population pundits could learn. There seems to be somewhat of a contradiction in suggesting that economic advance can take place in spite of speedy population growth and at the same time saying that "mastering the major problems of economic and social progress involves a considerable decrease in the birth rate." But what does seem true, at least so far, is that a certain amount of economic and social progress is needed to make family-planning programs really successful.

What is really interesting and important is the acceptance of the idea that the Soviet Union should take its part in "supporting" the developing countries. This idea, contained in Mr. Podyashchikh's article, is made more explicit by a Soviet scientist, Andrei Sakharov, in his book *Progress, Coexistence, and Intellectual Freedom:*

Unquestionably, control of the birth rate is important and the people, in India for example, are taking steps in this direction. But these steps remain largely ineffective under social and economic backwardness, surviving traditions of large families, an absence of old-age benefits, a high infant mortality rate, until quite recently, and a continuing threat of death from starvation.

It is apparently futile only to insist that the more backward countries

[72] "Soviet Population Theory from Marx to Kosygin," *Population Bureau,* Population Reference Bureau, Washington, D.C., Vol. 23, No. 4, Oct. 1967.

restrict their birth rates. What is needed most of all is economic and technical assistance to these countries. This assistance must be of such scale and generosity that it is absolutely impossible before the estrangement in the world and the egotistical, narrow-minded approach to relations between nations and races is eliminated. It is impossible as long as the United States and the Soviet Union, the world's two great superpowers, look upon each other as rivals and opponents.

This attitude is really the key to full world cooperation for coping with the problems of food supply and economic progress, complicated by increasing population pressures, in the developing countries.

If it means that both the United States and the Soviet Union would cooperate, forgetting ideological differences and political advantages in the interests of the general welfare, this is a situation to be wholeheartedly worked for. At the moment it seems rather Utopian, although Soviet aid to developing countries is increasing.

The fact that this Utopian situation has not arrived, and that it does not depend only on the West, does not absolve the West from its responsibility to make the most strenuous efforts in partnership with the developing countries to cope with the problems of progress and population increase.

THE UNITED NATIONS AND ITS AGENCIES AND POPULATION GROWTH United Nations agencies have been increasingly concerned with population growth and its relation to the various fields of human welfare. They stress in their work programs the importance of the problem of population increase and the need to deal with it by population-restriction policies. However, there have been controversies and reservations in some agencies about different aspects of these programs, and some have not accepted the need for United Nations aid to family-planning programs, or even the need for family-planning programs in any form.

The most urgent conflict confronting the world today is not between nations or ideologies, but between the pace of growth of the human race and the insufficient increase in resources necessary to support mankind in peace, prosperity, and dignity. The present population of 3.5 billion is expected to practically double by the year 2000. With the current unsatisfactory growth of resources the world will become more hungry, more crowded, more pressed in every sense. Half of those now living and two thirds of those still to be born in this century face the prospect of malnutrition, poverty, and despair.

All parents, rich or poor, should have, or be provided with, the facilities needed to effectively decide their own family size. I feel that there is no right more basic to humanity and more important to each individual than the right to enter this world as a wanted human being who will be sheltered, cared for, educated, loved, and provided with opportunities for constructive life.

On Human Rights Day, December 10, 1966, twelve world leaders signed a statement affirming the importance of family planning both to the individual and to their nations. On the same day in 1967 eighteen signatures were added to this noteworthy document. The heads of thirty states representing two fifths of the population of the world have now set their names to this declaration.[73]

The United Nations Population Division (formerly the United Nations Population Commission) is responsible for the vast mine of population information contained in each year's *Demographic Yearbook* and for other vital material used to assess the population situation. The work of the Population Commission is assisted by subcommittees in Santiago, Bangkok, and Beirut.

Population and its relation to economic and social development engaged the attention of the Economic and Social Council at its forty-fifth session in July 1968. The secretary-general opened the discussion. He pointed out that the population increase in the 1960's of 626 million people, with a yearly increase of over 60 million and a rapid increase in the younger age groups, necessitated special emphasis in the Second Development Decade on the critical relationship between population and resources. Population growth, he said, had emerged as the most critical and urgent of the world's population problems, and was now being linked more frequently to questions of fundamental human rights and the quality of life. He mentioned that national family-planning programs had been launched in twenty developing countries and had become an integral part of national development efforts.

In fact, all the relevant UN agencies, in preparing for the Second

---

[73] See Appendix 2: Declaration of World Leaders on Population Control.

Development Decade, and especially the Tinbergen Committee, which is planning the Decade, stress the importance of the population element in the Decade and of population policies. Seventy percent of developing countries belonging to the United Nations already have population policies and programs of some kind.

CONCLUSION There are several points with regard to family-planning programs that may be usefully stressed in concluding the treatment of them.

Such programs must be regarded from a totally human point of view. In other words, they should be intended to improve human life individually and socially, threatened as it is by an overly rapid increase in population. They should not be motivated, however unconsciously, by an anti-life bias, which some extreme proponents seem to have, or by a lack of love for children or lack of respect for the sacred privilege of passing on new life. The purpose must be that those who are born may have a chance of a life more in keeping with their human dignity and right to seek happiness. This applies also to the women who bear the children.

There is something abhorrent in proposing birth control to reduce the numbers of people in developing countries and at the same time refusing to support measures, e.g., of more aid or more equitable terms of trade. One distinguished senator in recent years was one of the principal advocates of family planning for developing countries and at the same time, as his Congressional record shows, was one of the chief supporters of cuts in foreign aid. Family-planning measures can only, it seems to me, be honestly advocated by those who are willing to make every effort to help the developing countries positively with respect for the value of every individual human being.

This human dignity must be respected in the means by which the programs are carried out. We are dealing with the human beings behind the statistics of demographers. For this reason I was shocked by the argument of a delegate at the UN Population Commission meeting in March 1965. He said, in supporting a motion for the UN to make available advice on family-planning programs, that just as plantations of young trees are thinned out, so should the increase of human beings be cut down. Apart from the fact that the simile suggests infanticide rather than contraception, or even abortion, this is surely a rather inhuman way to look at the question.

The aim of these programs must not be merely to make available certain techniques that will prevent so many births and therefore reduce numbers and rate of population increase by so much, as if these were abstract mathematical calculations. It is a matter of promoting such programs in the context of a dignified education in sex, love, marriage, and family life. In this respect, the Family Action program in Mauritius is ideal and is much superior to some mass programs. Even if other methods are adopted than the rhythm method, which was the basis of that program, it should still be possible to embody the positive features of that movement in population-restriction policies.

Here the example of the West German federal government is very encouraging. The government is prepared to give financial and technical assistance to developing countries who ask for it, but on condition that the birth-control programs have a built-in educational element stressing all these points. This policy resulted from discussions the Ministry for Economic Cooperation organized in 1968 on measures of population policy. The participants in these talks were representatives of the sciences (demography, anthropology, etc.), as well as representatives of marriage counseling organizations (those of Christian Churches among them) and representatives of other appropriate ministries (Foreign Office, Ministry of Health, Ministry for the Family and Youth Affairs).

The following standards, among others, for the cooperation of the federal government in measures of population as aid to the developing countries were agreed upon: complete freedom of the receiving country to adopt or reject measures of population policy; promotion of contraceptives only where there is a guarantee that those who receive them have the chance of receiving information and advice and can discuss the problem in such a way that they really achieve a sound basic attitude toward responsible parenthood; promotion of socio-political and economic conditions that provide the necessary socio-cultural background for a convinced acceptance of the population policy, e.g., such a policy should be formulated in agreement with the representatives of the culture of a country. Provision for training of suitable personnel from Germany and developing countries on all questions of love, marriage, and the family, as well as contraceptive techniques, was made, with the cooperation of the Churches, and the collaboration of the medical profession was sought.[74]

Such cooperation, of course, especially when it involves Christian Churches, needs to be exercised with delicacy and respect for non-Christian religious and moral feelings. However, the basic ingredients of a truly Christian concept of marriage do find an echo in the minds of most men of goodwill who are concerned about healthy family life.

This is especially true if one stresses that large numbers of children, especially in circumstances of great poverty, are not the only problems threatening marriage and the family. Other evils affecting married happiness should be combatted at the same time as a family-planning program is advocated. Such evils are: promiscuity (as distinct from consensual unions, which have a stability similar to real marriage); prostitution (especially the veritable slave trade in girls); infidelity; attitudes to marriage that make women basically inferior to men and virtually chattels of the husband; the double standard of morality, by which married women are supposed to be above reproach sexually, although the husband may take as many mistresses and engage in as many extramarital adventures as he likes. This "machismo," as it is called in Latin America, judges the virility of a man by the number of sexual conquests he makes, without real concern for the women who are the victims of the system. Abortion, especially when performed by non-qualified people in unhygienic conditions, and rape are other evils that bring untold misery and cannot be ignored by those who advocate family-planning programs to improve the quality of life.

Above all, family-planning programs must not be used as an excuse by developing countries for not relieving their own intolerable living conditions and for postponing the implementing of measures of social justice. On a visit to the slums of Lima, I was struck by the ambivalence of family-planning programs. Women living in miserable conditions obviously had need of birth-control measures so as to avoid bringing into the world many children who would complicate the problems of the slums. At the same time, it was abhorrent that social injustice should put them in the position where all they could foresee for their children was a life of pov-

[74] This material is taken from an unpublished paper of Msgr. P. Adenauer, director of the Zentral Institut für Ehe und Familie Frage in Cologne, with his gracious permission.

erty. It is conceivable that family-planning programs could, perhaps unintentionally, be used to plaster over the cracks of an outmoded and unjust social system.

All these considerations should not, of course, be used to block
needed population policies, but they should be kept in mind to ensure that such policies are truly human and do not mask the need
for social reform.

Chapter 7

PARTNERSHIP FOR DEVELOPMENT

THE FAMILY-PLANNING PROGRAMS WE have been considering must not be viewed in isolation. They must be part of integrated population policies and programs that include study and research into the whole population situation in the context of family life and family welfare. In turn, as the Caracas Conference insisted, these population studies and action programs must be seen in the wider context of economic and social development.

The population situation and population policies should be kept in perspective. Too often one aspect, e.g., the population explosion, is used as a scapegoat for lack of development traceable to many other causes. Family planning is then pursued with crusading zeal as if it were a panacea.

It is necessary to be aware that the population expansion is one very important factor, but only one, in the problem of development. A balance must be kept. Positive measures to overcome the other causes of poverty are absolutely essential. Any population policy must be integrated in an interdisciplinary manner with these measures to promote economic and social progress. To concentrate on population-restriction policies and neglect positive improvements in agriculture, reform of social structures, land reform, and so on, is as wrong and unrealistic as to concentrate on positive measures and ignore the population problem.[1]

[1] Hoffman, Paul, *World without Want*, p. 66. London: Chatto & Windus, 1962. It may be useful here to comment on the sentence in President Johnson's speech to the UN General Assembly, June 25, 1965, which has been widely quoted and as widely misunderstood: "Less than five dollars invested in population control is worth a hundred dollars invested in economic growth." It is clear from the speech and from subsequent action and policy statements of the President and the policy of AID (cf. "AID's Population Policy" by William S. Gaud, in *War on Hunger*, Vol. II, No. 3, March 1968, p. 3) that he did not mean that family planning could take the place of, or would be substituted for, aid for economic growth. He was merely stating the comparatively very small cost of large-scale family-planning programs per head compared to other programs. Perhaps it was unfortunate he said this, as the calculation is a very rough and ready one.

The United Nations Population Commission, in its meetings in New York in March 1965 and in Geneva in November 1967, was notable for this balanced approach. The papers and reports of these meetings [2] and the forthcoming revised version [3] of the seminal study of the commission's *Determinants and Consequences of Population Trends,* first published in 1953, give the whole range of relevant demographic factors in the context of agricultural, industrial, health, and family development and provide the best guidelines for population policies for developing countries.

This holistic approach is the best safeguard against extreme and narrow views on the population expansion. Sometimes the impression is given by proponents of such views that unless population control is energetically pursued—and this is often regarded as immediately possible and of greater necessity and feasibility than agricultural or general economic development—it is not worthwhile doing anything. This adds to a general feeling of despair with regard to the whole situation of the developing countries. But it must be clearly seen that agricultural and economic advance are not factors which can be "canceled" by population increase. They have a validity of their own.

Nevertheless, as we have stated so often, population increase does complicate the problems of world poverty, and it is for this reason that population policies, family-planning programs, and the need for immediate action—in which the technical cooperation of the developed countries can be of great assistance—has been emphasized.

But the problems of population shade into the wider problems of development. The urgency of these problems, which is too little realized even now, may be gauged by the fact that some of the disasters that the more pessimistic population writers threaten may well be the penalty for failure to achieve world cooperation for development.

Dr. B. R. Sen, former director-general of the FAO, significantly put the choice before the nations very clearly, in a speech to the United Nations Population Commission on March 24, 1965.

For it has been recognized that there will be no lasting peace or security in the world until hunger and want can be eliminated. In fact what

[2] Available from the Population Division, United Nations, New York.
[3] I was given the advanced draft chapters of this authoritative work by the kindness of Miss Edith Adams of the Population Commission, for use in the preparation of this book.

is in danger is not merely the health and happiness of individuals but the very basis of free and democratic society. The next thirty-five years, till the end of the century, will be, as I have said, a most critical period in man's history. Either we take the fullest measures both to raise productivity and to stabilize population growth, or we will face disaster of an unprecedented magnitude. We must be warned that in the present situation lie the seeds of unlimited progress or unlimited disaster, not only for individual nations but for the whole world. I myself feel optimistic that mankind will not stand aloof from the drama of life and death that is unfolding before our eyes but will come forward to achieve that miracle of organized will which seems to be distant today. This indeed must happen if freedom and dignity are to survive.

It is tragic that with such issues at stake, and with the possibility of winning the race between population increase and food production, at least in the short-term, within our grasp, the willingness of developed countries to play their role seems to be slackening. Assistance, foreign aid—or, as I would prefer to call it, the contribution of the more affluent countries to the partnership to create a better world, where glaring economic inequalities between and within nations would be wiped out—is an essential condition of the success of the developing countries.

The partial failure of the United Nations Conference on Trade and Development of spring 1968, the reluctance of the more affluent countries to move quickly towards the target of one percent of the Gross National Product,[4] the general apathy and disillusionment with regard to aid, are all ominous signs that the central problem of our age is still a marginal concern of the developed countries compared to their domestic concerns and problems.

The savage cut in America's foreign aid proposals of September 1968 of $1.3 billion dollars was a great blow to the developing countries. This was offset to a slight extent by the greater concern of some European countries, but the "heroic" effort of Great Britain to *increase* its aid contribution in spite of its economic difficulties was more of a gesture than a great lift to the aid effort: a rise from £205 million per year in 1967 to £215 million in 1968 and £226 million in 1969 is hardly in keeping with the seriousness of the crisis.

---

[4] It is interesting to compare with the one percent target the percentage spent on armaments by the developed countries. No country spends less than one percent of national income; the United States spends over 10 percent, Great Britain about 7 percent. In the case of the United States this is over $100 billion.

There is no space here for a lengthy treatise on the progress of the developing countries or of the duties of both developed and developing countries to make this a top priority of their policies. In any case, in indicating the situation solutions have also been proposed that could not be implemented without massive, technically assisted, adequately controlled aid from the developed countries and wholehearted efforts toward their own development on the part of the developing countries.[5]

Still, it may be useful to point to some recent events that give hope that wiser counsels may prevail and that the developed countries will measure up to the gravity of the situation and be moved to constructive and adequate action.

The first of these events was undoubtedly the historic speech of Robert S. McNamara, as newly appointed president of the World Bank Group, to the board of governors in Washington on September 30, 1968.[6] It was historic for two reasons. The first reason was its purpose: to rally to the cause of development those who for one reason or another had become fainthearted and were slackening their efforts. Mr. McNamara declared that this was his deliberate intention:

I am not despondent about the difficulties that lie ahead because I have faith in our ability to overcome them. That is why I have proposed a program of greatly increased activity by the World Bank Group, so that by taking a lead in development assistance we may encourage all those, rich and poor alike, who have begun to lose heart and slacken their pace.

If we in the Bank are able to double our effort, this could be the signal for others to rally again to the struggle, determined to use our overwhelming strength for the betterment of all mankind, and the fulfillment of the human spirit.[7]

[5] Such a partnership will mean a rethinking of the motivation for foreign aid. The use of aid as a means of combatting Communism in the cold war will have to give place to a fuller commitment to President Kennedy's motive for aid: "because it's right." Cf. a very significant article by Senator Edward Kennedy, "World Poverty and World Peace," Johns Hopkins University, Baltimore, May 2, 1967. But the idea of some economists that aid is a "myth" can be very damaging to the cause of the developing countries, as the whole argument of this book indicates.

[6] See Appendix 4. It is published in pamphlet form by the Bank for International Reconstruction and Development (World Bank), Washington, D.C.

[7] McNamara speech, pp. 13, 14.

The second reason why it was historic was because in this speech Mr. McNamara announced a new dynamism in the policy of the World Bank. He made it obvious that he intended to pursue an aggressive policy of raising and distributing funds. He announced that globally the Bank Group during the next five years would lend twice as much as during the previous five years. This means, as he said, that between 1968 and 1973 the Bank Group would lend in total nearly as much as it has lent since it began operations twenty-two years ago:

This is a change of such a degree that I feel it necessary to emphasize that it is not a change of kind. We believe that we can carry out these operations within the high standards of careful evaluation and sound financing that my prececessors have made synonymous with the name of the World Bank.[8]

The reputation of the World Bank stands high, together with that of its affiliate, the International Development Association, which deals with the needs of poorer countries that cannot accept loans on the commercial terms the World Bank offers. When the history of aid over the last twenty years comes to be written, the role the World Bank has played in the success stories of these two decades will be seen to be considerable, not only because of the amount of money advanced but also because of the invaluable technical assistance that went with it. Much of the success of the Pakistan economic "miracle" must be attributed to the funds and advice of the World Bank. This is by no means to minimize the part that the government and people of Pakistan have played. It illustrates in a very happy way the cooperation between outside agencies and a developing country, mainly using the funds of the developed world.

The fact that this highly respectable institution, at a time when the cause of aid was at its lowest ebb, should embark under its new president on such a bold policy is very important from the point of view of morale. This is all the more so because Mr. McNamara has a reputation as a hardheaded business man who has had a meteoric career in achieving results. He is not noted for backing lost causes. In the ninety days Mr. McNamara was in office up to

[8] *Ibid.*, p. 5.

the time of his speech the World Bank raised more funds by borrowing than in the whole of any single calendar year in its history.

In this speech, remarkable for its condensed wisdom, there are three points that in my opinion stand out. First of all, in one paragraph Mr. McNamara cut down to size the alibi of the developed countries with regard to balance of payments.[9] As he said, the balance of payments difficulty is a problem of balance among the rich economies and not a balance between those countries as a group and the rest of the world. Very little of the money lent in aid stays in the developing countries; almost all of it returns quickly in payment for the goods purchased in the richer countries.

The second significant point is that the five-year plan Mr. McNamara announced involves considerable changes in the allocation of resources, both to geographic areas and to economic sectors, to suit the considerably changed circumstances of today and tomorrow. With regard to Asia, the World Bank lending should rise substantially by 1973. In Latin America it was proposed to double the investment rate. In Africa, just coming to the threshold of major investment for development, the greatest expansion of World Bank activities was contemplated. There, by 1973, with effective collaboration from the African countries, according to Mr. McNamara, the World Bank will have increased its investment threefold.

It has often been said about the World Bank that its main aid effort is toward the more developed of the developing countries, who can afford, or who think they can afford, the World Bank terms, and that the really poor countries are neglected. It is a fact that many of the poorest countries, despite their great need, have had the least technical and financial assistance from the Bank Group. About ten of these have had no loans or credit at all. This is largely because of their inability to prepare projects for consideration. The Bank, said Mr. McNamara, has proposed in these cases to provide special assistance to improve economic performance and to identify and prepare projects acceptable for group financing. It should be remembered that although the World Bank functions as a bank on a commercial basis, its profit is largely available for the I.D.A. to help the poorer countries.[10]

[9] *Ibid.*, p. 6.

[10] A reasonable return for such good securities is offered on World Bank bonds. Could not the Churches—now much more concerned about helping poorer countries—invest some of their capital in the World Bank? The point

The third significant point is the place given in Mr. McNamara's speech to the subject of special interest here, namely the participation by the World Bank in programs of family planning. It was a bold and courageous decision for the Bank to become involved in this controversial subject.[11] A certain amount of criticism was expected, and this was perhaps made all the more likely because the speech took place within a few months of the publication of *Humanae Vitae*, when controversy, especially in the United States, was at its height. But the criticism on the whole was muted, even though in South America some quite adverse reactions were recorded. Some of this criticism was due to the fact that naturally enough this item was taken out of its context by the communications media, and it was also seized on by the keener advocates of family planning as the main point of Mr. McNamara's speech. What was missed by some of his critics and his supporters was precisely the balanced treatment of the subject and the perspective given to it as part of a many-pronged attack on world poverty. One might take issue with one or two of the sentences in the treatment of the subject; for example, it is doubtful whether one could say that "more than anything else it is the population explosion which, by holding back the advancement of the poor, is blowing apart the rich and poor and widening the already dangerous gap between them." Nevertheless, the entry of the World Bank into this field, and the way it has chosen to announce that entry, is a valuable contribution to the solution of the problems we have been considering in this book. This is all the more the case because one can expect the same very high standards in dealing with these programs and evaluating them as the Bank has shown with regard to its other socioeconomic efforts.

Another very encouraging event with regard to the aid position is the report of the commission set up under Lester Pearson to examine the whole aid effort, with regard to both donor and recipient countries, over the past twenty years, in order to assess its successes and failures and to learn how aid—cooperation between developed and developing countries—can be made much more

---

was put to me by George Bull, editor of the *Director*, the periodical of the British Institute of Directors (with a membership of 40,000 directors of British companies). This would be apart from the one percent income of the Churches suggested to be devoted to aid.

[11] McNamara speech, pp. 11–13.

effective.[12] This "Grand Assize" could be of the highest importance. Often enough, the impression is given by those who are keenest to stress the special responsibility of the developed countries that it is only lack of will, lack of generosity, or lack of plain commonsense that prevents these countries from doing their full and adequate share in aiding the developing countries. But very often this reluctance is not a sign of weak will, although it is perfectly true that the real will to help the developing countries does not measure up to the need. There are real misgivings about whether aid is properly used and whether developing countries have put themselves in a position to make best use of it. However much one may wish to do so, it is not right to discount this feeling. But this should not offset the great successes that have taken place, which receive far less publicity. It should not take away from the fact that a huge effort is necessary, and that when failures are pointed out this is not an argument against the aid program but an argument for its more effective organization. It is insufficiently realized that one of the effects of poverty in the developing countries is that they lack the personnel who can give honest and efficient service in the various sectors affected by aid programs. But neither public grants drawn from taxpayers nor private charity can long survive in an atmosphere of suspicion generated by stories, some of them well-founded, of abuse of grants and loans intended to help the poorer countries and the poor within those countries.

The Pearson inquiry, therefore, a multilateral project supported by developed and developing countries alike, under the aegis of the World Bank, comes opportunely to enable a more objective assessment of the aid situation to be obtained as a basis for a further leap forward. There is a tremendous reservoir of goodwill, of desire to do something to help less materially fortunate peoples, but donors want to be sure that their aid, and even their sacrifices, are put to good account.

In spite of the disillusionment and slackening of effort, to which I have already referred, this huge reservoir can be tapped. For example, the British Overseas Development Ministry of the United Kingdom gets letters in favor of aid to developing countries in a proportion of twelve to one.

Another hopeful sign, at least for the United States effort, is the

[12] The Lester Pearson Commission was set up in August 1968, and its report was published by the World Bank in October 1969. See Appendix 5 for a summary.

possibility of peace in Vietnam. But Vietnam has too often been used by the developed countries as an alibi. Opponents of the war often very loosely say that the war is the main obstacle to helping the developing countries. There does not seem to be sufficient basis for this. First of all, if the United States really wanted to, it could manage to give more aid to the developing countries in spite of the war in Vietnam. Secondly, the other countries of the Development Assistance Committee of the OECD (sixteen of them) are not hampered by this war; in fact, some have been made much more prosperous by it, and therefore theoretically are in a better position to give aid. Also, the population of North and South Vietnam is just over 37 million, compared to the population of the developing world of about 2.4 billion. But there is no doubt that peace in Vietnam, with an end to the tremendous expenditure on the war effort there, would create a much better psychological climate and also a greater financial potential for increased aid.

It has been reckoned that the amount of money spent on the war in Vietnam in a year would be enough to rehouse all the slum dwellers of South America. This is of course a mathematical calculation with no relation to real life. No one expects that when the war ends all the saving in expenditure will be devoted to the poor of the world. But the ending of the war in Vietnam could be the signal for renewed generosity: the allocation of a good proportion of released resources to foreign assistance. This could be the target of political pressure for those who feel that American aid should be restored to, and even surpass, previous levels.

Another very hopeful sign is the increasing involvement of the Churches in the war against world poverty. At the World Council of Churches meeting on Church and Society, in Geneva in 1966, considerable attention was paid to the issue, and nearly forty pages of the report [13] of this conference were devoted to the economic growth of the developing countries and the need for the Christian Churches to be committed to assist it. The World Council of Churches Assembly at Uppsala in 1968 showed a very great awareness of the problems of world poverty and of the need of the Churches to become committed as a moral Christian duty. Both as institutions and through their individual members the Churches were pledged to a realistic and well-informed campaign to form

[13] *Official Report,* World Council of Churches, pp. 52–93. Geneva: 1967.

public opinion in their respective countries so that world cooperation for development might take place. In a number of countries
the idea is being spread of one percent of Church income and of
members' personal income to be pledged to aid for the developing
countries—partly as a positive contribution to development but
also as an example to government and public opinion.

The paper prepared for the Uppsala conference [14] on this issue
modestly called itself a stimulant to further discussion, but it was
in reality a masterly treatise on the Church and development and
was welcomed as such by the Assembly. Barbara Ward, in a splendid ecumenical gesture, was allowed to address the Assembly on
world poverty. The reception given to her was confirmation of the
fact that world poverty was one of the chief issues of the conference.

The Catholic Church is awakening to its obligations in this field,
which have been stressed by the Popes since Pius XII, in the first
year of his reign in 1939, issued his encyclical *Summini Pontifica-
tus.*

More than seventy speeches were made during the Second Vatican Council drawing attention to the problems of the developing
countries and Christian responsibility with regard to them. As the
result of this concern, Pope Paul made two very significant moves,
which have not received the publicity accorded some of his other,
less popular statements. On January 6, 1967, he established the
Pontifical Commission on Justice and Peace (in answer to the re-
quests of the Vatican Council Fathers expressed in the Vatican
document *The Church in the Modern World*) as a body in the central organization of the Catholic Church—the Curia—to focus on
the problems of world poverty and to mobilize the whole Church
to be concerned with them. Then on March 26, 1967, he issued the
encyclical *Populorum Progressio* (On the Development of Peoples), which was a very simple direct appeal for action with regard
to world poverty and may well be called the "Charter of the Developing Countries."

The great strength of Christians numerically in the world means
that if they were really mobilized in this crusade, a tremendous
pressure could be brought to bear.

In fact, neither the Catholic Church nor other Christian

[14] Richard Dickinson, *Plummet & Line*, World Council of Churches, Geneva: 1968.

Churches envisage their efforts in isolation. This is *par excellence* an ecumenical venture, and one of the first fruits of this was a conference held in Beirut, April 21–27, 1968, on World Cooperation for Development, sponsored by a joint Committee for Society, Development, and Peace (SODEPAX) of the World Council of Churches and the Catholic Church. At this conference fifteen top experts of the World Council and of the Pontifical Justice and Peace Commission met with more than thirty observers from secular and governmental bodies, to consider the role that the Christian Churches could play. The Beirut Report that emerged has been given wide publicity within the Churches. It was officially accepted at Uppsala and is serving as a basis for ongoing action. It was a historic document as the first agreed statement of a combined conference on the subject. The fact that the report was drawn up with the assistance of observers from so many secular bodies showed that the Christian Churches do not regard their role as introverted, but rather as an outgoing effort to join with all men of goodwill in solving this greatest problem of our age.

The report of the Beirut conference stresses not only the need for much more aid but also the need for better terms of trade. Lester Pearson has said, "Perhaps the best form of aid is trade; we have not made nearly enough progress in helping developing countries by putting them in a position where they could add to their own resources by trading with others on a competitive basis, in their own products, primary and industrial."[15]

The contents of the Beirut Report will be spread throughout developed and developing countries by National Commissions of Justice and Peace from the point of view of the Catholic Church and by the member churches of the World Council of Churches.[16]

But perhaps the most hopeful events in the past few years are the success stories of countries such as Pakistan, Ceylon, Taiwan, and others, which have proved the value of enlightened, technically assisted aid matched by the energy, resourcefulness, and hard work of developing countries. In the long run, this is one of the most powerful incentives for the developed countries to measure

[15] Pearson, Lester, "Bitter Contrasts," *World Hunger*, Vol. 1, No. 7, Jan. 1969. London: U.K. Freedom from Hunger Campaign.

[16] The Statement of the Beirut conference is reproduced in Appendix 3. The full report of the conference is available from the Joint Committee on Society, Development, and Peace, 150 Rue de Ferney, Geneva, Switzerland.

up to their responsibilities, and the Grand Assize of Lester Pearson has made public such success stories, which will offset the more publicized failures.

CONCLUSION The population explosion gives urgency to the need to cope with the problems of the developing countries. The moral issues have been recognized by the United Nations and by statesmen of many individual nations, and have been accepted by governments; they have been pointed out by writers such as Barbara Ward [17] and have been underlined by world religious leaders and concerned humanists. And there is a commitment to what is one of the central tasks of our age, but it is a halfhearted one. We have not yet made the definite choice—and backed it with sufficient effort—between a world increasingly seen to be in the process of becoming better, with every human being entitled to and receiving the minimum conditions for a life in keeping with his human dignity, and a world where the increasing gap between poverty and riches will eventually, as Pius XII warned twenty years ago, explode into new wars.

Justice, charity, prudence, expediency, all combine to urge a massive effort in the war against world poverty and for the development of the developing countries. Barbara Ward, a member of the Pontifical Commission on Justice and Peace, put the matter very clearly in a recent article. She said that if history is any guide, the Atlantic world of today is poised between two variants of its own future. It can follow the route of drift, indifference, complacency, and inaction and watch the world's crisis slip beyond the point at which rational solutions can still be applied. This is a perfectly possible route. The past is strewn with the wreckage of regimes and societies that could not stop in the middle of their fun and feasting to read the writing on the wall in time.

Or the Atlantic Powers can take thought and action in time, looking carefully at the policies and expedients that have helped them to avoid disaster in the past and adopting the strategies that permit human society to secure control of its own destiny. This, too, is a possible route, since in spite of all its past errors and dis-

---

[17] Cf., for example, *Spaceship Earth*, pp. 63–122, New York: Columbia University Press, 1966, one of the whole series of books she has devoted to this subject. *World Poverty and the Christian*, by the present writer, New York: Hawthorn Press, 1963, deals with the special Christian responsibility.

order, the Atlantic world today is more stable, more open to human opportunity, wealthier, more competent, than would have seemed conceivable even twenty years ago.

Barbara Ward goes on to ask the crucial question: Which route will be taken? Now, she says, it is a matter of choice, just as it was in 1947 when the United States government, through General Marshall, made its first tentative commitment to European recovery and nineteen European nations responded with the effort to look at their problems jointly and to make joint recommendations— through the Franks Report—for a cooperative and coordinated program. In 1947 the Americans could have decided not to act, the Europeans not to respond—in which case, the next historical catastrophe would undoubtedly have occurred in Europe.

Barbara Ward's conclusion puts the problem of world poverty and the developing countries in its global and historic setting. At present, she maintains, the potential shape of crisis takes the new form of the gap between developed North and aspiring, poverty-stricken South. Its pattern is clear, its threats increasing, its locus could be the whole of human society. What is lacking is any sign of the new "Recovery Program," the new Marshall-type strategy designed to give the next twenty years the vigor, direction, and success of the last. Clearly the initiative for such an effort, she says, can come from either side of the Atlantic, but, perhaps as a symbol of their own recovered power and resources, the European nations might more appropriately invite their old benefactor to join them in a new, effective, yet visionary effort to apply the old lesson to the new challenge. Barbara Ward concludes:

In the wide arena of power, of strategy and missiles and proliferation and confrontation, the voice of smaller nations is hardly heard above the stentorian shouts of the great contenders. But the world of development is the quiet world of work and bread, where children can live and families flourish and men build the opportunities for coming generations. Here the voice of conscience and faith can be heard, whether it comes from large Powers or small. The essential point is that it should be heard, and heard in time so that the works of peace no longer occupy the last place on the agenda of survival and mankind reverses its present sleepwalking drift to deeper and more irreversible catastrophe.[18]

[18] Offprint from the *Liber Amicorum* published in tribute to August de Schryver, Minister of State, Holland, May 1968.

The population explosion, as part of the wider issues of world cooperation for development, is seen not as a menace but as a challenge, not as a phenomenon necessarily leading to catastrophe but as a manageable problem, if the spirit, the goodwill, and the resources necessary to its solution are forthcoming.

FURTHER STATISTICAL DATA ON THE POPULATION SITUATION

TABLE 1: WORLD POPULATION DATA CHART [1]

Region and country	Population estimates mid-1968 (millions)	Current rate of population growth	Number of years to double population	Birth rate per 1,000 population	Death rate per 1,000 population	Life expectancy at birth (years)	Population density per sq. km. [2]	Per capita national income (dollars)
WORLD	3,479	2.0	35	34	14	53	. . .	493
AFRICA	333	2.3	31	45	22	43	. . .	123
Northern Africa								
Algeria	12.9	2.8	25	46–50	1–14	. . .	5	195
Libya	1.8	3.0	24	. . .	. . .	. . .	1	636
Morocco	14.6	3.3	21	46–50	15–19	50–55	30	174
Sudan	14.8	2.8	25	49–55	22–27	. . .	6	90
Tunisia	4.7	2.8	25	45	17	. . .	27	179
United Arab Republic	31.8	3.0	24	44	15	50–55	30	130
Western Africa								
Dahomey	2.5	1.7	41	50	33	30–35	21	60
Gambia	0.4	2.1	33	37–42	19–23	. . .	30	75
Ghana	8.4	2.6	27	47–52	22–26	40–45	33	245

[1] Source: Population Reference Bureau, Washington, D.C. Given as 1968 statistics, but derived mainly from United Nations, *Demographic Yearbook*, 1967.

[2] Density figures supplied by the author from *Demographic Yearbook*, 1967.

TABLE 1: WORLD POPULATION DATA CHART (*Continued*)

Region and country	Population estimates mid-1968 (millions)	Current rate of population growth	Number of years to double population	Birth rate per 1,000 population	Death rate per 1,000 population	Life expectancy at birth (years)	Population density per sq. km. ²	Per capita national
Guinea	3.8	1.1	63	50	38	25–35	15	6
Ivory Coast	4.1	1.9	37	52	33	30–35	12	18
Liberia	1.1	1.7	41	. . .	. . .	. . .	10	14
Mali	4.8	2.0	35	52	33	30–35	4	5
Mauritania	1.1	1.7	41	47–53	26–30	40–45	1	10
Niger	3.6	2.4	29	53	29	35–40	3	7
Nigeria	62.0	2.5	28	45–53	25–32	. . .	63	6
Senegal	3.8	2.0	35	40–45	23–29	35–45	18	14
Sierra Leone	2.5	2.4	29	. . .	. . .	. . .	33	12
Togo	1.8	2.3	31	52–58	27–32	30–40	30	8
Upper Volta	5.2	1.4	50	47–53	28–33	30–35	18	4
Eastern Africa								
Burundi	3.4	2.0	35	46–51	25–30	35–40	118	4
Ethiopia	23.8	1.8	29	. . .	. . .	. . .	19	4
Kenya	10.2	2.9	24	48–55	18–23	40–45	17	7
Madagascar	6.4	2.1	33	42–48	22–26	. . .	12	8
Malawi	4.2	2.4	29	. . .	. . .	. . .	34	3
Mauritius	0.8	2.6	27	35.3	8.8	48–65	407	27
Mozambique	7.2	1.7	41	. . .	. . .	. . .	9	4
Rwanda	3.4	2.0	35	52	. . .	. . .	121	4
Somalia	2.8	1.9	37	. . .	. . .	. . .	4	4
Southern Rhodesia	4.7	3.2	22	44–50	13–16	50–55	11	20
Tanzania	12.4	1.9	37	40–46	22–26	35–45	. . .	6
Uganda	8.1	2.5	28	42–48	18–23	. . .	33	7
Zambia	4.1	3.0	24	49–54	17–21	40–45	5	17
Middle Africa								
Angola	5.5	1.7	41	. . .	. . .	40–50	. . .	5
Cameroon	5.6	2.2	32	48–52	25–28	35–40	11	10
Central African Rep.	1.5	1.5	46	46–50	25–31	35–40	2	12
Chad	3.5	1.5	47	44–48	29–33	30–35	3	6
Congo (Brazzaville)	0.9	1.6	44	41–45	24–26	35–40	2	12
Congo (Dem. Rep.)	16.7	2.3	31	40–45	20–25	35–45	7	6
Gabon	0.5	0.3	233	35–42	27–32	25–45	2	33

Region and country	Population estimates mid-1968 (millions)	Current rate of population growth	Number of years to double population	Birth rate per 1,000 population	Death rate per 1,000 population	Life expectancy at birth (years)	Population density per sq. km.²	Per capita national income (dollars)
Southern Africa								
Botswana	0.6	2.0	35	. . .	. . .	. . .	1	55
Lesotho	0.9	2.0	35	40	. . .	40–50	29	50
South Africa	19.2	2.6	27	38–44	12–16	50–60	15	509
South-West Africa	0.6	2.0	35	. . .	. . .	. . .	1	. . .
ASIA	1,943	2.2	32	39	17	50	. . .	128
Southwest Asia								
Cyprus	0.6	1.5	47	24–26	6–8	70	65	623
Iraq	8.9	3.1	23	42–48	12–16	. . .	19	193
Israel	2.8	2.2	32	25.4	6–7	72	127	1,067
Jordan	2.2	3.2	22	44–50	13–16	. . .	21	179
Kuwait	0.5	5.1	14	47–49	6–7	. . .	31	3,184
Lebanon	2.6	2.5	28	32–36	7–11	. . .	237	335
Saudi Arabia	7.1	2.0	35	. . .	. . .	. . .	3	165
Southern Yemen	1.2	2.3	31	. . .	. . .	. . .	. . .	. . .
Syria	5.8	3.0	24	. . .	. . .	. . .	29	156
Turkey	33.8	2.9	24	43	. . .	50–60	2	244
Yemen	5.2	1.6	44	. . .	. . .	. . .	26	75
Middle South Asia								
Afghanistan	16.0	2.2	32	. . .	. . .	. . .	25	70
Bhutan	0.8	2.1	33	. . .	. . .	. . .	16	50
Ceylon	12.2	2.8	25	33	8	62	175	130
India	523.0	2.5	28	41	18	45	163	86
Iran	26.5	3.0	24	50	20	. . .	15	211
Nepal	10.7	2.1	33	39–43	18–22	. . .	73	66
Pakistan	126.0	3.1	23	50	20	45	111	89
Southeast Asia								
Burma	26.4	2.2	32	46–52	25–31	45–50	37	56
Cambodia	6.6	2.4	29	40–46	17–22	45–50	35	112
Indonesia	112.8	2.3	31	40–45	18–22	. . .	72	85
Laos	2.8	2.4	29	45–49	22–24	. . .	11	56
Malaysia	8.7	3.2	22	37–39	7.6	57–65	63	250
Philippines	35.9	3.5	20	44–50	10–15	50–60	112	219

TABLE 1: WORLD POPULATION DATA CHART (Continued)

Region and country	Population estimates mid-1968 (millions)	Current rate of population growth	Number of years to double population	Birth rate per 1,000 population	Death rate per 1,000 population	Life expectancy at birth (years)	Population density per sq. km. [2]	Per capita national
Singapore	2.0	2.5	28	30	5.5	. . .	3,293	50
Thailand	33.7	3.1	23	44–48	13–14	65–70	61	10
Vietnam (North)	20.8	. .	. .	. . .	. . .	. . .	123	. .
Vietnam (South)	17.4	2.6	27	35–42	13–18	. . .	97	11
East Asia								
China (Mainland)	728.0	1.5	47	. . .	. . .	. . .	74	8
China (Taiwan)	13.5	2.7	26	32.5	5.5	65–70	356	18
Hong Kong	3.9	2.7	26	24.9	5.0	65–75	3,601	29
Japan	101.0	1.1	63	13.7	6.8	71	267	69
Korea (North)	13.0	2.8	25	35–40	10–14	. . .	103	18
Korea (South)	30.7	2.8	25	38–44	10–14	55–60	295	8
Mongolia	1.2	3.0	24	38–42	10	. . .	1	19
AMERICA								
Northern America	222	1.1	63	19	9	71	. . .	2,79
Canada	20.7	1.6	44	19.4	7.5	72	2	1,82
United States	201.3	1.1	63	18.5	9.5	71	21	2,89
Latin America	268	3.0	24	40	10	60	. . .	34
Middle America								
Costa Rica	1.6	3.5	20	44–46	7.7	62–65	29	35
El Salvador	3.3	3.7	19	47–49	9.9	57–61	142	23
Guatemala	4.9	3.1	23	46–48	16.6	50–60	42	28
Honduras	2.5	3.5	20	47–50	15–17	. . .	21	194
Mexico	47.3	3.5	20	44.1	9.6	58–64	22	41
Nicaragua	1.8	3.5	20	47–50	14–16	. . .	13	298
Panama	1.4	3.2	22	41–42	10–11	. . .	17	42
Caribbean								
Barbados	0.3	1.7	41	25.3	8.2	63–68	570	36
Cuba	8.2	2.6	27	34–36	8–9	. . .	68	31
Dominican Republic	4.0	3.6	20	45–48	14–16	57–60	77	212
Haiti	4.7	2.5	28	45–50	11–21	35–45	162	8
Jamaica	1.9	1.8	39	38.8	7.7	63–68	168	407

Region and country	Population estimates mid-1968 (millions)	Current rate of population growth	Number of years to double population	Birth rate per 1,000 population	Death rate per 1,000 population	Life expectancy at birth (years)	Population density per sq. km.²	Per capita national income (dollars)
Puerto Rico	2.7	1.5	47	28.3	5.9	68–73	300	959
Trinidad and Tobago	1.0	2.8	25	37–39	6.9	63–68	195	501
ropical S. America								
Bolivia	3.9	2.4	29	43–45	20–24	. . .	3	144
Brazil	88.3	3.2	22	41–43	10–12	. . .	10	217
Colombia	19.7	3.2	22	40–45	11–13	. . .	16	237
Ecuador	5.7	3.4	21	45–50	12–14	. . .	19	183
Guiana	0.7	2.9	24	39.9	8.1	60–65	3	248
Peru	12.8	3.1	23	44–45	11–13	55–60	9	218
Venezuela	9.7	3.6	20	46–48	9–10	65–70	10	745
emperate S. America								
Argentina	23.4	1.5	47	21.5	8.2	63–70	8	740
Chile	9.1	2.2	32	32.0	10.7	. . .	12	515
Paraguay	2.2	3.2	22	42–45	12–14	. . .	5	185
Uruguay	2.8	1.2	58	23–25	8–9	65–70	15	537
UROPE	455	0.7	100	18	10	70	. . .	1,069
Iorthern Europe								
Denmark	4.8	0.8	88	18.4	10.3	72	111	1,652
Finland	4.7	0.7	100	16.7	9.4	69	14	1,399
Iceland	0.2	1.7	41	23.9	7.1	73	2	1,870
Ireland	2.9	0.4	175	21.6	12.1	70	41	783
Norway	3.8	0.8	88	18.2	9.5	73	12	1,453
Sweden	7.9	0.8	88	15.8	10.0	74	17	2,204
United Kingdom	55.8	0.5	140	17.8	11.7	71	225	1,451
Vestern Europe								
Austria	7.4	0.4	175	17.6	12.5	70	87	970
Belgium	9.7	0.6	117	15.8	12.0	71	312	1,406
France	50.4	1.0	70	17.4	10.6	71	90	1,436
Germany (West)	60.3	0.6	117	17.6	11.5	71	232	1,447
Luxembourg	0.3	0.5	140	15.5	12.1	68	130	1,498
Netherlands	12.7	1.1	63	19.2	8.1	74	371	1,265
Switzerland	6.2	1.2	58	18.3	9.3	71	147	1,928

TABLE 1: WORLD POPULATION DATA CHART (Continued)

Region and country	Population estimates mid-1968 (millions)	Current rate of population growth	Number of years to double population	Birth rate per 1,000 population	Death rate per 1,000 population	Life expectancy at birth (years)	Population density per sq. km. ^{2}	Per capita
Eastern Europe								
Bulgaria	8.4	0.7	100	14.9	8.3	70	74	4
Czechoslovakia	14.4	0.5	140	15.8	10.0	71	111	8
Germany (East)	17.1	0.2	350	15.8	13.3	71	148	1,2
Hungary	10.2	0.3	233	13.6	10.1	70	109	7
Poland	32.3	0.8	88	16.7	7.3	68	101	7
Romania	19.4	0.6	117	14.3	8.2	68	81	3
Southern Europe								
Albania	2.0	2.5	28	34.0	8.6	65	67	3
Greece	8.8	0.7	100	18.1	7.9	69	65	5
Italy	52.8	0.6	117	18.9	9.5	70	172	8
Malta	0.3	. .	. .	16.8	9.0	69	1,002	4
Portugal	9.5	0.7	100	22.3	10.9	64	100	3
Spain	32.4	0.8	88	20.9	8.6	70	63	5
Yugoslavia	20.2	1.1	63	20.2	8.0	65	77	4
OCEANIA	18.5	1.8	39	20	9	71	. . .	1,6
Australia	12.0	1.8	39	19.3	9.0	71	2	1,6
New Zealand	2.8	1.8	39	22.4	8.9	71	10	1,7
U.S.S.R.	239	1.1	63	18.2	7.3	70	10	9

TABLE 2: COUNTRIES WITH HIGH RATES OF POPULATION INCREASE [3]

Country	Population (millions)	Rate of population increase	Population density per sq. km.
AFRICA			
Algeria	12.9	2.8	5
Kenya	10.2	2.9	17
Libya	1.8	3.0	1
Mauritius	.8	2.6	1
Morocco	14.6	3.3	30
Nigeria	62.0	2.5	63
S. Rhodesia	4.7	3.2	. . .
Sudan	14.8	2.8	6
Tunisia	4.7	2.8	27
United Arab Republic	31.8	3.0	30
Zambia	4.1	3.0	5
ASIA			
Ceylon	12.2	2.8	175
China (Taiwan)	13.5	2.7	356
Hong Kong	3.9	2.7	. . .
India	523.0	2.5	163
Iran	26.5	3.0	15
Iraq	8.9	3.1	19
Jordan	2.2	3.2	21
Korea (North)	13.0	2.8	103
Korea (South)	30.7	2.8	. . .
Lebanon	2.6	2.5	237
Malaysia	8.7	3.2	7
Mongolia	1.2	3.0	1
Pakistan	126.0	3.1	111
Philippines	35.9	3.5	112
Singapore	2.0	2.5	3293
Thailand	33.7	3.1	61
Turkey	33.8	2.9	41
South Vietnam	17.4	2.6	. . .
SOUTH AMERICA			
Bolivia	3.9	2.4	3
Brazil	88.3	3.2	10
Colombia	19.7	3.2	16
Costa Rica	1.6	3.5	29
Cuba	8.2	2.6	68
Dominican Republic	4.0	3.6	77

[3] Source: *Demographic Yearbook,* 1967.

TABLE 2: COUNTRIES WITH HIGH RATES
OF POPULATION INCREASE (*Continued*)

Country	Population (*millions*)	Rate of population increase	Population density per sq. km.
Ecuador	5.7	3.4	19
El Salvador	3.3	3.7	141
Guatemala	4.9	3.1	42
Guiana	.7	2.9	3
Haiti	4.7	2.5	162
Honduras	2.5	3.5	21
Mexico	47.3	3.5	22
Nicaragua	1.8	3.5	13
Panama	1.4	3.2	17
Paraguay	2.2	3.2	5
Peru	12.8	3.1	9
Trinidad and Tobago	1.0	2.8	195
Venezuela	9.7	3.6	10
SOUTHERN EUROPE			
Albania	2.0	2.5	67

TABLE 3: COUNTRIES WITH LOW RATES
OF POPULATION INCREASE [4]

Country	Population (*millions*)	Rate of population increase	Population density per sq. km.
EUROPE			
Austria	7.4	.4	87
Belgium	9.7	.6	312
Bulgaria	8.4	.7	74
Czechoslovakia	14.4	.5	111
Denmark	4.8	.8	111
Finland	4.7	.7	14
France	50.4	1.0	90
Germany (East)	17.1	.2	148
Germany (West)	60.3	.6	232
Hungary	10.2	.3	109
Ireland	2.9	.4	41
Luxembourg	.3	.5	130
Norway	3.8	.8	12
Poland	32.3	.8	101
Romania	19.4	.6	81
Sweden	7.9	.8	17

[4] Source: *Demographic Yearbook,* 1967.

Appendix 2

DECLARATION OF WORLD LEADERS ON POPULATION CONTROL AND STATEMENT BY U THANT, DECEMBER 10, 1966

ON HUMAN RIGHTS DAY, DECEMBER 10, 1966, with the active support of the secretary-general of the United Nations, a Declaration on Population was signed by twelve heads of state and presented to U Thant. On the same day, a year later, eighteen more signatories added their names. This is a comparatively small proportion of the United Nations' 132 member nations. But the importance of some of the countries and the number of people represented (900 million) make the signatures of these countries very significant, especially when we are dealing with a subject of great sensitivity, which is inclined to inhibit world leaders from open commitment. The Declaration is as follows:

The peace of the world is of paramount importance to the community of nations, and our governments are devoting their best efforts to improving the prospects for peace in this and succeeding generations. But another great problem threatens the world—a problem less visible but no less immediate. That is the problem of unplanned population growth.

It took mankind all of recorded time until the middle of the last century to achieve a population of one billion. Yet it took less than a hundred years to add the second billion, and only thirty years to add the third. At today's rate of increase, there will be four billion people by 1975 and nearly seven billion by the year 2000. This unprecedented increase presents us with a situation unique in human affairs and a problem that grows more urgent with each passing day.

The numbers themselves are striking, but their implications are of far greater significance. Too rapid population growth seriously hampers efforts to raise living standards, to further education, to improve health and sanitation, to provide better housing and transportation, to forward cultural and recreational opportunities—and even in some countries to assure sufficient food. In short, the human aspiration, common to men everywhere, to live a better life is being frustrated and jeopardized.

As heads of governments actively concerned with the population problem, we share these convictions:

We believe that the population problem must be recognized as a principal element in long-range national planning if governments are to achieve their economic goals and fulfill the aspirations of their people.

We believe that the great majority of parents desire to have the knowledge and the means to plan their families; that the opportunity to decide the number and spacing of children is a basic human right.

We believe that lasting and meaningful peace will depend to a considerable measure upon how the challenge of population growth is met.

We believe that the objective of family planning is the enrichment of human life, not its restriction; that family planning, by assuring greater opportunity to each person, frees man to attain his individual dignity and reach his full potential.

Recognizing that family planning is in the vital interest of both the nation and the family, we, the undersigned, earnestly hope that leaders around the world will share our views and join with us in this great challenge for the well-being and happiness of people everywhere.

STATEMENT BY U THANT ON THE OCCASION OF THE DECLARATION I am very pleased to receive this declaration on population growth and human dignity and welfare. I want to express my particular appreciation to Mr. John D. Rockefeller III, Chairman of the Board both of the Population Council and of the Rockefeller Foundation, for his untiring efforts to secure ever wider acceptance of the Declaration. This document has now been signed by thirty Heads of State or Government.

There are important links between population growth and the implementation of the rights and freedoms proclaimed in the Universal Declaration of Human Rights. It is therefore wholly appropriate that the date chosen for this ceremony should follow so closely Human Rights Day.

It is also appropriate because, nowadays, population planning is seen not only as an integral part of national efforts for economic and social development but also as a way to human progress in modern society.

We observe today rapidly changing attitudes towards the population problem, particularly in the developing countries where the rates of population increase are usually so high. There now exists in many countries an express desire to limit the size of families, as illustrated by the fact that highly dangerous and illegal means are increasingly used for this purpose. The desire to limit the size of the family is not surprising. With an ever-higher percentage of new-born children assured of healthy and productive lives, parents do not, as in the past, see the need for a very large family to be assured of good care in their old age.

The Universal Declaration of Human Rights describes the family as the natural and fundamental unit of society. It follows that any choice and decision with regard to the size of the family must irrevocably rest with the family itself and cannot be made by anyone else. But this right of parents to free choice will remain illusory unless they are aware of the alternatives open to them. Hence, the right of every family to information and to the availability of services in this field is increasingly considered as a basic human right and as an indispensable ingredient of human dignity.

The work of the United Nations itself in the population field has so far been relatively limited, given the importance of the problem. Against this background, I invited, in July of this year, Governments, non-governmental organizations, and private individuals to contribute to a new trust fund for population activities. I renew this invitation today. Our aim is to expand our work in those countries where it is more needed and which request our help.

We are concerned with the number of human beings on earth. We bear an immense responsibility for the quality of human life in future generations. I have no doubt that we can succeed. Man has shown increasing ability to master his environment. He is now acquiring the knowledge, as well as the means, to master himself and his own future. It is his duty to do so—for his own sake and for the sake of succeeding generations to whom we must bequeath a life worthy of human beings.

Appendix 3

STATEMENT OF THE BEIRUT CONFERENCE, APRIL 27, 1967

THE WORLD CONFRONTS A "NEW HIStory." For the first time, science and technology have vanquished the distances of space and time and placed super-abundant and growing wealth at man's disposal. At the same time, a single aspiration for human emancipation and dignity inspires the whole human family. These developments point to the emergence of a single planetary community.

Yet the resources of this community are so distributed—80 percent of them being at the disposal of only 20 percent of the people, living in the main around the North Atlantic—that while one segment of humanity is rich and growing richer, the rest still struggle in varying degrees of poverty and have little certainty of breaking out of their stagnation in the next decades.

Why are these facts of particular concern to the Christian community? This is the question considered at Beirut at the Conference on World Cooperation for Development sponsored by the World Council of Churches and the Roman Catholic Church and hence the first international conference to be organized and held on such a wide ecumenical basis.

The one primary reason is that the majority of Christians live in the developed North and if this area is wealthy far beyond the general level of world society, they profit from this unbalanced prosperity and must in conscience account for their stewardship. A second reason is that all Christians bear heavy responsibility for a world in which it can seem "normal" to spend $150,000 millions a year on armaments, yet difficult to mobilize more than $10,000 millions for the works of economic and social cooperation. A third reason is that Christians are totally committed to the unity and equality of all mankind under the headship of Christ, the Son of Man, and hence to unity and justice in the world society in which the human family lives. A fourth reason is that they believe in man's God-given responsibility to use his resources to recreate and renew the face of the earth. And last, they meet at a time when the desire for cooperation in development shows signs of slackening in the wealthy North, while the need for growth grows steadily more urgent in the developing South. They must therefore as Christians, in developed and developing countries alike, renew their dedication to the tasks of worldwide justice and development.

This challenge to the Christian conscience demands action at two levels—at the deeper level of education to form public opinion and in its immediate mobilization to influence political decision-making. In education, the Conference urges the Christian Communions:

1. To introduce the concept and the fact of Christians' deep involvement in world unity, justice, and development into every level of education —from their catechisms to their graduate studies. Seminaries, teacher training, colleges, and missionary institutes are particularly asked to see that every student accepts the vision of human unity, justice, and cooperation as an integral part of Christian faith and that in missionary work, the concept of development be placed within the central strategy for work in the field.
2. To prepare, in cooperation with the international agencies and with local expert groups, material on justice and development to be used in adult education, literacy campaigns, and through the mass media; and to seek the active participation of all citizens in planning and carrying through these campaigns.
3. To reform their own Church structures and policy and their own personal commitment so as to respond to the challenge of world justice, for instance, by pledging fixed and increasing percentages of their income to world development.

In the field of political action, the Conference recommends that the following priorities be stressed for action during the Seventies:

A. *In the Developed Countries*

1. That a commitment to genuinely unrequited and productive transfers of resources equal to one percent of GNP be made by the developed nations, if possible by 1970, without prejudice to an increase later.
2. That a flow of private investment equal to at least another one percent be aimed at by that time.
3. That the rescheduling of debt be accelerated and the terms of credit be eased for the future.
4. That manpower for technical assistance be systematically expanded to match the increase in financial transfers.
5. That the UNCTAD resolutions on stabilizing the prices for selected primary products and on preferential access to developed markets be achieved by mid-decade.
6. That programs and policies pursued by developed countries respect the genuine needs and priorities of developing countries—reformed agriculture, not higher defense, labor-intensive industries, not industrial giants working at a quarter of capacity, schools and clinics, not prestige projects, the advancement of all the people, not the monopoly of the few.
7. That the needs of developing countries be given higher priority in all the new schemes for international liquidity.

B. *In the Developing Countries*

1. That removing the social and political obstructions to dynamic progress and bringing all the people into the efforts and benefits of modernization be given the highest priority in local political action.
2. That programs for the modernization of agriculture and appropriate policies to slow down accelerated population increases—policies which respect the rights and religious beliefs of each family—be given the priority they need to lessen the prospect of possible famine in the next two decades and to give the hope of better diets, health, education, and responsible family life.
3. That in the industrial and service sector priority be given to appropriate technologies, including, where suitable, labor-intensive enterprise, and strategies be reasonably related to the availability of local resources.
4. That education be geared to an adequate concept of the nations' needs for citizens with modern attitudes and capacities, with especial reference to agricultural, technical, and managerial training.
5. That all plans be linked to a systematic mobilization of financial resources by way of adequate taxation and stimulus to local saving.
6. That regional common markets be established to coordinate industrial investment so as to enlarge the base for effective industrialization, to increase the competitiveness of exports and to secure a steady increase in trade between developing nations.

Developed and developing peoples alike are concerned with more than their own policies and reactions. They are all members of a wider, ever more interdependent world economy.

All would benefit if the lawlessness of the world were reduced and men's energies turned from preparations for war to the works of peace. Both in development and in the pursuit of peace, men can underline their common partnership and commitment by steadily increasing their resort to international institutions and agencies.

The Conference, therefore, urges:

(i) that the United Nations family hasten its formulation of strategies for the Seventies; and that Christian communities mobilize themselves to support targets which are consistent with the growing Christian consensus on development and cooperation.
(ii) that a rising percentage of development transfers should be channelled through the international agencies.
(iii) that, where practicable, the rest of the bilateral transfers should be distributed within the framework of multilateral consortia or consultative groups.

(iv) that all governments, separately and jointly, re-examine their priorities and give development and cooperation the central attention and prestige traditionally allotted to defense.

The work of development will not be finished in a day or a year. This is a work for this century and beyond. The Conference asks Christian citizens everywhere to pledge their support to development as a settled commitment, to campaign or lobby for development by all means at their disposal, and to give governments, parties, leaders, and agencies no peace until the whole human race can live with reasonable ease and hope in its single planetary home. In order to encourage Christians to play their full part in this urgent work, the Conference recommends that the ecumenical Exploratory Committee which sponsors this meeting be established on a permanent basis and become an active agent of Christian education and action.

Appendix 4

SPEECH BY ROBERT MC NAMARA, PRESIDENT OF THE WORLD BANK, SEPTEMBER 30, 1968

THIS IS MY FIRST PUBLIC SPEECH as President of the World Bank, and I speak to you with some diffidence as a newcomer with only half a year's experience in this post—but perhaps the half year in my whole life in which I have felt myself most challenged by the prospect before me.

I have always regarded the World Bank as something more than a Bank, as a Development Agency, and when I came here six months ago I was not entirely a stranger to the problems of World Development. As American Secretary of Defense I had observed, and spoken publicly about, the connection between world poverty and unstable relations among nations; as a citizen of the world I had begun to sense the truth in Pope Paul's dictum that "Development is Peace." Yet I was uneasily aware that as the peoples of the world looked at the sixties—the United Nations' Development Decade—they felt a deep sense of frustration and failure. The rich countries felt that they had given billions of dollars without achieving much in the way of Development; the poor countries felt that too little of the enormous increases in the wealth of the developed world had been diverted to help them rise out of the pit of poverty in which they have been engulfed for centuries past.

How far is this mood of frustration and failure justified by the events of the past decade? I have sought to find out the truth about this, but, though there have been many voices only too anxious to answer my question, each with a panoply of statistics to prove its point, there is no agreed situation report, nor any clear joint strategy for the future.

There have been successes: many billions in aid have been forthcoming from the developed world, and as a result of that aid and of their own increased capacity to manage their affairs, the economic growth of the poorer countries has been stimulated.

Let us make no mistake: Aid does work, it is not money wasted, it is a sound investment. Even the ultimate goal of the Development Decade, an annual rise in national incomes in the poorer countries of 5 percent by 1970 is likely to be achieved: the average annual growth thus far has been 4.8 percent.

And yet . . . you know and I know that these cheerful statistics are cosmetics which conceal a far less cheerful picture in many countries. The oil rich nations of the Middle East have prospered economically; so have some small states in East Asia. But for the nations of Africa and South Asia—nations with a population of over one billion—the average increase in national income is, at most, 3.5 percent, and much of the growth is concentrated in the industrial areas while the peasant remains stuck in his immemorial poverty, living on the bare margin of subsistence.

Casting its shadow over all this scene is the mushrooming cloud of the population explosion. If we take this into account, and look at the progress for human beings rather than nations, the growth figures appear even less acceptable.

The annual growth of per capita income in Latin America is less than 2 percent, in East Asia only about 2 percent, in Africa only one percent, and in South Asia only about half a percent. At these rates, a doubling of per capita income in East Asia would take nearly thirty-five years, in Latin America more than forty years, in Africa almost seventy years, and in South Asia nearly a century and a half. Even in the most progressive of these areas, the amount of improvement would be imperceptible to the average citizen from year to year.

Such a situation cries out for a greater and more urgent effort by the richer countries to assist economic growth in these poorer countries. It is clear they are financially capable of such action. During the Development Decade so far, they have *added* to their *annual* real incomes a sum of about $400 billion, an addition itself far greater than the *total* annual incomes of the underdeveloped countries of Asia, Africa, and Latin America.

But I found, and I need hardly tell you this, that while the requirement for assistance was never higher, the will to provide it was never lower in many, though not all, of the countries which provide the bulk of economic aid.

And the disenchantment of the rich with the future of development aid was fed by performance deficiencies of many of the poorer nations. Blatant mismanagement of economies; diversion of scarce resources to wars of nationalism; perpetuation of discriminatory systems of social organization and income distribution have been all too common in these countries.

This then was the picture of the development world which I found in my first weeks at the World Bank. A confused but sharply disappointing picture, in which it was difficult to see what had gone wrong in the past (though something clearly had), or what was the right path ahead for us.

In these circumstances, I turned to a suggestion which had been put forward by my predecessor, Mr. George Woods—one of his many bits of wise advice from which we all, and I especially, have benefited. This was that we should establish a commission of men well versed in world affairs, and accustomed to influencing them, who would survey the past aid effort; seek out the lessons it can teach for the future; and then examine that future to see what needs to be done by rich and poor, developed and underdeveloped alike to promote the economic well-being of the great majority of mankind. As you know, Mr. Lester Pearson, formerly Prime Minister of Canada, has agreed to lead such a survey, which will now proceed independently of the Bank.

The Pearson Commission will be turning our eyes to the long future, marking out guidelines not just for a decade but for a whole generation of development that will carry us to the end of this century. But here are we now, living in 1968, with much that we can and must do today and tomorrow. It is already clear beyond contradiction that during the first four fifths of the Development Decade the income gap between the developed and the less developed countries has increased, is increasing and ought to be diminished. But it is equally clear that the political will to foster development has weakened, is weakening further, and needs desperately to be strengthened.

What can the Bank do in this situation? I have been determined on one thing: that the Bank can and will act; it will not share in the general paralysis which is afflicting aid efforts in so many parts of the world. I do not believe that the Bank can go it alone and do the job of development that needs to be done around the world by itself; but I do believe that it can provide leadership in that effort, and can show that it is not resources which are lacking—for the richer countries amongst them have resources in plenty—but what is lacking, is the will to employ those resources on the development of the poorer nations.

We in the Bank, therefore, set out to survey the next five years, to formulate a "development plan" for each developing nation, and to see what the Bank Group could invest if there were no shortage of funds, and the only limit on our activities was the capacity of our member countries to use our assistance effectively and to repay our loans on the terms on which they were lent.

As a result of this survey, we have concluded that a very substantial increase in Bank Group activities is desirable and possible.

It is toward this objective that I shall attempt to guide the Bank's activities in the next few years. In doing so I shall need the advice and support of you gentlemen, our Governors, expressed through the Board of Executive Directors. Therefore I think it prudent and fitting that I should now present to you an outline of my thinking.

Let me begin by giving you some orders of magnitude: I believe that globally the Bank Group should during the next five years lend twice as much as during the past five years. This means that between now and 1973 the Bank Group would lend in total nearly as much as it has lent since it began operations twenty-two years ago.

This is a change of such a degree that I feel it necessary to emphasize that it is not a change of kind. We believe that we can carry out these operations within the high standards of careful evaluation and sound financing that my predecessors have made synonymous with the name of the World Bank.

Our loans will be for projects as soundly based and appraised as ever in our history. However, more and more, in looking for projects to support we shall look for those which contribute most fundamentally to the development of the total national economy, seeking to break strangleholds on development; to find those growth opportunities that stimulate further growth. And our help will be directed to those poor nations which need it most.

This I believe to be sound development financing, but it is not risk-proof; nor do I believe that the utter avoidance of risks is the path of prudence or wisdom. For instance, I recently visited Indonesia where, for good reasons, the Bank has never made a loan of any sort in the past. What I found was the sixth largest nation in the world, rich in natural resources, striving in the wake of the most terrible disasters, both economic and political, to set itself straight on the path to development. Without external help Indonesia faces certain disasters; by giving help (as we have begun to do through the International Development Association and through the establishment of a permanent mission) we are running some risks. I do not believe you would wish it otherwise.

The parable of the talents is a parable about power—about financial power—and it illuminates the great truth that all power is given us to be used, not to be wrapped in a napkin against risk.

But if we are to lend at double the level of the past, can we raise the money? I will not speak now about the soft loan money which is raised by Government contributions—you all know how essential these funds are—but about the money we raise by bond issues in the capital markets of the world. I am confident that the money is there, because I have confidence in the immense capacity of the economies of the developed world; no country need fear bankrupting itself because it plays its full part in development.

There are, of course, certain constraints resulting from balance of payments difficulties, but I am fully aware that the balance of payments difficulty is a problem of balance among the rich economies and not of balance between those countries as a group and the rest of the world—very little of the money lent in aid stays in the developing countries, almost all of it returns quickly in payment for the goods purchased in the richer countries. It is our job in the World Bank to look at the world money markets as a whole, and see where there are surpluses, where there are reserves that can be tapped. Following this line we have gone to the Middle East, and successfully raised funds there, as well as in the more conventional markets of the world—in particular Germany and America.

As a result, in the past ninety days the World Bank has raised more funds by borrowing than in the whole of any single calendar year in its history.

I would stress that in doubling the Bank Group's lending activities we shall not depart from our high standards of investment policy. But I would not want you to think that our policy is simply "more of the same."

Our five-year prospect calls for considerable changes in the allocation of our resources, both to geographic areas and to economic sectors, to suit the considerably changed circumstances of today and tomorrow.

First as to area: in the past the Bank Group has tended to concentrate its effort on the South Asian subcontinent. Much has been achieved—the harnessing of the waters of the Indus River system for power and irrigation for instance—and much remains to be achieved. I believe World Bank lending to Asia should rise substantially over the next five years. But it is not to Asia alone that our new effort will be directed. It is to Latin America and Africa as well, where in the past our activities have been less concentrated, and to some countries in great need of our help, such as Indonesia and the United Arab Republic, where our past activities have been negligible.

In Latin America, I foresee our investment rate more than doubling in the next five years. But it is in Africa, just coming to the threshold of major investment for development, where the greatest expansion of our activities should take place. There, over the next five years, with effective collaboration from the African countries, we should increase our rate of investment threefold.

Further changes will flow from our shift to a greater emphasis on Africa and Latin America. The states of these two continents are smaller than the giants of Asia. There will be many more but smaller projects, demanding much more staff work per million dollars lent than in the past.

The work of the Bank will also be increased because in many of the countries in which we will now be investing, there is no well-established Development Plan or Planning Organization. We shall try, in conjunction with other sources of funds, to help these countries to develop plans and to adopt wise and appropriate policies for development—in some cases by establishing resident missions as we have done in Indonesia— but always remembering that it is their country, their economy, their culture, and their aspirations which we seek to assist.

In particular, we will exert special efforts to right one upside-down aspect of Bank Group operations: the fact that many of our poorest members, despite their greater need, have had the least technical and financial assistance from the Bank Group. About ten of these have had no loans or credits at all. This is largely because of their inability to prepare projects for consideration. In these cases we will provide special assistance to improve economic performance and to identify and prepare projects acceptable for Bank Group financing.

With the doubling of Bank Group lending and with the increase in the complexity of our operations, there will clearly be need for an increase in the total professional staff of the Bank, as well as for some streamlining of our procedures. We are now engaged in a worldwide recruiting drive to find people with the high standards of expertise and dedication that have always been the attributes of its staff. I am anxious that this should really be an International Bank, in fact as well as in name, and I intend to ensure that we move steadily in the direction of the widest possible distribution in the nationalities of our staff.

Not only should our lending double in volume and shift geographically, but we can foresee, as well, dramatic changes among sectors of investment. Great increases will occur in the sectors of Education and Agriculture.

Education is a relatively new field for the Bank on which my predecessor George Woods, with his wise sense of priorities, began to place increased emphasis. In recent years the Bank has been seeking, hesitantly but with a growing sense of urgency, to find its optimum role in this field.

We are aware of the immense numbers of illiterates in the developing world: about 30 percent in Latin America, 60 percent in Asia, 80 percent in tropical Africa. We know too that education is relevant to all aspects of development: it makes a more effective worker, a more creative manager, a better farmer, a more efficient administrator, a human being closer to self-fulfillment.

The need is clear, but it has been less clear how the Bank's resources can be brought to bear on this labyrinthine problem. Now, after some years of collaboration with Unesco, we believe we see a way ahead for increasing Bank investment in education—investment which we hope will call forth further investment by the governments of the developing countries themselves.

Our aims here will be to provide assistance where it will contribute most to economic development. This will mean emphasis on educational planning—the starting point for the whole process of educational improvement. It will mean assistance, particularly in teacher training, at *all* levels, from primary to university. It will mean expansion of our support for a variety of other educational activities, including the training of managers, entrepreneurs, and of course of agriculturalists.

It is important to emphasize that education, normally one of the largest employers in any country, is one of the few industries which has not undergone a technological revolution. We must help to move it out of the handicraft stage. With the terrible and growing shortage of qualified teachers all over the developing world we must find ways to make good teachers more productive. This will involve investment in text books, in audio-visual materials, and above all in the use of modern communications techniques (radio, film, and television) for teaching purposes.

To carry out this program we would hope over the next five years to increase our lending for Educational Development at least threefold.

But the sector of greatest expansion in our five-year program is Agriculture, which has for so long been the stepchild of development. Here again there has never been any doubt about its importance. About two thirds of the people of the developing world live on the soil, yet these countries have to import annually $4 billion of food from the industrialized nations. Even then their diet is so inadequate, in many cases, that they cannot do an effective day's work and, more ominous still, there is growing scientific evidence that the dietary deficiencies of the parent are passed on as mental deficiencies to the children.

The need has stared us in the face for decades past. But how to help?

In the past, investment in agricultural improvement produced but a modest yield; the traditional seeds and plants did better with irrigation and fertilizer but the increase in yield was not dramatic. Now, as you know, research in the past twenty years has resulted in a breakthrough in the production of new strains of wheat and rice and other plants which can improve yields by three to five times. What is more, these new strains are particularly sensitive to the input of water and fertilizer; badly managed they will produce little more than the traditional plants, but with correct management they will give the peasant an unprecedented crop.

Here is an opportunity where irrigation, fertilizer, and peasant education can produce miracles in the sight of the beholder. The farmer himself in one short season can see the beneficial results of that scientific agriculture which has seemed so often in the past to be a will-o'-the-wisp tempting him to innovation without benefit.

Our task now is to enable the peasant to make the most of this opportunity and we, with the continuing assistance of FAO, intend to do so at once and in good measure. Irrigation schemes, fertilizer plants, agricultural research and extension, the production of pesticides, agricultural machinery, storage facilities—with all of these we will press ahead in the immediate future. Indeed in the coming year we plan to process more than twice the value of Agricultural loans as in the last, and our Agricultural dollar loan volume over the next five years should quadruple.

There is an element of risk in all this, of course. The seeds were issued before all the tests had been completed; the resistance of the crops to local diseases or pests cannot yet be assured; the splendid harvests in India and Pakistan this year cannot all be attributed to the new seeds. But I have no doubt, though setbacks may lie ahead, that we are now on the brink of an Agricultural revolution as significant as any development since the Industrial revolution. It is one that gives us a breathing spell in the race between man and his resources.

This leads me to yet another area where the Bank needs to take new initiatives—the control of population growth. This is a thorny subject which it would be very much more convenient to leave alone. But I cannot, because the World Bank is concerned above all with economic development, and the rapid growth of population is one of the greatest barriers to the economic growth and social well-being of our member states.

This is the aspect of the population problem with which I shall deal, because it is this aspect which most closely concerns the World Bank and its members. It makes it impossible for any of us to brush the subject aside, however strong our inclinations to do so may be.

I do not need before this audience to deal with the terrifying statistics of population growth as a whole, which show that although world population totaled only one-quarter billion in the first century A.D. and required 1,650 years to add another quarter billion, it added one billion in the next 200 years, a second billion in the following century, and a third billion in the next thirty years. It is now expected to add three more billion by the end of the century. By then, at present rates, it will be increasing one billion each eight years. Nor do I need to deal with the personal tragedies and dangers to health of unwanted births, though these were suddenly illuminated for me by an item in a newspaper last month which recorded that in the two largest cities of one European country live births were outnumbered by illegal abortions which imperiled the life of each unhappy mother.

As a development planner, I wish to deal only with the hard facts of population impact on economic growth. Recent studies show the crippling effect of a high rate of population increase on economic growth in any developing country. For example, take two typical developing countries with similar standards of living, each with a birth rate of 40 per 1,000 (this is the actual rate in India and Mexico) and estimate what would happen if the birth rate in one of those countries, in a period of twenty-five years, were to be halved to 20 per 1,000, a rate still well above that in most developed countries. The country which lowered its population growth would raise its standard of living 40 percent above the other country in a single generation.

In terms of the gap between rich countries and poor, these studies show that more than anything else it is the population explosion which, by holding back the advancement of the poor, is blowing apart the rich and the poor and widening the already dangerous gap between them.

Furthermore these economic studies show that this drag of excessive population growth is quite independent of the density of population. This is something that needs emphasizing in view of the fact that many policy makers in the developing countries attach only minor importance to reducing population growth. It is a false claim that some countries need more population to fill their land or accelerate their economic growth. There are no vacant lands equipped with roads, schools, houses, and the tools of agricultural or industrial employment. Therefore, the people who are to fill those lands, before they can live at even the current low standard of living, must first eat up a portion of the present scarce supply of capital—it is this burden which defeats a nation's efforts to raise its standard of living by increasing its population.

No one can doubt then that very serious problems of population growth face most of the developing nations today; what are the chances of their being mastered by natural causes? The answer lies in understanding the nature of the population explosion. It is not caused by an increase in the birth rate, but by a dramatic drop in the death rate due mainly to medical advances. It is this death control which has created the present emergency, and I do not believe that anyone would wish to reintroduce pestilence—or any other of the four horsemen of the apocalypse—as a "natural" solution to the population problem.

We are therefore faced with the question of what action we at the Bank, as a Development Agency, should take to lift this burden from the backs of many of our members. I propose the following three courses:

First: to let the developing nations know the extent to which rapid population growth slows down their potential development, and that, in consequence, the optimum employment of the world's scarce development funds requires attention to this problem.

Second: to seek opportunities to finance facilities required by our member countries to carry out family planning programs.

Third: to join with others in programs of research to determine the most effective methods of family planning and of national administration of population control programs.

With these three proposals for immediate action, I hope we may contribute to the success of the UN system which is already working in this field and to the well-being of the developing nations.

Gentlemen, I have spoken long enough. Let me conclude by saying that in the next few days, while we examine the innumerable and daunting problems which face you who exercise control over so much of the world's financial and economic power, I hope that none of us will yield to despair as we see how much there is to do, how little time in which to do it.

There is no cause for despair. There is every reason for hope. In the past few generations the world has created a productive machine which could abolish poverty from the face of the earth. As we lift up our eyes from contemplating our troubles, who can fail to see the immense prospects that lie ahead for all mankind, if we have but the wit and the will to use our capacity fully.

I am not despondent about the difficulties that lie ahead because I have faith in our ability to overcome them. That is why I have proposed a program of greatly increased activity by the World Bank Group, so that by taking a lead in development assistance we may encourage all those, rich and poor alike, who have begun to lose heart and slacken their pace.

If we in the Bank are able to double our effort, this could be the signal for others to rally again to the struggle, determined to use our overwhelming strength for the betterment of all mankind, and the fulfillment of the human spirit.

Appendix 5

SUMMARY OF THE LESTER PEARSON REPORT [1]

THE REPORT OF THE COMMISSION ON International Development, set up by the World Bank in August 1968 under the chairmanship of Mr. Lester Pearson, was published on October 1, 1969. . . . The sponsors of AWD share the Prime Minister's view that "it will become one of the most important documents of the twentieth century."

The Commission recommends a ten-point strategy for the strengthening of international co-operation for development, in which the following are the principal objectives:

1. To create a framework for free and equitable international trade.
2. To promote mutually beneficial flows of foreign private investment.
3. To establish a better partnership, a clearer purpose, and a greater coherence in development aid.
4. To increase the volume of aid. (The Commission recommends that donor nations should increase their aid to one percent of GNP as rapidly as possible, and in no case later than 1975, and that not less than 0.7 of the one percent should be official aid.)
5. To meet the problem of mounting debts. ("Debt relief should be recognized as a legitimate form of aid.")
6. To make aid administration more effective. (Among other improvements, the Commission recommends the progressive untying of aid.)
7. To redirect technical assistance. (The Commission recommends that national and international corps of technical assistance personnel should be given adequate career opportunities.)
8. To slow the growth of population.
9. To revitalize aid to education and research.
10. To strengthen the multilateral aid system. (The Commission recommends that the proportion of resources allocated to multilateral aid should be doubled by 1975.)

The Commission declares that the objective of its conclusions and recommendations is "a durable and constructive relationship between developing and developed nations in a new and interdependent world economy."

The report has this to say about population: ". . . no other phenomenon casts a darker shadow over the prospects for international develop-

[1] From *Power to End Poverty*, 1969, published by Action for World Development, 69 Victoria St., London, S.W.1.

ment than the staggering growth of population. It is evident that it is a major cause of the large discrepancy between rates of economic improvement in rich and poor countries."

It makes the following specific recommendations:

That developing countries identify their population problem, if they have not already done so; recognize the relevance of population growth to their social and economic planning; and adopt appropriate programs.

That bilateral and international agencies press in aid negotiations for adequate analysis of population problems and of the bearing of these problems on development programs.

That developed countries initiate or strengthen their own facilities for population studies.

That international organizations extend their training of population and family-planning specialists in all relevant categories.

The Commission therefore endorses the proposal to appoint a Commission for Population in the United Nations.

The Commission therefore recommends that the World Bank, in consultation with the WHO, launch immediately a wide-ranging international program for the direction, coordination, and financing of research in the field of human reproduction and fertility control.

In addition, the Commission urges action on population matters by the rich countries themselves, stating that "developing countries which have not done so should bring their legislation and social policy into line with the practice of family planning among their own populations."

The Pearson Commission recognizes that steps beyond family planning are essential, since fertility is influenced by social and economic conditions that militate either for or against the desire for large families. It specifically states that "wherever possible all agencies, bi-lateral and multi-lateral, should encourage and support social policies with fertility-reducing implications." Particularly important, the report notes, are factors such as the level of education and educational opportunities for women, and social security.

BIBLIOGRAPHY

THE FOLLOWING IS A SHORT SELECT BIBLIOG-raphy. In this vast field any bibliography is bound to be incomplete. It will reflect the interests and the gaps in knowledge of the author. This is even more the case here, where the effort has been not to overload the text with highly scientific or difficult-to-acquire works. The more serious student will also find in the books listed useful bibliographies for further reading.

Books

Agency for International Development. *Population Program Assistance*. Washington, D.C.: 1968.
——*The A.I.D. Story*. Washington, D.C.
Appleman, Philip. *The Silent Explosion*. Boston: Beacon Press, 1966.
Baade, Fritz. *The Race to the Year 2000*. London: The Cresset Press, 1963.
Barrett, Donald N. (ed.). *The Problem of Population*. Vol. 1, *Moral and Theological Considerations*, 1964; Vol. 2, *Practical Catholic Applications*, 1964; Vol. 3, *Educational Considerations*, 1965. Notre Dame, Ind.: University of Notre Dame Press.
Bauer, P. T. *Indian Economic Policy and Development*. London: George Allen & Unwin, 1961.
Benson, Don (ed.). *Dialogue on Poverty*. New York: Bobbs-Merrill Co., 1966.
Bockle, Franz (ed.). *War, Poverty, Freedom*. New York: Paulist Press, 1966.
Borgstrom, Georg. *The Hungry Planet*. New York: Collier Books, 1965–67.
Bowe, Gabriel. *The Third Horseman*. Dayton, Ohio: Pflaum Press, 1967.
Bracher, Margery. *Overpopulation and You*. Philadelphia: Fortune Press, 1966.
Calder, Ritchie. *Commonsense About a Starving World*. London: Victor Gollancz, 1962.
CELAP (Centro Latino Americano de Población y Familia). *Población y Familia*, Vol. 2. Santiago: June 1968.
Cépède, Michel; Houtart, François, and others. *Population and Food*. New York: Sheed & Ward, 1964.
Clark, Colin. *Population Growth and Land Use*. New York: The Macmillan Company, 1967.

Clarke, W. M. *Private Enterprise in Developing Countries*. New York: Pergamon Press, 1966.

Coale, Ansley J. *The Growth of World Population*. Washington, D.C.: National Academy of Sciences, 1963.

——, and others. *Family Planning in Kenya*. A report submitted to the government of Kenya by advisory mission of the Population Council of the United States, published in Nairobi, 1965.

——, and Hoover, Edgar M. *Population Growth and Economic Development in Low-Income Countries*. Princeton, N.J.: Princeton University Press, 1958.

Congar, Yves, O.P. *Power and Poverty in the Church*. London: Geoffrey Chapman, 1964.

Correia-Afonso, John. *The Church and the Developing Nations*. Rome: Gregorian University, 1968.

Day, Lincoln H. and Alice Taylor. *Too Many Americans*. Boston: Houghton Mifflin Co., 1964.

De Castro, Josue. *The Black Book of Hunger*. Boston: Beacon Press, 1969.

Drogat, Noel. *Challenge of Hunger*. London: Burns & Oates, 1962.

Dunne, George H. (ed.). *Poverty in Plenty*. New York: P. J. Kenedy & Sons, 1964.

Durand, John D. (ed.). *World Population*. The Annals of the American Academy of Political and Social Sciences. Philadelphia: 1967.

Ehrlich, Paul R. *The Population Bomb*. New York: Ballantine Books, 1968.

Fagley, Richard M. *The Population Explosion and Christian Responsibility*. New York University Press, 1960.

Faris, Donald K. *To Plough with Hope*. London: Victor Gollancz, 1958.

Federation of German Scientists. *World Food Crisis, or Is Famine Inevitable?*. Hamburg: Rowohlt paperback, 1968.

Food and Agriculture Organization of the United Nations. *World Food Program*. Rome: 1967.

Freeman, Orville L. *World Without Hunger*. New York: Frederick A. Praeger, 1968.

Gabor, Dennis. *Inventing the Future*. London: Martin Secker & Warburg, Ltd., 1963.

Galbraith, John Kenneth. *Economic Development*. Cambridge, Mass.: Harvard University Press, 1964.

Greep, Roy O. (ed.). *Human Fertility and Population Problems*, proceedings of seminar sponsored by American Academy of Arts and Sciences. Cambridge, Mass.: Schenkinan Publishing Co., Inc., 1963.

Guy, Drs. François and Michèle. *Île Maurice*. Lyon: Éditions Xavier Mappus, 1968.

Hardin, Clifford (ed.). *Overcoming World Hunger*, American Assembly volume. Englewood Cliffs, N.J.: Prentice-Hall, 1969.

Hardin, Garrett (ed.). *Population, Evolution, Birth Control*, 2nd ed. San Francisco and London: W. H. Freeman & Co., 1969.

Harrar, J. George. *Strategy Towards the Conquest of Hunger*. New York: Rockefeller Foundation, 1967.

Hauser, Philip M. (ed.). *The Population Dilemma*. Englewood Cliffs, N.J.: Prentice-Hall, 1963.

Hirschman, Albert C. *The Strategy of Economic Development*. New Haven: Yale University Press, 1958.

Hoffman, Paul. *World Without Want*. New York: Harper & Row, 1962.

Hopcraft, Arthur. *Born to Hunger*. London: Pan Books, 1968.

Hunter, Guy. *The Best of Both Worlds*. London: Oxford University Press, 1967.

Huxley, Aldous. *Brave New World Revisited*. London: Chatto & Windus, 1959.

Iowa State University Press. *Food—One Tool in International Economic Development*. Ames: 1962.

Johnson, Harry G. *Economic Policies Towards Less Developed Countries*. London: George Allen & Unwin, 1967.

Jones, Joseph Marion. *Does Overpopulation Mean Poverty?*. Washington, D.C.: Center for International Economic Growth, 1962.

Kelly, George A. *Overpopulation: A Catholic View*. New York: Paulist Press, 1960.

Kennedy, Senator Edward. *World Poverty and World Peace*. Baltimore: Johns Hopkins University, May 2, 1967.

King, Maurice. *Medical Care in Developing Countries*. London: Oxford University Press, 1966.

Kingsley, Davis. *Theory of Change and Response in Modern Demographic History*. Princeton, N.J.: Population Index, Office of Population Research, Princeton University, 1963.

Lacey, Janet. *Meeting Human Need*. Edinburgh: Edinburgh House Press, 1965.

Lebret, L. J. *The Last Revolution*. New York: Sheed & Ward, 1965.

Little, I. M. D., and Clifford, J. M. *International Aid*. London: George Allen & Unwin, 1965.

Llewellyn, Bernard. *The Poor World*. London: Zenith Books, Hodder & Stoughton, 1967.

McCormack, Arthur (ed.). *Christian Responsibility and World Poverty*. London: Burns & Oates, 1963.

——*People, Space, Food*. London: Sheed & Ward, 1960.

——*Poverty and Population*. Oxford: Catholic Social Guild, 1963.

——*World Poverty and the Christian*. New York: Hawthorne Press, 1963.

Moncrieff, Anthony (ed.). *Second Thoughts on Aid*. London: BBC Publications, 1965.

Montemayor, Jeremiah U. *Ours to Share*. Philippines: Rex Book Store, 1966.

Moomaw, I. W. *The Challenge of Hunger*. New York: Frederick A. Praeger, 1966.

——*Crusade Against Hunger*. New York: Harper & Row, 1966.

Moran, Jr., William E. (ed.). *Population Growth—Threat to Peace*. New York: P. J. Kenedy & Sons, 1965.

Moussa, Pierre. *The Underprivileged Nations*. London: Sidgwick & Jackson, 1962.

Myrdal, Gunnar. *Asian Drama,* 3 Vols. New York: Pantheon Books, 1968.

Nevett, A., S.J. *Population—Explosion or Control?.* London: Geoffrey Chapman, 1964.

Ng, Larry K. Y., and Mudd, Stuart (eds.). *Population Crisis— Implications and Plans for Action.* Bloomington: Indiana University Press, 1965.

Ohlin, Goran. *Population Control and Economic Development.* Paris: OECD, 1967.

Osborn, Fairfield. *Our Crowded Planet.* London: George Allen & Unwin, 1964.

Oser, Jacob. *Must Men Starve?.* London: Jonathan Cape, 1956.

Paddock, W. and P. *Famine—1975.* Boston: Little, Brown & Co., 1967.

——*Hungry Nations.* Boston: Little, Brown & Co., 1964.

Paul XI, Pope. *On the Development of Peoples (Populorum Progressio).* Washington, D.C.: United States Catholic Conference, 1312 Massachusetts Avenue, 1967.

Pierre, Abbé. *Man Is Your Brother.* London: Geoffrey Chapman, 1958.

Population Institute. *First Conference on Population, 1965.* University of the Philippines Press, 1966.

Prochnow, Herbert V. (ed.). *World Economic Problems and Policies.* New York: Harper & Row, 1965.

Reay, Hugh. *Arms or Aid for War on Want.* London: Housmans, 1967.

Rogers, Edward. *Poverty on a Small Planet.* London: S.C.M. Press, 1964.

Rottenberg, Simon. *Technical Co-operation in Latin America.* Washington, D.C.: National Planning Association, 1957.

Sauvy, Alfred. *Fertility and Survival.* London: Chatto & Windus, 1961.

Savile, A. H. *Extension in Rural Communities.* London: Oxford University Press, 1965.

Schaaf, C. Hart, and Fifield, Russell H. *The Lower Mekong: Challenge to Cooperation in South-East Asia.* Princeton, N.J.: D. Van Nostrand Co., 1963.

Shonfield, Andrew. *The Attack on World Poverty.* London: Chatto & Windus, 1961.

Shriver, Sargent. *Point of the Lance.* New York: Harper & Row, 1964.

Spaull, Hebe. *The World Unites Against Want.* London: Barrie & Rockliff, 1961.

Stamp, Dudley. *Our Developing World.* London: Faber & Faber, 1960.

Stamp, Elizabeth. *The Hungry World.* Leeds: E. G. Arnold & Son, 1967.

Still, Henry. *Will the Human Race Survive?.* New York: Hawthorn Books, 1966.

Stycos, J. Mayone. *Human Fertility in Latin America.* Ithaca: Cornell University Press, 1968.

Ward, Barbara. *It Can Be Done.* London: Geoffrey Chapman, 1965.

——*The Lopsided World.* New York: W. W. Norton & Co., 1968.

——*Nationalism and Ideology.* New York: W. W. Norton & Co., 1966.

——*The Rich Nations and the Poor Nations.* New York: W. W. Norton & Co., 1962.

——*Spaceship Earth.* New York: Columbia University Press, 1966.

Zimmerman, Anthony. *The Catholic Viewpoint on Overpopulation.* New York: Hanover House, 1961.

Speeches, Articles, Periodicals, Reports, Government Publications

American Association for the Advancement of Science. Report of symposium, *World Food/Population,* Dec. 26–27, 1968. Washington, D.C.

Boerma, Dr. Addeke H. Report of Sixteenth General Conference of International Federation of Agricultural Producers, Tunis, April 29, 1968. Rome: Food and Agriculture Organization, 1968.

British Association. *Hunger: Can It Be Averted?.* London: Aug. 1961.

Brown, Lester R. "A New Era in World Agriculture." Presented at first annual Senator Frank Carlson Symposium on World Population Problems, Kansas State University, Manhattan, Kans., Dec. 3, 1968.

Central Food and Technological Institute Report. Mysore: 1968.

Coale, Ansley J. "Population Trends and Population Control," *Science and the Modern World,* ed. Jacinto Steinhardt. New York: Plenum Press, 1966.

Congress Symposium No. 1, *Population Problems in the Pacific,* Aug. 22–26, 1966. Background Paper No. 1. University of Tokyo.

Cutajar, Michael Zammit, and Franks, Alison. *The Less Developed Countries in World Trade.* London: Overseas Development Institute, 1967.

Development Studies Association. *International Cooperation for Development,* International Round Table, First National Development Conference, April 16, 1966.

Divine Word Publications. *Annual Report.* Techny, Ill., 1968.

Food and Agriculture Organization, Rome. *Impact of Population on Food Supplies of the United Nations,* by B. R. Sen. 1965.

——*Millions Still Go Hungry.* 1964.

——Report of Fifth Regional Conference for Africa, Kampala, Nov. 18–30, 1968.

——Report of *Pane per il Mondo* Conference, Rome, 1968.

——*The Basic Freedom—Freedom from Hunger.* 1960.

——*The Problem of Population and Resources of the United Nations.* Sept. 1969.

——*The State of Food and Agriculture.* 1967, 1968, 1969.

——*The World's Food Supplies.* Jan. 30, 1969.

——"Population Growth and Agricultural Development," by K. C. Abercrombie. *Bulletin of Agricultural Economics and Statistics,* Vol. 18, No. 4, April 1969.

——"On the Problems of Our Planet," by Alberto Lleras Camargo. McDougall Lecture at Fifteenth Session, FAO Conference, Sept. 26, 1969 (Paper 69/LIM/1).

Food and Drug Administration, Advisory Committee on Obstetrics and Gynecology. *Report on the Oral Contraceptives.* Washington, D.C.: Aug. 1966.

——*Report on Intrauterine Contraceptive Devices.* Washington, D.C.: Jan. 1968.

Ford Foundation. *Population Newsletter: On Agriculture, Science, and the Developing World.* May 1969. Available from Ford Foundation Office, 320 East 43d St., N.Y.C., N.Y. 10017.

General Electric Center for Advanced Studies, Santa Barbara, Calif. Monograph prepared for United States Agency for International Development. *Turkey: The Effects of Falling Fertility,* Vol. I, Aug. 1969.

——*Guatemala: The Effects of Declining Fertility,* Vol. II, Aug. 1969.

——*Description of the Economic-Demographic Model.*

——*Economic Benefits of Slowing Population Growth,* Vol. I.

International Conference on Family Planning Programs, Proceedings. Geneva: Aug. 1965.

International Labor Office Governing Body, Paper G.B. 173/4/7, 173d Session. Geneva: Nov. 12–15, 1968.

International Planned Parenthood Federation. See Victor-Bostrom Fund.

International Union for the Scientific Study of Population. Conference paper, London, Sept. 1969. "Chile," by Roman Romero.

——"The Economics of Population Control," by Paul Demeny.

——"Population Policies in the Light of the Papal Encyclical *Humanae Vitae,*" by John Marshall.

——"Relationship Between Family Planning and Maternal Health," by A. H. Denny.

——"Why Does Contraception Meet So Many Difficulties in Superseding Abortion?", by Frank Novak.

Martelet, Gustave, S.J. "Pour mieux comprendre l'encyclique *Humanae Vitae*" (For A Better Understanding of the Encyclical *Humanae Vitae*), *Revue Nouvelle Théologique,* Nov. and Dec. 1968.

Mayer, Jean. "Food and Population—the Wrong Problem," *Daedalus,* Summer 1964.

——"Toward a Non-Malthusian Population Policy." *Columbia Forum,* Vol. XII, No. 2, Summer 1969.

McNamara, Robert S. Address to the Board of Governors, World Bank. Washington, D.C.: Sept. 30, 1968.

——Address to University of Notre Dame. Notre Dame, Ind.: May 1, 1969.

——Address to Inter-American Press Association. Buenos Aires: Oct. 18, 1968.

Miro, Carmen. *La población de America Latina en il siglio XX* (The Population of Latin America in the Twentieth Century). Cali, Colombia: Paper presented to the first Pan-American Assembly on Population, 1965.

National Policy Panel Reports. *World Population: A Challenge to the UN and Its System of Agencies.* New York: May 1969.

National Secretariat for Social Action. *Conclusions of the National Congress for Rural Development.* Manila: 1967.

Organization for Economic Cooperation and Development, Paris. *Development Assistance.* 1968.

——*Development Plans and Programs.* 1964.

——Report of First Population Conference of the Development Center, Paris, Dec. 3–5, 1968.

——*The Food Problems of Developing Countries.* 1967.

——*Population Control and Economic Development.* 1967.

——*The Development Center Report on Population,* October 1969.

Organization of American States. Final Report of the First Meeting of the Advisory Committee on Population and Development, July 29–31, 1968.

Overseas Development Institute. *French Aid.* London: 1964.

Oxford Committee for Famine Relief. *The OXFAM Story.* New York: The Macmillan Company, 1964.

Pakistan International Family Planning Conference. *Education and Family Planning.* Dacca: Jan. 28, 1969.

——*Implications of Population Growth for Employment.* Dacca: Feb. 4, 1969.

Population Council, New York. *Annual Report.* 1967.

——*Studies in Family Planning.* Cf. especially No. 40 (April 1969) and No. 42 (May 1969).

——Report to the Kenya Government. Aug. 1965.

——*The Economic Effect of Declining Fertility in Less Developed Countries,* by Gavin W. Jones. Feb. 1969.

——*Muslim Attitudes to Family Planning,* by W. Parker Maudin. Aug. 1967.

——and Rockefeller University. *Biological Aspects of Fertility Regulation,* by Sheldon J. Segal. 1968.

Population Institute, Manila. *Population Redistribution; Population of the Philippines.* Unpublished articles by Mercedes B. Concepcion, communicated to the author in 1968.

Population Institute of the University of the Philippines. First Conference on Population, 1965. Quezon City: 1966.

Population Reference Bureau. *Population Bulletins.* Washington, D.C.

Pradervand, Pierre. "La Course Démographie–Développement Économique" (Population Growth and Economic Development), *Développement et Civilisation.* Paris: International Training and Research Center for Development (IRFED), Dec. 1968.

Presidential Message on Population, July 18, 1969. Available from Population Crisis Committee, 1730 K St. N.W., Washington, D.C., 20006.

President's Committee on Population and Family Planning. *Population and Family Planning.* Washington, D.C.: Nov. 1968.

President's Science Advisory Committee. *Report on the World Food Problem.* Vols. 1, 2, 3. Washington, D.C.: May 1967.

Princeton University Office of Population Research. *The Demography of Tropical Africa.* Symposium by William Brass, Ansley Coale, Paul Demeny, Don F. Heisel, Frank Corrimer, Anatole Romaniuk, Etienne Van De Walle. Princeton, N.J.: 1968.

Royal Institute for International Affairs, London. Chatham House Conference, *New Directions for World Trade.* Sept. 16–24, 1963.

Science. Feb. 23, 1968, and May 24, 1968.

Scott, John. *Hunger—Must We Starve?* Report on World Food Crisis to the Publisher of *Time.* New York: Time, Inc., 1966.

Technology Review. "World Food Crisis." June 1968.

United Nations. *War on Want.* Report of conference on the UN Development Decade. New York: Pergamon Press, 1962.

——Population Commission. *Long-Range Program of Work in the Fields of Population.* Thirteenth Session, Feb. 2, 1965. *World Population Prospects Up to the Year 2000.* Thirteenth Session, Jan. 20, 1965. *Proceedings of the World Population Conference,* 4 Vols. 1965. *Population Newsletter* series, starting in 1968.

——Publications. *Demographic Yearbook.* New York: 1967. *Historical Outline of the World Population Growth.* New York: 1967. *Pre-investment and Productivity.* New York: 1967. *Towards A Dynamic Development Policy for Latin America.* New York: 1963. *World Population Prospects as Assessed in 1963.* New York: 1966. *World Population Prospects 1965–85 as Assessed in 1968.*

United States Agency for International Development. *Population Program Assistance.* Sept. 1968. Available from Population Service, Washington, D.C., 20523.

——*U.S. Economic Assistance Programs, 1966.* Washington, D.C.

United States *Congressional Record,* 1968.

United States Department of Agriculture. *Increasing World Food Output,* by Lester R. Brown. Washington, D.C.: 1965.

——Economic Research Service. *Accelerating India's Food Grain Production, 1967–68 to 1970–71.*

——Foreign Agricultural Economic Report No. 40.

——*Growth of Crop and Livestock Output in Selected Developing Nations, 1948–1965.*

——*Man, Land, and Food: Looking Ahead at World Food Needs.* 1963.

Victor-Bostrom Fund, International Planned Parenthood Federation, New York. *Can Mass Starvation Be Prevented?* Report No. 7, Fall 1967.

——*How Family Planning Programs Work—Will They Succeed?* Report No. 10, Fall 1968.

——*India.* Report No. 2, 1966.

——*The Santiago Conference.* Report No. 6, Summer 1967.

——*South America.* Report No. 3, 1966.

——*The United Nations and the Population Crisis.* Report No. 8, Spring 1968.

Wahren, Carl. "International Assistance in Family Planning." Paper presented at International Union for the Scientific Study of Population, London, September 1969.

World Council of Churches, Geneva. Report of Conference on World Cooperation for Development, Beirut, April 1968.

——Official Report. 1967.

——Report of Uppsala Conference. 1968.

World Food Congress, Second, Report of, The Hague, June 16–30, 1970.

World Health Organization. *Basic and Clinical Aspects of Intrauterine Devices.* Technical Report Series No. 332. Geneva: 1968.

——*Biology of Fertility Control by Periodic Abstinence.* Technical Report Series No. 360. Geneva: 1967.

——*Clinical Aspects of Oral Gestogens.* Technical Report Series No. 326. Geneva: 1966.

World Justice, issues of. Louvain, Belgium.

Worlock, Bishop Derek; Pratt, Oliver; and others. *You and the World.* London: Living Parish Pamphlets, Dec. 1968.

INDEX